Modern Vegetable Protein Cookery

Modern Vegetable Protein Cookery

Joan Kendig and Keith Kendig

ARCO PUBLISHING, INC.
NEW YORK

Published by Arco Publishing, Inc.
219 Park Avenue South, New York, N.Y. 10003

Library of Congress Cataloging in Publication Data

Kendig, Joan
Modern vegetable protein cookery.

Includes index.
1. Vegetarian cookery. I. Kendig, Keith, 1938- joint author. II. Title.
TX837.K46 641.5'636 79-21127
ISBN 0-668-05098-5 (Paper Edition)
ISBN 0-668-04617-1 (Cloth Edition)

Printed in the United States of America

Acknowledgments

I would like to thank my mother, Rose Nowicki, not only for passing along her cooking skills, but also for the time she spent taking care of my domestic details while the manuscript was being prepared; and also my father, sister and brothers, as well as many people outside my family who supported and encouraged this book. Most of all, I want to thank my husband for working out the data I needed to create these recipes.

—J.K.

It is a pleasure to express my gratitude to:

G. Theodore Wood, for all the enjoyable times we had working out and perfecting various computer programs.

Richard Black, for several helpful conversations on linear programming.

The Cleveland Garden Center, for allowing me to reproduce the woodprints from a rare book by P. Mattioli (Venice, 1583).

My wife, for her talent and persistence in transforming unlikely computer print-outs into gourmet vegetarian meals.

—K.K.

Finally, both of us would like to acknowledge our indebtedness to Frances Moore Lappe's *Diet For A Small Planet*, which first brought to our attention the idea of balanced vegetable protein.

Preface

There is an increasing awareness in the United States that a heavily meat-oriented diet has shortcomings. In the 1970's, Lappe's *Diet For a Small Planet* helped us become more aware of its ecological faults. We saw how inefficient converting the world's limited plant food resources into meat is, and how a steer typically eats 16 pounds of whole grains and legumes to produce only *one* pound of animal protein. We learned that intelligent use of the earth's land could feed the world—a wholesome, more vegetarian diet could nourish us all—but that the earth *simply isn't big enough to feed everyone on meat*.

Then in 1977, the U.S. Senate released a publication with far-reaching implications. Entitled *Dietary Goals for the U.S.*, this report, by a special panel of leading U.S. nutritional experts, focuses less on ecology and more on our health. The study especially looks at our nation's big "killer diseases" in light of our eating habits. Their findings point to a number of fundamental weaknesses in our current diet, and the report outlines specific goals for which we, as a nation, should aim.* It is once again a wholesome, more vegetarian diet which can so naturally fulfill the goals outlined in the report.

The remarkable thing is that the viewpoints of leading nutritional thinkers so closely agree with those of leading ecological thinkers. In harmony with ecological considerations, the simple act of diverting the world's plant food resources from raising animals to feeding people could not only better nourish the world and save millions of lives in developing countries, but it could save more millions of lives *right here at home*.

The fact is that people here, and in other affluent heavy meat-eating nations, are dying at unprecedented rates from heart attacks and other diseases resulting from plugged arteries—arteries filled with cholesterol made

* See Appendix 2.

by animals, which is interspersed through all their meat. But plants *never* contain cholesterol. If we bypass animals and eat closer to the bottom of the food chain, we can significantly decrease the intake of both cholesterol and saturated fats. Wholesome vegetarian food can offer a very real measure of protection against many of the major diseases that kill us today.

In switching to a meatless diet, there are two main problems. This book is our answer to them.

HOW DO YOU GET ENOUGH PROTEIN?

This is the first problem.

One response is to increase substantially the use of eggs and cheese. However, both contain cholesterol, and most cheeses are high in saturated animal fats and calories. Another response is to complement incomplete proteins by "mixing legumes with cereals." This often results in rice-and-legume dishes, casseroles and bean soups which, for most families, means a major change in eating style. Americans expect a piece of steak, chicken, fish, or *something* that's basically "the protein item" on the plate. If it's not there, families typically feel deprived or put off, and a meaningful transition to a more vegetarian diet fails. This leads to the second problem.

HOW DO I GET THE FAMILY TO ACCEPT VEGETARIAN FOODS?

Just what, for instance, is going to replace that T-bone steak? And is the replacement reliably going to supply an active, on-the-go family with plenty of good, solid protein? Our book contains solutions to both problems.

First, the proteins in the recipes have all been computer-tested for strength and are guaranteed to supply plenty of well-balanced, usable protein—enough for even the most active family. Second, the recipes have a more familiar form. You will find a big selection of "American favorites," all meatless, that many families will readily accept—vegetarian spaghetti and meatballs, meatless patties and burgers, rich-tasting vegetarian meatloaves, main-dish pies, elegant crepes, and so on. Changing eating habits has never been easy for anyone, but these recipes, with their strong protein and popular forms, should make it easier for many people to start. The advantages of a low-cholesterol, low-fat, and more vegetarian diet are tremendous. We hope you enjoy these recipes as much as we have.

Contents

Modern Vegetable Protein Cookery

Almonds

Introduction

This book is the unexpected result of combining our experiences from two widely different areas—one of us as a mathematician, the other as a cook. Here are the stories from each of us on how this book came to be.

From the mathematician:

For a long time I knew that people who ate little or no meat were less afflicted by many of the big modern diseases than the rest of the population. I also knew that all the well-known, long-lived cultures—the Hunzas in the Himalayas, the Georgians in Russia, the Vilcabambans in Ecuador—ate practically no meat. These facts seemed to suggest cutting down on or eliminating meat. The beef boycott in 1973 acted as a catalyst for both of us and we made our first small venture into vegetarian eating.

In those days I didn't know very much about balancing proteins, and that first venture lasted exactly 24 hours. After reading about complementing proteins, we tried again, but usually ended up feeling unsatisfied. By that time, I appreciated the first problem—getting enough protein.

Now I knew that protein consists of amino acids, that eight of these amino acids are essential, and that the human body uses them in certain quite specific proportions. I found out just what these proportions are, and I then made some rough calculations of the amino acid proportions in the combinations I had been using. I found them to be quite far away from the ideal. In retrospect, I realized that in mixing plant proteins such as rice, beans, wheat, and so on to get combinations with proportions closer to the body's needs, my ratios were very approximate. My instinct was to try to find the best combinations possible from plant sources. This meant writing down equations, which I did. But to *solve* them!

Computation using a hand calculator proved to be unbelievably slow, and at the end of four hours, I seemed to be no closer to finding any "ideal combinations'' than at the beginning. After a time I realized that this problem was the perfect candidate for a really giant computer. I fed data of the amino acid contents of forty different seeds, grains, legumes, and nuts into a computer and instructed it to find the best combinations of every ingredient with every other ingredient. This ''linear programming'' problem would have taken several years to do by hand. The giant computer did the whole job in 19 minutes, producing a two-inch stack of information all beautifully printed out on 11 × 15-inch computer sheets. The information I brought home with me that day was to change my life.

The next morning I selected two of the strongest combinations and mixed them together, making a cereal. I ate it with some milk and fruit, and even had my customary three-mile run. I felt great! By lunch time I felt normally hungry. After mixing various combinations for two weeks, I felt I was on the right track. My wife, who is a superb cook and who recognizes a computer print-out gruel when she sees one, wasn't quite so sure. It seemed clear that there was no way to program the computer for aesthetics and taste. However, we were intrigued by the possibilities which had opened up, and we started on the long road which finally culminated in this book.

From the cook:

I grew up on a diet of balanced meals and good foods, very few desserts, and few junk food snacks. For dinner we had meat with potatoes, rice, or noodles, and one or two cooked vegetables, plus a large, raw mixed salad. All these years we had mostly beef as our meat course.

After a while I got tired of beef, so that when the time came for me to make my own household I was not sorry to serve beef only once or twice a week. My husband was from California, in those days the vanguard of the ''health food'' movement, and he was filled with thoughts of cutting down on animal fats, eggs, and beef, and replacing red meat with chicken and fish. I liked chicken and fish, so we had that the rest of the week, with the same basic menu pattern from my childhood days.

As the months went by I found myself leaning more and more toward fish because I hated ripping the skin off the chicken, cutting apart the ligaments and bones, and all the nasty little cadaverous operations involved in preparing flesh for the table. Yet I never thought of vegetarian meals.

In 1973, when the beef boycott started because of high beef prices, people around us seemed to be more interested in meatless meals. There were recipes printed in the newspaper. A friend showed us a copy of *Diet For a Small Planet*. How nice, I thought, to be independent of flesh for protein! Was it really possible? Few people I knew actually believed it. We were products of an age which believed that meat equals protein. Milk, eggs, and cheese were breakfast and lunch proteins. Meat (or chicken or fish) was for dinner. And that was it. In those days, experimenting with vegetarian foods was a radical move. But we decided to try it, even though for us it meant only giving up mostly fish and occasionally turkey and chicken.

We tried balancing vegetable proteins, eating big plates of rice and vegetables with beans. Or cabbage leaves stuffed with rice and a tiny bit of soy grits. Result? Hunger—only an hour or two after dinner. We just couldn't feel satisfied, and we worried about our nutrition. Was there really enough protein in those dishes? Theoretically, there was supposed to be. But we were discouraged early, and eagerly went back to that piece of fish. Or else we relied heavily on cheese and milk, an unsatisfactory solution.

Yet there was still that pull in the direction of vegetable protein. We tried again, this time with soybeans. I remember making eggplant stuffed with soybeans and experimenting with soybean casseroles. I began to appreciate the virtues of soybeans, but my recipe repertoire was very limited. A casserole or two with those same little beans became tiresome. I started to collect vegetarian cookbooks, leaf through them in stores, study them in libraries. I believe that I have viewed, judged, and learned from nearly every vegetarian cookbook presently available to the American public. I could not find a book that did exactly what I wanted it to do.

I finally came to this conclusion: What I wanted was a vegetable protein piece of "meat." I wanted that because I would not then have to calculate grams of protein from beans and grains. I would not have to change my basic cooking habits or my expectations of nutrients from the meal pattern so familiar to me.

We had tried commercial canned vegetable protein "meats" but they didn't suit us because of saltiness, additives, or wrong flavors. And we preferred homemade food. Why couldn't we devise patties that were made of balanced vegetable proteins? Ones that had the kind of protein you could get from the same size piece of meat? It was not that we desired to imitate meat, only to *represent* it. There would also be a certain psychological satisfaction in seeing that piece of protein in its proper place on the plate.

About this time, my husband began to explore the computer aspect of the problem, and after seeing how well his early combinations worked, I decided to try using them to make homemade patties and burgers. That decision marked the beginning of the long road ahead of us.

I began to learn both the protein-combining and physical characteristics of our ingredients so that solid, balanced vegetable protein meatballs and burgers would stick together without eggs, so that loaves would slice nicely, and so on. I discovered a way of using soybeans that would eliminate the monotony of serving the bean in the shape of a bean, making possible cutlets, new kinds of loaves, and eggless quiches. By getting to know these ingredients I was able to combine them to bring out the advantages of each. The end result is this book—the one I had wanted on my own kitchen shelf half a dozen years ago.

The main-dish recipes are meant to take the place of meat on the table, in the sense that you can include a salad and vegetable to make up a traditional dinner, just as you would with meat. Generally speaking, you can judge the amount of protein as you would with ordinary meat dishes. For instance, the meatballs in spaghetti and meatballs contain approximately the same amount of protein as ordinary meat meatballs.

Food habits are hard to change, as any dieter can attest. What dieter would not rather have a low-calorie version of a favorite food, and feel psychologically satisfied, than have none at all and feel deprived? When you see a special recipe, you will feel much better because you can make it with our soy-granule burger rather than depriving yourself because you don't eat meat! Substitution often works magically for those of us who are still involved with the romance of food. Sometimes it's not that we crave the taste of flesh in those dishes we like, but it's the symbolic significance and form of the food—its associations—that give us satisfaction. That is why I have devised these recipes. They allow you to make a more pleasant transition to vegetarian fare than just eating a plate of rice and beans.

We have discovered a number of bonuses in changing to a vegetarian diet. Here are some of them:

- The cost of eating goes down. Meat, fish, and fowl are expensive and are getting more so.

- Vegetarian foods keep longer and are easier to store. Dried beans, for example, can be stored in a dark, dry place almost indefinitely. Under refrigeration, cooked vegetarian foods keep their taste and freshness better than flesh.

- There is less worry about fat and cholesterol. The amount of saturated fat and cholesterol we ingest is a very small fraction of the American average of 600 milligrams per day, and is well within the limits set by every study we have ever seen.

- Cooking is cleaner. There is less fat and certainly no grease in the kitchen. The fat we do eat is almost all unsaturated.

- We never have a feeling of deprivation. Since vegetarian food tends to have more fiber, the calories aren't so concentrated as they are in meats. When we've finished eating, we have a normal feeling of fullness.
- Weight control is easier because of the high-fiber, low-fat, low-calorie composition of the foods.

If you still associate steak with the good life, you may never want to give it up, but you may want to cut down on it, either because of the cost or because you are convinced it would be better for your health to consume less. People have said to me, "I would like to cut down on meat, but I don't know what to serve instead." If you are like these people, then this book is for you.

Cooking Hints

In this chapter we give some information about the foods we use, especially soybean products, and substitutes for foods we limit, such as eggs and cheese. There is an important section on the various ways of cooking beans, with a timetable for different kinds of beans. We explain uses of the pressure cooker in the vegetarian kitchen, and special uses of other kitchen equipment for these recipes.

INFORMATION ON FOODS AND FOOD SUBSTITUTES

Soy flour and soy powder. There is some confusion between these terms. Technically, a flour is made from the ground grain or bean. If raw, dried soybeans are ground, the resulting flour has a raw, beany taste. *It must be thoroughly cooked to destroy the trypsin-inhibiting factor* which prevents digestion of protein in the body. Often you can buy such "raw" flour in bulk in certain health food stores. It is especially useful for making breads that will be *well cooked*. Most commercial soy flour is called *soy powder*. (Sometimes, though, it is labeled *soy flour*.) It is always heat-treated to destroy the anti-trypsin factor. It can then be used in lightly cooked dishes and foods. It is preferable for making soy curd, especially if the curd will not be used in a cooked dish but in something like salad as cottage cheese is used. You can recognize heat-treated soy flour or powder by its taste: mild and slightly sweet, with no sharp, raw aftertaste.

Soy nuts. Sometimes called per-nuts or pro-nuts, these are roasted soybeans used like peanuts. *The kind we use in the recipes in this book are dry-roasted* (no oils are used in their preparation), *unsalted soy nuts*. They can be bought in many health food stores. Bottled soy nuts, even the unsalted ones, have some oil in them. They will not work as well as dry-roasted soy nuts in the recipes where the ground soy nuts are needed to absorb moisture and hold ingredients together. The oil in them inhibits moisture absorption.

Soy granules. These are bits of textured vegetable protein made from a soy flour mixture produced by the expeller process without the use of solvents or other additives. They are pre-cooked and can be eaten as they are. They taste slightly sweet and crunch in the mouth because they are dry, ready to absorb liquid in the recipes. Though they are textured, they are not called TVP, but are something different. They are not the same as *soy grits*, which are usually cracked raw soybeans. Such soy grits must be cooked before eating. They are best added to whole grain cereals during the cooking process. Sometimes people call soy granules soy grits. Make sure that they are made by a process that cooks them, otherwise they will not work in our Soy Granule Burger.

Soy flakes or rolled soybeans. These are soybeans that have been soaked, then heated somewhat and rolled flat so that cooking time is less than that of the whole soybean. They need to be cooked and cannot be eaten as they are over a long period of time. Some people eat them as they are as a cereal or in home-made uncooked granola-type cereal, but this can be harmful because of the anti-trypsin factor which needs to be thoroughly cooked out.

Supplementing with soy powder, soy granules, and soy nuts. These soy items are edible just as they are since they have been heat-treated to destroy the anti-trypsin factor. They do not have the "soybeany taste." Add a tablespoon of soy powder or soy nuts to your bowl of granola if it is made mostly of oats. You will then get a superior protein for breakfast.

When cooking oatmeal, for every ⅓ cup of dry oatmeal plus 1 cup of water (one serving) add 2 tablespoons of soy granules in the cooking pot. Bring to a boil and simmer, covered, for 5 minutes. The soy granules will take up the extra water in the oatmeal, giving a pleasant texture to the cereal. Add skim milk for an even more nutritious cereal dish.

For a meatless spaghetti sauce that compares favorably with a regular meat sauce, add soaked soy granules to our basic Italian Tomato Sauce (*see* Basic Recipes), or to your own favorite spaghetti sauce recipe. Just mix ¾ cup soy granules with 1½ cups of hot water or tomato juice and a tablespoon or so of soy sauce. When the granules have absorbed the liquid, stir them into the sauce during the last five minutes of cooking. The soy protein complements your whole wheat spaghetti. Add some cheese and you have an even stronger protein.

One of the best uses for soy flour is in making whole grain bread. Experts at Cornell University have shown that a mixture of 5 parts of soy flour and 95 parts of wheat flour contains 19% more usable protein than wheat flour alone. The mixture also has twice the growth-promoting value of wheat flour alone. To achieve this combination, when using 6 cups of whole wheat flour for making bread, replace ½ cup plus 1 tablespoon of whole wheat flour by soy flour. For an even better protein combination, see our bread recipe (page 48). Use some soy flour in making your quick breads, pancakes, and waffles.

When making soups containing pasta, add some soy granules for the same complementary protein effect.

Butter and eggs. We minimize the use of butter in this book because of its high animal fat content, but you will find a bit used occasionally.

Eggs should be limited to three or four a week per person because of their concentration of cholesterol. Only about half our recipes use eggs, and in those we use only one or two. If a recipe uses one egg, the four to six people eating the food are getting only a small amount—one-quarter to one-sixth of an egg. Eating four to six servings of such recipes a week still gives the person a total of only about one egg a week from those dishes.

Egg replacer is a commercial leavener found in health food stores to replace eggs in flour products. We use it in our Basic Crust Mix for those who wish to limit eggs.

Eggless recipes. Many vegetarian recipes depend on dairy products for complete protein, especially eggs. There are many recipes for quiches and crepes based on eggs that you can find elsewhere, but in this book we have concentrated on main-dish pies made with soy batter custard and various vegetables in a high-protein crust. We also have a number of recipes for thin pancakes made with whole-grain flours and soaked soybean batters, cooked in the manner of crepes. They can be filled with creamed vegetables or beans with sauce, rolled and baked in a shallow casserole or on individual platters, and garnished with extra sauce, just as crepes are. Though we include recipes made with eggs, we have tried to reduce our dependence on them, both for the sake of variety and also for possible health reasons, since the cholesterol controversy is still unresolved.

Some vegetarians, called vegans, prefer not to use animal products at all. These eggless recipes are for them also. (Vegans should be sure to get extra vitamin B_{12} supplements in the form of tablets or enriched foods, such as nutritional yeast or soy milk.)

We have a number of cutlets, patties, skillet burgers, skillet dishes, and loaves as well as "crepes" and "quiches" that are made without eggs. In every category of recipes there are a good number of them, amounting to more than half the recipes in this book. Some recipes using eggs are easily modified with egg substitutes such as chick-pea-flour binder.

Cheese and cheese substitutes. Cheese is delicious but it contains up to 40% animal fat and usually contains large amounts of salt. On the plus side, it is high in protein (20 to 35%) and certain vitamins (A, Riboflavin, B_{12}, K). Many vegetarian main dish recipes *depend* on cheese for their protein content, using as much as half a pound or 2 cups of grated cheese, as in some quiches. We prefer to use smaller amounts of cheese both for flavor and to increase protein quality of our vegetable proteins, which provide the basic protein content of our dishes. Thus we reduce our dependence on cheese as a protein source, cutting down on a lot of unwanted extra calories and fat.

Some people, especially vegans, like the flavor of a cheese spread substitute made with the best-tasting nutritional yeast available to them. (See the recipe in the section of Basic Recipes.) This spread can be used on sandwiches or thinned with water for a "cheese" sauce on patties or loaf slices.

We use cottage cheese in some of our recipes because it is a good source of protein, but often we substitute soy curd (or tofu) in such recipes. Seasoned, cooked soy curd can also be used the way cottage cheese is used in salads, or spread on lasagna noodles like ricotta cheese. (See Basic Recipes for instructions on making soy curd from soy flour.)

Milk. We use skim milk in our recipes to limit fat. We often make a "cream" sauce with thickened vegetable cooking water, seasonings, and a bit of skim milk powder.

Liquid lecithin. Liquid lecithin is an oily emulsifier and B-vitamin substance that comes from soybeans. It also comes in granules to use in cereals or in baking. Rubbed around the sides and bottom of loaf pans and muffin tins, with a little unrefined soy oil to help it spread better, liquid lecithin will allow the cooked food to be removed easily. It is the same substance used in commercial pan sprays, but in the liquid form you eliminate the propellant.

Oils and frying. Fried foods should be limited because of excess calories relative to the amount of other nutrients in the foods that are fried. We use small amounts of oil (usually only a tablespoon) to sauté vegetables or to brown cutlets and other foods with only moderate heat.

To eliminate frying an oil-absorbing vegetable like eggplant, you can steam the slices in a steam rack. Or for breading eggplant, instead of frying it spread the slices thinly with a little mayonnaise, drop them in crumbs, and bake them on an unoiled baking sheet at 425° for 15 minutes. Then lower the oven temperature to 375° for baking the eggplant in a casserole dish with tomato sauce and cheese slices, or use the prepared eggplant as necessary in your particular recipe.

Baking powder. For the leavening of crusts and quick breads (pancakes, muffins), we use the phosphate baking powder which can be obtained in health food stores. This kind of baking powder leaves residues of calcium phosphate and disodium acid phosphate. Since calcium and phosphorus are nutrients for the bones and teeth and are required for proper body function, this baking powder seems logical to use. Other kinds of baking powder, made with alum or cream of tartar, have residues that are not natural mineral constituents of the body.

Condiments and salt. We recommend catsup made without refined sugar or corn syrup. You can get catsup made with honey at health food stores. If you use pickles, relishes, mustard, and the like, we think the best comes from the same place (no preservatives or additives). We recommend Tamari, a soy sauce made with natural ingredients by a process of fermentation, rather than supermarket soy sauce made with sugars, corn syrup, and additives.

We try to limit the use of salt, but we do use some. (Too much salt is implicated in high blood pressure.) Vege-Sal is nice to use because every teaspoon of it contains dried vegetables to replace some of the sodium chloride that would be in a teaspoon of plain salt. Thus you get less actual salt per teaspoon, plus some minerals from the dried vegetables.

Flavorings and soup bases. We use Vegex, a type of vegetarian bouillon cube made from plant protein, yeast extract, natural flavorings, vegetable fat, onion, parsley, and spices. It contains vitamin B_1. We also use Emes Instant Soup Base, a low-sodium chicken-style or beef-style vegetarian flavoring containing wheat protein and dried vegetables. Vege-Sal is added to it for additional saltiness, if desired. Of all the kinds we have examined, these products contain the most natural, least objectionable ingredients. Of course, their use is optional. (If you substitute any other flavorings containing salt, eliminate the Vege-Sal from the recipe and taste the food before you salt it.) We also use a nutritional yeast which has been hickory smoked. It simulates a ham-like or bacon-like flavor (Bakon Yeast or Sovex). Such yeast contains protein, B-complex vitamins, and minerals. These products can be found in health food stores.

For a brown color in meat substitutes we sometimes mention using Kitchen Bouquet or Gravy Master, made from caramel, water, dried vegetables, salt, and spices. We also sometimes include cereal coffee, such as Postum, which is roasted powdered bran and wheat with molasses. You will find the occasional use of Worcestershire sauce, cocktail onions, pimientos, olives, and the like in small amounts. These options are used to give the foods variety, interest, and acceptability for some people.

Sauces and gravies. We use vegetable ingredients to take the place of meat juices and drippings as gravy bases. Simple light brown sauces for patties can be made by dissolving Vegex cubes in hot water, seasoning with a bit of crushed thyme or marjoram, and thickening with cornstarch or whole wheat pastry flour. (Use ratio of 1 Vegex cube to 1 cup of hot water plus 1 tablespoon of cornstarch or 2 tablespoons of whole wheat pastry flour.)

Tomato sauce is delicious with soybean foods. You can use canned sauce or make your own with fresh or canned tomatoes, or a combination of them. (There are several recipes in the Basic Recipes Section.) An excellent spaghetti sauce can be made simply with tomato paste, water, and seasonings, or more elaborately with extra tomatoes, onions, parsley, garlic, even diced carrot or potato, Italian herbs, and soy sauce in the blender, then simmered on the stove until the flavors are blended and the vegetables are cooked, 20 to 30 minutes. Or pressure cook it for just a few minutes. Tomato juice thickened with whole wheat pastry flour (1½ to 2 tablespoons per cup) or cornstarch (1 tablespoon per cup) with a few crushed Italian herbs also makes a nice simple sauce.

You can use your vegetable cooking water to good advantage for the liquid base of a sauce. Put 1 cup in the blender, add 2 tablespoons of whole wheat pastry flour and ½ teaspoon of your preferred herb (thyme, marjoram, basil) and Vege-Sal to taste (approximately ½ teaspoon). Blend until smooth, then pour the mixture into a non-stick saucepan. Stir constantly over moderate heat until the mixture thickens and bubbles. Stir in a few tablespoons of powdered milk for a white sauce, use a bit of grated Cheddar for cheese sauce, or just stir in ½ teaspoon of Gravy Master or Kitchen Bouquet for a brown sauce. Eliminate the herb and add a touch of curry powder for another kind of sauce.

Interesting vegetable sauces can be made with cooked potatoes for thickening instead of flour or cornstarch. Cook a small diced potato in a cup of water, perhaps with a little diced onion or celery, or even some grated carrot. Season to taste, add a little powdered milk and process in the blender until smooth. Use it as it is or as a base for brown sauce or cheese sauce as described above. (See the recipes for Cashew-Carrot, Marjoram-Walnut, and Basil-Almond Cutlets in the Skillet Burger Section.)

A good sauce to serve over cooked brown rice, whole wheat noodles, cooked millet, or whole wheat can come from seasoned cooked beans puréed in the blender with enough of their cooking water to make the sauce as thin as you desire. Stir in some toasted sesame seed meal for flavor and increased protein complementarity, or sprinkle it on top of the sauce over your grains.

You can make a nice cashew nut gravy to substitute for a cream sauce. Put ¼ cup of cashew nuts in the blender container with 1 cup of water and 1 tablespoon of oil. Blend until smooth. Add ½ teaspoon each of onion powder and Vege-Sal. Thicken with 1 tablespoon of cornstarch (or 2 tablespoons of whole wheat pastry flour), stirring constantly over moderate heat in a non-stick saucepan.

COOKING BEANS

There are several methods of cooking beans. Use the one most convenient for you.

Soaking beans overnight. Soak washed and picked-over beans in a covered Pyrex bowl in twice their volume of water. Refrigerate them in warm weather to prevent fermentation. (Split peas, lentils, and blackeyed peas do not need soaking before cooking.)

To determine the number of hours ahead of serving time to start cooking the beans you have chosen, look at the chart on page 13 and follow the instructions. Bring the beans and soaking water to a boil in a heavy saucepan, cover, lower heat, and simmer until tender. (Add enough water to cover the beans if necessary.) Remember that older beans that have been stored a long time are tougher and may take longer to cook than the specified times in the chart.

Pressure cooking beans. Soak beans overnight as directed above. Look at the chart on page 13 to determine how long before serving time to start cooking them. Then put them in the pressure cooker with soaking water (and additional water, if necessary) just to cover. (You may prefer to discard *soybean* soaking water, cooking them in fresh water.) Bring cooker up to pressure, lower heat, and pressure cook for the specified time in the chart. You may have to experiment a bit with suggested cooking times to find the best amount of time for the kind of beans you buy and store.

Short-soaking beans. In a saucepan bring washed beans and 2½ to 3 times their volume of water to a boil. Boil for 1 minute. Remove from heat, cover, and let stand for 1 hour. Then cook by simmering in a regular pot, covered, or pressure cook as directed in the chart on page 13.

Quick no-soaking method. Wash a cup of dried beans and drop them with a spoon, just a few at a time, into a pot containing a quart of boiling water. Add only enough beans at a time so that the boiling does not stop. This method allows the starch grains to burst, breaking the outside skins of the beans. The beans then cook more quickly because they can absorb the hot water more rapidly. When all the beans have been put in the pot, cover, lower heat, and let the beans simmer until they are tender—about the same time as that given in the chart below. Or pressure cook according to times given in the chart.

Slow-cooker method. Beans soaked overnight or by the 1-hour method may be cooked in the slow-cooker for 10 to 12 hours at low heat, or 5 to 6 hours at high heat. First pre-cook them for 1 hour by simmering on top of the stove.

Seasoning beans. Only after the beans are cooked should you add salt, oil, tomatoes, molasses, or other seasonings. If you add any of these before cooking is finished, they can interfere with the cooking or toughen the beans.

Bean Cooking Timetable

The cooking times given are approximate. Beans vary in the time needed for tenderizing because of age or storage conditions. They get drier and tougher if stored long. Times given are for soaked beans (except for split peas, lentils, and blackeyed peas, which do not require soaking).

Type of Bean	*Ordinary Cooking Pot*	*Pressure Cooker (15 lbs.)*
Split Peas	30 minutes	10 minutes
Lentils	30 minutes	10 minutes
Blackeyed Peas	30 minutes	20 minutes
Pink Beans	45 minutes	15 to 20 minutes
Small Limas	45 minutes	15 to 20 minutes
Whole Peas	1 to 1½ hours	20 to 30 minutes
Great Northern Beans	1 to 1½ hours	20 to 30 minutes
Brown Beans	1 to 1½ hours	20 to 30 minutes
Large Limas	1 to 1½ hours	20 to 30 minutes
Pinto Beans	2 hours	25 minutes
Kidney Beans	2 hours	25 minutes
Navy Beans	2 hours	30 minutes
Red Beans	2 hours	30 minutes
Black Beans	2 hours	35 minutes
Chick-peas	2 hours or more	40 to 45 minutes
Soybeans	2 hours or more	45 minutes

Eliminating flatulence. If you want to minimize digestive problems with the beans, you can discard the soaking water (and, if desired, the first cooking water). The basic cause of flatulence associated with beans is the absence of enzymes in our systems which break down into simple sugars the trisaccharides (raffinase and stachyose) normally found in beans. The undigested trisaccharides provide food in the lower intestine for the natural bacterial flora which produce the carbon dioxide and hydrogen that cause flatulence.

Since the trisaccharides are water soluble, they may be removed from your bean dishes by discarding the soaking water after the beans have soaked at least three hours. There will be some loss of protein, minerals, and water soluble vitamins, but you can compensate for this somewhat by adding two tablespoons of nutritional yeast to the finished dish after the beans are cooked. (You can go even further and discard the fresh water used to cook the beans for 30 minutes. Add new water and finish cooking.)

Dried beans must be well cooked. Most fruits and vegetables can be eaten raw for their best nutritional value. But the legume family of vegetables should not be eaten raw or only partially cooked because of their toxic potential.

When dried legumes are thoroughly cooked (soft inside, *not crunchy*), they contribute protein and B vitamins to the diet. If they are raw or undercooked they can be dangerous for several reasons. Most raw legumes contain substances sometimes called "toxalbumins." When they are cooked, the heat of cooking changes the toxic chemicals into harmless substances, burns them up, or dilutes them in water.

Some of these substances are the trypsin inhibitors, which prevent the action of the enzyme trypsin (in the digestive tract) in the process of protein absorption. If trypsin inhibitors are ingested over a long period of time, no matter how much protein you take in, it would be worthless to the body and normal growth could not take place. Raw soybeans and raw soy flour made from ground soybeans without heating contain these trypsin inhibitors. Soybeans must be thoroughly cooked so that they can be mashed between your tongue and the roof of the mouth. Otherwise they are not cooked enough. Untreated soy flour must be thoroughly cooked in homemade breads. Otherwise use soy powder, soy flour which has been heat-treated, to remove these enzyme inhibitors.

Legumes also contain hemagglutins, which inhibit growth by combining with cells lining the intestinal walls, preventing the intestinal absorption of nutrients. Insufficiently cooked beans or inadequately heated bean flour can produce nausea, vomiting, and diarrhea because of hemagglutins.

Raw legumes, particularly soybeans, have a factor which can block the uptake of iodine by the thyroid. Some people recommend taking kelp as food or in tablets as a precaution if the diet is high in soybeans. Such seaweed products contain abundant iodine.

Lima beans contain a complex glycoside that yields hydrocyanic acid, a poison. Chick-peas contain a trypsin inhibitor which is somewhat resistant to heat, but probably in very small amounts.

Most of the anti-nutritional or toxic elements of legumes can be partially or wholly eliminated by appropriate methods of cooking, so that they have become wholesome dietary staples in many parts of the world.

We stress that cooked legumes should not be the least bit crunchy. Do not think you are getting better nutrients from crisp, dried legumes as you are from crisp, succulent vegetables like zucchini or asparagus. Make sure your soybeans, chick-peas, and lima beans are *soft* inside.

Soaking and freezing soybeans. Soybeans can be used to make all kinds of attractive foods without the slightest resemblance to beans, and even without that "soybeany taste." You can form patties, cutlets, loaves, or muffin-shaped foods with a blender batter made from soaked soybeans and a whole-grain flour (millet, oats, wheat) with seasonings and minced vegetables. This soybean batter can be baked in the oven in tins of different shapes, steamed in the pressure cooker, or baked on an electric skillet.

To prepare the beans for these versatile foods, wash them thoroughly and soak them overnight in a little over twice their volume of water (2½ cups of water to 1 cup of beans). The next day, drain the beans, rinse them, and use them as they are given in the recipes. (The soaking water dissolves out the trisaccharides which cause flatulence. Discarding the soaking water also removes the strong bitter-bean taste that some people complain about in cooked soybeans.)

For last-minute meals, keep a supply of soaked soybeans, well drained, in one-cup freezer containers. Then you can briefly defrost just the right amount for a recipe, or even use it frozen. Just pop it into the blender with the specified amount of water in the recipe, blend until smooth, and continue with the recipe. Once the blender batter has been prepared, a process consuming only about 5 minutes, cutlets can be served in half an hour. (See the recipe for Soy-Millet Cutlets in the Skillet Burgers Section.)

USE OF THE PRESSURE COOKER

Cooking dried beans. There are several methods of cooking dried beans, but we prefer pressure cooking, especially for soybeans. The pressure cooker makes them really tender in a short time. A timetable for pressure cooking beans is included in the section on Cooking Beans in this chapter (*see* page 13).

Fresh vegetables. We use the pressure cooker virtually every day for cooking vegetables to perfection. Instead of allowing the vegetables to touch the water in the bottom of the cooker, we put them in a circular folding steam rack with one-inch metal feet. Vegetables like green beans and broccoli will come out crisp-tender and succulent, yet will retain their vibrant green color. White potatoes, sweet potatoes, and winter squash quickly become tender with delicious flavors.

Vitamins and minerals are better perserved with quick pressure cooking than longer boiling in water or even longer conventional steaming in a regular pot with a steam rack. Ideally, vegetables should be cooked in the absence of air and light and with as little liquid as possible. A pressure cooker fulfills these conditions. It is true that exposure to any heat results in some loss of vitamins, but since cooking times are shorter in a pressure cooker (only one to five minutes) there will be less loss than in longer regular cooking.

The pressure cooker comes with a recipe booklet giving a timetable for cooking vegetables in certain sizes. We have often used the table, but have found that we like to vary the sizes of the vegetable pieces so that the cooking time is usually only *one* minute. We have found that we like one-inch pieces of green beans cooked for two minutes instead of three. Experiment yourself to determine your preferences. Remember always to rinse the cooker in cold running water to stop the cooking process on these precisely-timed vegetables.

Vegetable combinations. The pressure cooker is excellent for making your own fresh vegetable combinations such as cauliflower chunks, carrot slices, and broccoli florets, or frozen peas with fresh-diced potatoes. After having determined the one-minute size vegetable pieces from each variety, you can mix them in the steam rack and cook them together. Occasionally we use frozen vegetables such as corn, peas, or mixed vegetables—the kind that pour out from a resealable bag. Undefrosted, they take only one minute to cook in the steam rack. They mix nicely with diced fresh vegetables that cook in the same amount of time.

Vitamin cooking water. For a delicious "cream sauce" to use on your vegetable combinations, use the cooking water in the pressure cooker. Mix a little powdered milk in the water, adding more liquid if you want more sauce. Thicken it with a bit of cornstarch (1½ teaspoons per ½ cup of liquid) or whole wheat pastry flour (1 tablespoon per ½ cup) and season to taste. Serve this sauce over the vegetables. This way you are serving whatever nutrients have been dissolved in the cooking water.

If we don't make sauce with the vegetable water we always pour it into a one-quart freezer container with a tight-fitting lid. The liquid accumulates over a period of a week or so in different-colored frozen layers. Then, this quart of vitaminized water (spring water, which we prefer to use) is used for a nice soup base, or for cooking washed lentils or split peas. To do this, rinse the outside of the container with hot water so that the frozen chunk slides out into the cooking pot. Melt it over medium heat, covering it with a lid. Have the soup ingredients ready to put in when the liquid comes to a boil. We have even used smaller quantities of this frozen cooking water for cooking whole wheat macaroni or spaghetti.

Whole grains and pasta. Whole-grain pasta from the health food store usually takes longer to cook than white flour varieties. If you want them in a shorter time, the pressure cooker does a good job. The pressure cooker timetable in the instruction booklet usually pertains to refined flour products and polished rice. Longer times are required for whole-grain products—about 5 minutes for whole wheat pasta, and 20 minutes for brown rice, barley, and other medium-cooking grains. Whole wheat berries, whole rye, whole oats, and hard grains taker longer—about 35 minutes as opposed to 1 hour or more of regular cooking.

Quick soups. We like the pressure cooker for whole wheat alphabet noodles when our small son wants alphabet soup in a hurry. They take about 5 minutes. When they are done, we add some frozen mixed vegetables and a Vegex cube, then pressure cook for another minute. Usually some cold tomato juice is mixed into the bowl of hot noodles and vegetables to get the right eating temperature for our little boy.

You can cook your own soups with chopped fresh vegetables and cooking water or other liquid in just one minute. Add leftover cooked beans, rice, grains or pasta. If you want to cook the pasta at the same time as the vegetables, cut the vegetables in much larger chunks than the one-minute size. Pressure cook five minutes, cool under running water, then mash the vegetables a bit with a potato masher after cooking.

SPECIAL USES OF KITCHEN EQUIPMENT

Use of the blender. A blender is an invaluable aid in a vegetarian kitchen for making batters, grinding bread into crumbs, making whole-grain flours in small quantities, making chopped nuts and nut-meals, and preparing smooth, quick-cooking sauces.

The blender really simplifies soybean cooking, making available their protein and other nutrients in many delicious forms. By soaking soybeans overnight, then draining and rinsing them, you can make a superb meat and egg substitute in the blender with water or cooking liquid, seasonings, and some whole-grain flour. The resulting smooth batter is baked in a variety of shapes and sizes.

We especially like the blender for quick sauces that enhance the pleasure of eating vegetarian loaves and patties. Two tablespoons of whole wheat flour combined with a cup of vegetable cooking water in the blender will produce a smooth liquid that thickens in about 3 minutes over moderate heat in a non-stick saucepan. Flavor it with Vege-Sal, herbs, and a little instant powdered milk for creaminess.

The blender is great for a nice spaghetti sauce that doesn't have to be simmered for hours. Onions, whole tomatoes, garlic, parsley, even minced carrots or other vegetables puréed in the sauce do not need long cooking—only 20 minutes at the most, or no pre-cooking at all if used in a baked dish. This method preserves vitamins and gives a piquant taste.

We usually use a small electric grain grinder for making bread crumbs, nut meals, and small amounts of flour, but the blender can be used to make these foods. Sometimes it is actually better for making walnut meal, which tends to make an oily walnut butter in the grinder. Pushing the start button for a few seconds, then pressing the off button so that the nut particles fall back toward the blades, then pressing the on button again, is a method that gives good results.

Grain grinder. We use a small electric coffee and grain grinder to prepare ingredients for many recipes—small quantities of whole grain flours (millet, oat, wheat), nut and seed meals, and bread crumbs from torn up slices of bread. The grinder is more efficient and more effective than a blender, because you can lift it up and shake it for uniform grinding, while the blender often has to be started and stopped, opened and stirred. The blender also has the disadvantage of inefficiency with small quantities that will not rise above the blades. With the grinder you can shake the particles up into the whirling blades.

The grinder requires a longer time for making millet flour (a full minute of non-stop grinding) than for making, for instance, oat flour from rolled oats (a few seconds). The harder the grain, the longer the time needed. Some nuts or seeds grind quickly (dry-roasted soy nuts), while others need a longer time and considerable shaking (almonds). Some make a dry meal (sunflower seeds) and others an oilier mixture (walnuts) that needs to be scooped away from the sides of the grinder bowl with a spoon.

Special use of the electric skillet. We use the electric skillet for soybean-batter vegetarian cutlets because the heat can be regulated and controlled so efficiently. The heat can be counted on to be uniform. It can be turned up to moderate for browning the cutlets at the beginning of the cooking, then it can be lowered to only 200° for the last 10 minutes to bake them through. The lid also has vents to allow steam to escape so that the cutlets can bake without puffing up too much. Stovetop cooking of soybean-batter cutlets gives irregular results on our electric stove, because the heat is not evenly distributed on the curved bottom of the pan. A flat, non-stick griddle might work better, if you could get a lid that fits properly.

Non-stick pans and bakeware. These are excellent for vegetarian cooking, especially for foods using soybean batter. Since vegetable protein is somewhat drier than ground meat, which contains fat to baste itself, unrefined soybean oil or liquid lecithin must be used to grease ordinary tins so that the food can be removed easily. The non-stick baking sheets, loaf pans, and muffin tins can eliminate this oiling, or minimize it. This saves time and calories.

Non-stick skillets are excellent for crepes and thin pancakes, and for various patties cooked on top of the stove. They require nylon, plastic, or wooden spatulas to preserve their smooth surface.

A non-stick electric skillet gives much better results with soybean batter cutlets than one with a regular metal surface, which is more efficient for meat that gives off fat or that is cooked in gravy. The vegetarian cutlets tend to crust and stick to the regular pan. With a non-stick skillet the crust sticks to the cutlet instead of to the surface of the skillet. Such cutlets are not usually cooked in sauce, but are served with sauce prepared separately. For those vegetarian foods that are simmered in sauce, such as soy granule burger recipes, the non-stick electric skillet is still better, because the granule burger chunks are first browned in a bit of oil before the sauce is added. They do not stick and have to be scraped off, leaving messy bits in the sauce.

Variety of baking tins. Loaf tins come in many sizes and shapes to provide different advantages and an interesting variety of dishes. The large loaf shape takes longer to bake—at least 1 hour—but it is good when you want to get the food in the oven quickly so that you can go out for an hour or so. It is good for providing a few days of sandwich slices for lunch, or for a big family meal.

The small loaf shape (1½ pints), often used for little loaves of bread, is excellent for a small family like ours, and it takes only 30 to 40 minutes to bake. It is attractive turned out on a platter, surrounded with colorful vegetables, and garnished with sauce.

Tiny loaf tins, often used for individual servings of corn bread, make beautiful individual soy-meat loaves. So do muffin tins. These utensils have the advantage of quicker cooking time also—20 to 30 minutes. You can make nice little soy-muffin morsels with miniature muffin tins. They are attractive for hors d'oeuvres, or use ½ dozen of them for an entrée serving. These will certainly cook in only 20 minutes, but the tin takes longer to oil than a large loaf pan, as do all the smaller tins filled with large amounts of batter distributed among them.

You can get interesting shapes by using rectangular cans from sardines or oval tins from salmon, for instance. Be sure to smooth down and avoid the cut edges when oiling the tins. Certain molded cooked tins, corn stick pans, popover pans, and other utensils you might find also allow you to make attractive foods with soybean batters.

Using the freezer for cooked foods. We always prefer to make our foods from fresh ingredients, but there are times when the freezer becomes necessary. If you work outside the home or have other obligations that limit your preparation time for dinner, some freezer supplies will help you.

When you have time to cook dried beans, apportion them among freezer containers in the quantities (1 or 2 cups) that you will use in your meals. If you don't like to use canned beans (many contain sugar and preservatives) this could be your method. Let them defrost in the refrigerator overnight for use in the next day's dinner. (Cook large quantities of beans to be frozen in your slow-cooker while you are away.)

Some of our casseroles, especially pasta dishes, can be frozen after assembly, then taken out for baking without defrosting. An assortment of these dishes prepared on weekends will help a homemaker with outside employment.

You can make balanced vegetable protein macroburgers in quantity and store them in the freezer between squares of freezer paper. They can be heated in a few minutes over moderate heat in a non-stick skillet, then served on whole wheat bread or buns. (The recipe for Macroburgers is in the Skillet Burgers Section.)

The food taking up most space in our freezer is homemade whole-meal bread. We bake up to 5 loaves at a time, then store four, well wrapped, in the freezer. Allowing a loaf to defrost overnight in the regular refrigerator section prepares the bread for use in the morning.

You can make waffles and pancakes in quantity and freeze them for quick breakfasts. Heat them in the toaster when you need them.

Using the freezer for quick-meal ingredients. Some of our recipes are basically a mixture of dry ingredients and seasonings, to which liquid ingredients are later added. They can be made up in quantity and then stored in freezer containers with tight-fitting lids. For quick meals, this method can eliminate up to 15 minutes of grinding and mixing certain recipes.

Our best convenience mix is Soy Granule Burger, a combination of soy granules, rolled oats, whole wheat flour, soy nut meal, wheat germ, and bran with finely chopped walnuts. These ingredients will keep pretty well mixed together in a large freezer container. We usually prefer to make it up fresh when substituting ground sunflower seeds for the walnuts, since sunflower seed meal can deteriorate fairly rapidly. (Instructions for Soy Granule Burger are in the Basic Recipes Section.) Soy granule burger dishes can often be cooked in less than half an hour.

Other quick meals can be made with soaked soybeans that have been drained and stored in the freezer. These soybeans make 30-minute vegetable protein cutlets from a blender batter. (See the recipe for Soy-Millet Cutlets in the Skillet Burgers Section.)

Recipes

The following recipes are divided into 10 sections with about 2 dozen recipes in each section.

The first section, *Basic Recipes,* contains recipes for meat substitutes prepared beforehand to make other recipes in the book, and a few cheese substitutes or sauces used in other recipes. We also include a recipe for whole-grain bread here.

Oven Loaves is a section of balanced vegetable protein combinations for meat loaf substitutes and other kinds of baked loaves both plain and fancy.

Oven Patties and Individual Forms are recipes to be baked as patties or cutlets on cookie sheets, or in interesting shapes like upside-down muffin croquettes or filled vegetable protein cups.

Skillet Burgers are individual portions of balanced protein in burger or patty shapes, cooked in the electric skillet or on top of the stove.

Pies and Crust Items contains basic high-protein crusts for main-dish pies such as quiche substitutes with soybean batter and vegetables, pizzas and pizza variations, and filled crust items to eat out of hand.

Crepes and Thin Pancakes contains basic recipes for balanced protein whole-grain crepes or eggless pancakes to be filled with meat substitutes, vegetables, and sauces for main dishes.

Casseroles and Oven Dishes use combinations of meat substitutes and vegetables or beans and grains baked together in the oven.

Skillet Dishes include meals of vegetable protein patties, mini-loaves, "steaks," balls, or chunks cooked in the skillet with vegetables.

Stuffed Vegetables use basic recipes of soy granule burger, sesameat, vegemeat, or soy curd to fill vegetable shells for main dishes.

Pasta Dishes gives some homemade whole-grain pasta recipes and shows how to make vegetarian spaghetti and meatballs or other meat substitutes with various kinds of pasta and sauces.

The average number of servings and grams of *balanced protein* per serving are given with each recipe. The grams of balanced protein for the day should add up to about 43 for men and 36 for women.

The Peanut Plant

Basic Recipes

This section contains recipes for meat substitutes that you prepare beforehand to make many other recipes in the book. (Basic Recipes used in other recipes are marked with an asterisk*.) The most important is our Soy Granule Burger formula, a ground beef replacer based on soybean protein complemented by oats and wheat. You can make meatballs, "hamburgers," patties, loaves, "steaks," and many kinds of stuffed vegetables with granule burger and its variants. There is even a sausage-seasoned version. (See the index under Granule Burger for lists of such recipes.)

Other vegetable protein ground beef substitutes are Basic Vegemeat and Basic Sesameat. Another sausage substitute good with bean dishes is Soy and Grain Sausage. For a quick and flavorful meatball substitute try Soy Nut Meatballs.

For diced or sliced vegetable protein to be used in casseroles, quick skillet dishes, crepes, and pasta dishes, we have devised a number of soyloaf recipes. These are combinations of soy flour or soy batter and whole wheat flour with seed meals which are pressure cooked or steamed in cans or metal bowls in advance, then used for many foods from sandwich fillings to fancy recipes. There are several chicken-style and beef-style soyloaves for dishes like Chicken-style Tetrazzini or Parisian Pot Pies. A nice Ham-style soyloaf, flavored with hickory smoked nutritional yeast, is good with beans or pasta dishes and sauce. Some spreadable soyloaves like Peanut-Soy Loaf or Soft Chicken-style Soyloaf are especially suited for sandwiches or spread on other foods for special recipes like rolled stuffed crepes or rolled lasagna noodles.

We also include instructions for making a delicious tangy soy curd (a soft version of tofu) used so often in this book to fill crepes, pasta rolls or shells, and stuffed vegetables, or as a cottage cheese substitute.

If you wish to make your own tomato sauce there are two recipes in this section, and also a recipe for a mushroom sauce.

Finally, we include a recipe for a delicious whole-grain bread.

Wheat

Soy Granule Burger Mix

The vegetable protein equivalent of ground meat, this is a substantial textured moldable "dough" for turning out meatballs, loaves, stuffed cabbage or peppers and a variety of skillet dishes. It may be mixed in quantity for ease and speed of future meal preparation, and stored in a tightly covered refrigerator container, preferably in the freezer compartment.

Basic Recipe for One Pound

⅓ c. soy granules
⅓ c. whole wheat flour
⅓ c. soy nuts, ground
⅓ c. raw rolled oats
⅓ c. walnuts, finely chopped
¼ c. wheat germ
¼ c. wheat bran
1 c. hot water
1 T soy sauce
1 Vegex cube, ground or crushed
½ t Kitchen Bouquet or Gravy Master (optional)

Mix dry ingredients together in a bowl (soy granules through wheat bran).

In a Pyrex measuring cup, dissolve the Vegex cube in the hot water. Add the soy sauce and Kitchen Bouquet. Gradually stir the liquid into the dry ingredients and mix well. Allow the mass to stand while you make preparations for the recipe to be used.

This burger mix may be put together ahead of time and allowed to stand absorbing the liquid in the refrigerator. The longer it stands, the firmer and more moldable the mass of "meat."

To cook the granule burger, use one of the following methods:

Chunked Granule Burger. Place the firm mass in a metal bowl and separate it into irregular chunks with a fork. Pressure cook for 5 minutes on the pressure cooker rack in 1 inch of water. Cool pan under running water. Or steam on a rack in a regular covered pot for 20 minutes.

Granule Burger Balls or Sausage Shapes. Form ½-inch balls or 3-inch long sausage shapes. Pressure cook on a steam rack over 1 cup of water for 2 minutes. Cool cooker under running water. Or steam on a rack in a regular covered pot for 20 minutes.

Small Loaves. Form 6 small loaves, compacting them with your hands. Place the loaves on a rack over 1 cup of water in the pressure cooker. Cover, bring up to pressure and cook for 5 minutes. Cool the cooker under cold running water. Or steam the loaves on a rack in a regular covered pot for 20 to 30 minutes.

These loaves may be sliced to use in recipes. Or use the slices for sandwich fillings with homemade sandwich sauces, lettuce, and sprouts.

All the above cooking methods result in a firm granule burger product to be used in the recipes in this book. The granule burger may be eaten after cooking in these ways, but the products are meant to be served in sauce. Make a simple brown sauce from the cooking water (*see* Sauces in the Cooking Hints Section) to serve with these items, or use tomato sauce.

Browned Balls, Chunks, or Patties. Separate the mass of firm granule burger into 1-inch balls or chunks or 1½-inch patties. Firm them well with your fingers. Brown them on all sides in 1 tablespoon of oil in a large non-stick skillet over moderate heat. Add 1 cup (or more) of tomato sauce or 1 cup of water plus 1 teaspoon of soy sauce. Bring to a boil, cover, lower heat, and simmer for 20 minutes. Stir occasionally during the simmering to allow the burger to absorb the liquid evenly.

The Basic Granule Burger Recipe makes enough for 4 to 6 servings.

Variations of basic recipe: Substitute ¼ c. sesame seeds, ground, or ¼ to ⅓ c. sunflower seeds, ground, for chopped walnuts. For "sausage" shapes, add herbs and spices (*see* directions below).

Granule Burger Sausage Balls or Links

To the dry ingredients of the previous Basic Soy Granule Burger Mix Recipe (made with sunflower or sesame seed meal instead of walnuts) add:

1 T hickory smoked yeast
¼ t fennel seeds, ground
¾ t oregano, crushed
¼ t pepper
¾ t garlic powder
½ t allspice
¼ t dried mustard

Add liquid ingredients in the basic recipe, then mix well. Allow mixture to stand for 10 minutes to absorb moisture.

Make small balls or sausage link shapes. Brown them in a little oil and simmer in 2 cups of tomato sauce or other sauce for about 20 minutes.

Or use as directed in a recipe.

Soy Granule Burger Refrigerator Convenience Mix

To make the previous Soy Granule Burger Basic Recipe for 1 pound in quantity, use these proportions:

1⅓ c. soy granules
1⅓ c. whole wheat flour
1⅓ c. soy nuts, ground
1⅓ c. raw rolled oats
1⅓ c. walnuts, chopped fine
1 c. wheat germ
1 c. wheat bran

Makes about 8 cups, or 4 times the amount needed for the 1-pound recipe.

To use the Convenience Mix, measure out 2 cups into a mixing bowl. Add the chopped onion, parsley, or onion powder which may be called for in the recipe you are using. Then stir in the 1 cup of hot water mixed with the pulverized Vegex cube, 1 T soy sauce and ½ t Kitchen Bouquet (optional). This mixture gives the equivalent of the previous Basic Recipe for 1 pound. It may be halved or doubled, depending on the size of your family.

Store this Convenience Mix in a tightly covered freezer container. Take out the amount you need for whatever recipe you are making. It does not need defrosting.

Bulgar Wheat Granule Burger

Make the Basic Recipe for Granule Burger with two substitutions: Substitute ⅓ c. bulgar wheat for ⅓ c. whole wheat flour and use ¼ c. sunflower seeds, ground, instead of chopped walnuts.

Add liquid ingredients as directed in basic recipe, mixing all together in a stainless steel bowl. When the liquid is absorbed, place the bowl, uncovered, in the pressure cooker on the rack that comes with the cooker.

Pressure cook in ½-inch of water for 5 minutes. Let the cooker cool naturally. Or steam the mixture on a rack in an ordinary covered pot. Bring about ½-inch of water in the pot to a boil, lower the heat, and simmer for about 15 to 20 minutes, or until mixture tastes cooked and bulgar wheat particles are tender.

Bulgar Wheat Granule Burger Sausage

Make the Basic Recipe for Granule Burger, substituting bulgar wheat for whole wheat flour and ¼ c. sunflower seeds, ground, for walnuts. Add to the dry mix:

½ t sage
½ t allspice
1 T hickory smoked yeast
½ t garlic powder

Add liquid ingredients and cook as directed for Bulgar Wheat Granule Burger.

Chopped Ham-style Granule Burger

Make the Basic Recipe for Granule Burger, substituting ⅓ c. bulgar wheat for ⅓ c. whole wheat flour and ¼ c. sunflower seeds (or pine nuts, if desired) for walnuts. Grind the seeds or nuts before adding them to the dry ingredients.

For the liquid in the Basic Recipe substitute:

1 c. heated tomato juice
1 T soy sauce
2 t honey

Combine the tomato juice mixture with the dry mix and let stand until it is absorbed. Cook as directed for Bulgar Wheat Granule Burger.

Chopped Chicken-style Granule Burger

Make the Basic Recipe for Granule Burger substituting ⅓ c. bulgar wheat for ⅓ c. whole wheat flour and ¼ c. almonds or hazelnuts, ground, for walnuts.

For the liquid in the Basic Recipe substitute:

1 c. hot water
1 T low-sodium chicken-style soup base
1 t Vege-Sal

Combine the liquid mixture with the dry mix and let stand until it is absorbed. Cook as directed for Bulgar Wheat Granule Burger.

Soy and Grain Sausage

Vegetarian sausage links or patties are made from soy granules complemented by wheat and oats, with herbs and spices.

½ c. soy granules
¼ c. whole wheat flour
¼ c. rolled oats
¼ c. wheat germ
¼ c. bran
2 T nutritional yeast flakes
2 T hickory smoked yeast
1 T soy powder
¼ t fennel seed, ground
¾ t oregano, crushed
¼ t pepper
½ t salt or Vege-Sal
1½ t garlic powder
½ t allspice
1 c. hot water
1 T soy sauce
1 T honey
2 T oil
1½ t prepared mustard

Mix dry ingredients (soy granules through soy powder) in a bowl. Stir in herbs and spices (ground fennel seed through allspice).

Mix 1 T soy sauce with hot water. Pour the liquid into the dry mix in the bowl. Stir well.

Mix honey, oil, and prepared mustard in a little bowl. Pour the mixture into the soy granule mixture, stirring to distribute it well. Let the vegetarian sausage mixture stand for about 10 minutes to absorb the moisture so that it can be shaped.

The sausage mixture may be fried as patties, rolled as little link shapes, or packed into cans to be steamed and later sliced and browned in a skillet.

To make patties, scoop out a large spoonful of sausage mix from the bowl for each patty and shape it with your hands. Place the patties on an oiled non-stick skillet over moderate heat. Brown them on each side for 1 or 2 minutes, then add 2 T of water, cover, lower the heat, and let them steam for 5 to 10 minutes.

For steamed "sausage rolls" that can be sliced and browned for later meals, pack the sausage mix into 2 cans (2½ inches in diameter) that have been well oiled with soy oil and liquid lecithin. Cover the cans with pieces of aluminum foil wrapped tightly around the edges. Pressure cook on a steam rack over 1 inch of water for 5 minutes. Let the pressure drop naturally. After the cans cool, remove rolls by loosening them with a table knife inserted all around between the can and roll. The roll should then drop out of the can when the can is inverted and tapped on the bottom. Wrap the rolls in foil, refrigerate, and use them within 2 to 3 days.

For little links, divide the sausage mix into 12 to 14 portions that you roll on a plate or in your hands to form link shapes about 3 inches long. They may be browned like the patties described above or steamed in the pressure cooker on a rack over 1 inch of water for 5 minutes. To use a regular pot for steaming, the cooking time must be increased to about 20 minutes, or until the links are firm.

Makes 4 to 6 servings.

The Oat Plant

Basic Sesameat

A savory combination of sesame seed meal, soy nut meal, soy powder, and wheat germ with seasonings and an egg or chick-pea flour binder. Use it to make skillet patties or use as directed in other recipes.

⅓ c. fresh sesame seeds, ground
¼ c. soynuts, ground
¼ c. low-fat soy powder
¼ c. raw wheat germ
1 T nutritional yeast
1 T wheat bran
1 t gluten flour or whole wheat flour
1 t dried parsley flakes or 2 T chopped fresh parsley
¼ t garlic powder
⅛ t ground thyme
1 Vegex cube, ground
1 small onion, minced
1 egg or 2 T chick-pea flour mixed with 2 T water
½ c. water or vegetable liquid

Mix together dry ingredients (sesame meal through parsley) in a mixing bowl. Stir in garlic powder, ground thyme, and ground Vegex cube. Stir in the minced onion.

Beat the egg in a separate small bowl, or mix the chick-pea flour with water. Add the ½ c. additional liquid and mix well. Stir this liquid mixture into the dry mixture. Let stand for 10 minutes or so for the liquid to be absorbed.

Use a large spoon to smooth out 6 patties on an oiled skillet. Brown the patties on the first side over moderate heat, then turn them and finish cooking until firm. Or bake the mix in a small metal bowl or loaf tin oiled with unrefined soy oil for 25 minutes, cool and dice for use in other recipes.

Add seasonings to the dry ingredients for this mix as directed in other recipes and cook accordingly.

Sesameat Sausage

Savory vegetable protein "sausage" patties with sesame seed meal, soy nut meal, soy powder, and wheat germ blended with special herbs and spices.

To the dry ingredients in the above recipe (sesame meal through parsley flakes) add the following herbs and spices:

¼ t garlic powder
¼ t ground thyme
¼ t nutmeg
½ t paprika
½ t oregano
¼ t marjoram
¼ t sage
¼ t savory
¼ t caraway seeds

Add ground Vegex cube, onion, egg (or substitute), and liquid as directed above. Make 12 small sausage patties on an oiled skillet with a spoon and cook as indicated. Or use this mixture in other recipes.

Basic Vegemeat

A savory burger-like combination of soy nut meal, soy powder, sesame meal, rolled oats, and chopped walnuts with herbs, onions, and mushrooms. Bake or pan-fry patties from this mix, or use it as directed in other recipes.

½ c. ground soy nuts, packed
¼ c. lowfat soy powder
⅓ c. sesame seeds, ground
⅓ c. rolled oats
¼ c. finely chopped walnuts
1 T nutritional yeast flakes
½ t ground thyme
¼ t garlic powder
1 medium onion, chopped
2 t oil
3 large mushrooms, finely chopped
¼ c. parsley, minced
1 Vegex cube
2 T hot water
1 T catsup
1 T soy sauce
½ t Gravy Master (optional)
1 egg or 2 T whole wheat pastry flour plus 2 T water

Mix dry ingredients (ground soy nuts through chopped walnuts) together in a bowl. Stir in yeast flakes, thyme, and garlic powder.

Heat 2 t oil in a small skillet and sauté the onion briefly. Add the onion, chopped mushrooms, and parsley to the dry ingredients.

In a small bowl, dissolve the Vegex cube in 2 T hot water. Add catsup, soy sauce, and Gravy Master. Break the egg into the bowl (or mix the whole wheat flour and water into it) and beat all the liquid ingredients together with a fork. Pour the liquid combination into the dry ingredients and mix well until everything is evenly moistened.

Form the mixture into a small loaf and bake at 350° for 25 minutes, or make patties to be baked or pan-fried. Or use as directed in another recipe.

Soy-Nut Meatballs

Rich-tasting high-protein balls with the texture of real meatballs, made of dry-roasted soybeans ground to fine flour, balanced with oats and fortified with wheat germ. Egg is the protein binding, chopped nuts and bran give texture and fiber, and cream cheese gives richness.

1 c. soy nuts, ground fine (dry roasted soybeans)
¼ c. walnuts, chopped fine
¼ c. rolled oats
¼ t garlic powder
2 T wheat germ
2 T wheat bran
1 Vegex cube, pulverized
2 medium eggs, beaten
½ (3 ounce) package cream cheese
¼ c. tomato juice
1 small onion, minced
1 c. tomato juice
1 or 2 T oil

Mix the dry ingredients and seasonings (soy nuts to bran) in a bowl. Mash the cream cheese with the beaten eggs in another bowl. Dissolve the pulverized Vegex cube in the ¼ c. tomato juice and mix this liquid with the eggs. Stir in the minced onion. Gradually add the dry ingredients to the liquid mixture, stirring while adding until a dough is formed. Let it stand for 10 minutes for the oats and bran to absorb moisture.

Turn out the contents of the bowl onto a piece of waxed paper or pastry cloth and squeeze the mixture out to a long roll about 20 inches long. Cut the roll into 20 pieces and form each piece into a ball with your hands.

In a skillet, sauté the balls on all sides in 1 or 2 T of oil over medium heat, turning with tongs. (Soy browns quickly, so watch them carefully.) Add 1 c. of tomato juice, bring to a boil, then simmer for 20 minutes, covered. The balls will absorb the juice and flavor, puffing up somewhat, with a residue of sauce surrounding them.

These balls are excellent just dropped into soup or stew without first browning them in a skillet. They retain their shape and absorb the moisture and flavor of the soup stock, yet taste and act like substantial "meatballs." They may be simmered in spaghetti sauce instead of tomato juice and served as you do spaghetti and meatballs. Or simmer them in a beef-like gravy, thicken it, and serve over brown rice or wheat-soy noodles. Add sour cream or yogurt to the gravy for "Stroganoff."

Soft Chicken-style Soyloaf in Cans

A soft steamed soyloaf made of soaked soybeans and complementary whole wheat flour, fortified with sunflower seed meal and ground soy nuts. Good for sandwiches or for use in recipes.

2½ c. soaked soybeans, drained
1 c. water
¼ c. oil
2 t Vege-Sal
2 T low-sodium chicken-style soup base
¾ c. whole wheat flour
¼ c. sunflower seeds, ground
½ c. soy nuts, ground

Put the beans and water in a blender container with the oil, Vege-Sal, and soup base. Blend until the bean particles are very fine.

Put the whole wheat flour and ground sunflower seeds in a mixing bowl. Pour the soybean mixture in and blend together well. Stir in the ground soy nuts.

Pour the mixture into 2 cans oiled with unrefined soy oil. Place cans on a rack over 1 inch of water in a pressure cooker. Seal the cans with pieces of aluminum foil. Pressure cook for 25 minutes. Cool naturally. Remove the cans from cooker to cool.

Makes 2 soyloaves, or about 7 c. (loosely filled) diced.

Light Chicken-style Soyloaf

A firmer, steamed soyloaf made of soaked soybeans and complementary whole wheat flour. Good diced for use in recipes or sliced and browned in a skillet.

1¼ c. soaked soybeans, drained
¼ c. water
2 T oil
½ c. whole wheat flour
1 t Vege-Sal
1 T low-sodium chicken-style soup base

Put the drained soaked soybeans with the water and oil in a blender container. Blend in spurts, turning blender off periodically to redistribute the mass of food with a fork or spatula. Blend until smooth. Remove to a mixing bowl, extracting all of the batter with a flexible spatula.

Mix the flour, Vege-Sal, and soup base into the soy batter. Oil 2 cans or a metal bowl with unrefined soy oil. Pour the batter into the cans or bowl. Place aluminum foil over the tops of the cans or over the bowl, pressing it around the sides to seal.

Pressure cook for 30 minutes on a flat rack over 1 inch of water. Allow pressure to drop naturally. Cool cans before removing soyloaf. Insert a knife around the sides of the loaf between the loaf and the can to loosen it. Dice soyloaf for use in recipes.

Makes 2 soyloaves, or about 2½ c. of diced soyloaf.

Dark Chicken-style Soyloaf

A firm, steamed soyloaf made with soy flour and soy nut meal with complementary whole wheat flour, fortified with sunflower seed meal. Good diced for use in recipes or sliced and browned in a skillet.

⅔ c. soy flour
⅔ c. soy nuts, ground
1 c. whole wheat flour
⅔ c. sunflower seeds, ground
2 T low-sodium chicken-style soup base
1½ t Vege-Sal
1½ c. water

Mix ingredients together in a bowl. Divide batter into 2 cans oiled with unrefined soy oil, or use a metal bowl. Place aluminum foil over the tops of the cans or over the bowl, pressing it around the sides to seal.

Pressure cook for 30 minutes on a flat rack over 1 inch of water. Allow pressure to drop naturally. Cool and remove loaf by sliding a knife down between the can and loaf all the way around. Dice loaf for recipes requiring soyloaf.

Makes 2 soyloaves, or about 6 c. (loosely filled) diced.

Beef-style Soyloaf in Cans

A soft, steamed soyloaf made of soaked soybeans and complementary whole wheat flour, fortified with sunflower seed meal and ground soy nuts. Good for sandwiches or for use in recipes.

2½ c. soaked soybeans, drained
1 c. water
¼ c. oil
2 T soy sauce
2 T low-sodium beef-style soup base
1 c. whole wheat flour
¼ c. sunflower seeds, ground
½ c. soy nuts, ground

Place the soaked drained soybeans in a blender container with the water, oil, soy sauce, and soup base. Blend until smooth. Remove batter to a mixing bowl, extracting it all with a flexible spatula.

Mix flour, ground seeds, and ground soy nuts with the batter.

Pour the batter into 2 cans (3 inches in diameter), oiled with unrefined soy oil. Place aluminum foil over the tops of the cans, pressing it around the sides to seal the edges.

Pressure cook for 25 minutes on a flat rack over 1 inch of water. Cool the cooker naturally.

Makes 2 soyloaves, or about 7 c. (loosely filled) diced.

Ham-style Soyloaf

1⅓ c. soy flour
⅔ c. soy granules
1 c. whole wheat flour
2 T hickory smoked yeast
1½ c. tomato juice
1 T honey
¼ c. oil
1 t Vege-Sal

Mix the soy flour, soy granules, whole wheat flour, and yeast in a bowl. Stir in the tomato juice, honey, oil, and Vege-Sal. Mix well.

Put the batter in 2 cans oiled with unrefined soy oil, or in a metal bowl. Cover the cans or bowl with aluminum foil pressed on to seal. Pressure cook on a rack over 1 inch of water for 25 to 30 minutes. Let cooker cool naturally.

Makes 2 soyloaves, or about 3 c. (loosely filled), diced, for each soyloaf.

Peanut-Soyloaf or Deviled Sandwich Spread

For an entrée, bake this loaf of soybeans, oats, and peanut butter to be served in slices. For a softer sandwich spread, steam the batter in foil-covered cans.

1½ c. soaked soybeans, drained
1½ c. fresh tomatoes
⅓ c. peanut butter
3 T oil
3 T soy sauce
1½ t onion powder
¾ c. rolled oats, ground to coarse flour

Put the soybeans, tomatoes, peanut butter, oil, soy sauce, and onion powder in a blender container. Blend until smooth. Mix in the ground oats, stirring in thoroughly with a narrow spatula.

Pour the batter into a loaf pan (8½ × 4½ × 2½ inches), coated with liquid lecithin or unrefined soy oil. Bake at 350° for 1 hour, or until firm and a cake tester comes out clean from the center of the loaf.

Makes 6 servings.

Deviled Sandwich Spread

Add 1 or 2 T Bakon Yeast to the soy-oat batter. Oil 2 cans (3¼ inches in diameter × 4¼ inches tall) with a combination of liquid lecithin and unrefined soy oil. Pour the batter into the cans, filling each a little over half full. (The batter expands when steamed.) Cover the cans with pieces of aluminum foil, pressing the edges of the foil securely around the rims.

In a large pot or kettle with a cover, place the cans on a metal rack in water that reaches to within 1 inch of the top of the cans. Cover, bring to a boil, lower the heat, and simmer for 2½ hours. (Or pressure cook for ½ hour in only 2 inches of water with the cans on the rack that comes with the cooker.)

Remove from the heat. Allow the pot to cool. Remove the cans when they are cool enough to touch. (With the pressure cooker, allow the pressure to fall naturally.) The "meat" will come easily from the cans. Slice and spread it on sandwiches like liverwurst or deviled ham.

The round sandwich loaves may be frozen in foil or freezer paper, to be sliced after defrosting.

Soy Curd

A ricotta or cottage cheese substitute made from natural (whole fat) soy flour.

1 c. soy flour (heat-treated)
4 c. water
¼ c. lemon juice
1 t Vege-Sal

Combine the soy flour with water in a blender container. Blend until smooth. Pour mixture into the top half of a large double boiler. Cover. Have 1 inch of water in the lower half of the double boiler and bring it to a boil. Double-boil for 20 minutes.

Remove from the heat. Pour in lemon juice and Vege-Sal. Stir once or twice. Separate the upper half of the double boiler from the lower to speed cooling. The curd forms as the mixture cools, in about 20 minutes.

After the mixture has cooled, pour the curd into a cheesecloth-lined strainer or flour sifter resting in a large bowl to catch the liquid. Allow the curd to drain and cool for up to half an hour. Squeeze the cheesecloth around the curd to press out the excess liquid. (Save the liquid in a freezer container for soup or for cooking beans.)

Makes 1½ to 2 c. soy curd and up to 3 c. of cooking liquid.

Note: Do not use less water than the recipe calls for, since the soy milk does not curd properly if it is too thick.

Seasoned Soy Curd

1 T oil
1 medium onion
1 recipe for Soy Curd (1½ c.)
1 T soy sauce or Vege-Sal to taste

Heat the oil and sauté the onion until tender. Stir the onion into soy curd in a bowl. Mix the soy sauce or Vege-Sal into the soy curd.

Vegetable Protein "Cheese" Spread

A cheese substitute resembling processed dairy cheese spread, full of protein but containing less fat.

½ c. nutritional yeast flakes
3 T whole wheat flour
1 T plus 1½ t cornstarch
¾ t salt or Vege-Sal
1 c. water
2 T unrefined soy oil
1 t prepared mustard (optional)

Mix together the yeast flakes, flour, cornstarch, Vege-Sal, and water in a blender container. Blend at low speed until perfectly smooth. Pour the mixture into a non-stick saucepan. Stir constantly over medium heat, using a nylon or wooden spatula, until the mixture thickens and bubbles. Let bubble for just half a minute.

Remove from the heat and whip in the oil with the spatula. Stir in mustard, if desired.

Seasoned Coating Mix

1 c. whole wheat flour
1 c. whole wheat bread crumbs
1 t Vege-Sal
½ t garlic powder
½ t onion powder
2 t paprika
1 T oil

Mix all ingredients together and blend with a pastry blender to mix the oil evenly with the dry ingredients. Store in a covered jar in the refrigerator.

Makes about 2 c.

Seasoned Dipping Batter

3 T whole wheat flour
3 T chick-pea flour
¼ t Vege-Sal
⅛ t garlic powder
1½ t soy sauce
½ c. water

Combine the flours, Vege-Sal, and garlic powder in a wide shallow bowl. Mix soy sauce with water in a measuring cup. Pour the liquid gradually into the dry mix, beating with a fork until no lumps remain.

Use for dipping vegetables or gluten pieces before rolling them in crumbs.

Makes about 1 c. batter.

Italian-style Tomato Sauce

1 medium onion, minced
1 clove garlic, minced (or ¼ t garlic powder)
1 T oil
1½ c. water or vegetable water
1 Vegex cube
1 can (6 ozs.) tomato paste
2 T chopped fresh parsley
1 T grated Parmesan cheese
2 t honey (optional)
½ t Italian herb seasoning
½ t dried basil

For spaghetti sauce: Sauté onion and garlic in oil in saucepan over medium heat. (If you are using garlic powder, mix it in when you add the herbs.)

Crush Vegex cube and mix it into the vegetable cooking water. Pour the water into the pan and heat until Vegex is dissolved. Mix the tomato paste into the water, stirring until it is uniformly mixed. Add the remaining ingredients (parsley through basil).

Bring to a boil, lower heat, and simmer for 20 minutes, covered.

Makes 2 c. of sauce.

For use in a recipe to be cooked: Put all ingredients in a blender container. Blend until smooth, with bits of green parsley showing. Use in the recipe as directed.

Tomato Sauce

1 can (6 ozs.) tomato paste
1½ c. water or vegetable cooking water
1 T plus 2 t soy sauce, or to taste

Combine ingredients in a blender container and blend until smooth. Use wherever canned tomato sauce is required, if desired. One cup of this sauce is equivalent to 1 can (8 ozs.) of tomato sauce.

Makes about 2 c. of sauce.

Mushroom Sauce

1 T oil
1 small onion, chopped
1 c. sliced fresh mushrooms
1 c. vegetable cooking water
1 T low-sodium chicken-style soup base
2 T whole wheat pastry flour
½ t Vege-Sal
½ c. evaporated skim milk

Heat the oil in a large non-stick saucepan. Sauté the onion and mushrooms until tender.

Place vegetable cooking water in a blender container with the soup base, flour, and Vege-Sal. Blend until smooth. Add cooked onions and mushrooms to blender and blend just until the mushrooms are chopped.

Pour the mixture into the saucepan. Cook, over medium heat, stirring constantly, until mixture thickens and bubbles. Stir in evaporated skim milk.

Makes about 2 c. of sauce.

Note: Use this sauce as an option in recipes containing commercial condensed mushroom soup.

WHOLE-GRAIN BREAD

Bread is one of man's finest inventions, and should *still* be the staff of life. One loaf of the real thing contains a rich assortment of vitamins, minerals, and trace elements as well as protein, carbohydrate, and fiber—everything a wholesome diet stands for. It's easy to add in other good things, too—soy flour, oats, sunflower seeds, raisins, even cranberries—making the loaf all the more delicious and nutritious.

If you get into the routine of making your own bread, it will be hard to go back to the store-bought variety. And if you wonder why even 100% whole wheat bread bought at the supermarket somehow doesn't seem to measure up, here is one reason. The flour-milling industry has played the following word-tricks on us: 100% whole wheat bread, even if it says 100% whole wheat flour on the label, isn't actually 100%. It's only 95%, and the most valuable part—the germ—has been removed. (This is allowed by the Food and Drug regulations.) In cracked wheat bread, the flour is yet more refined. If you want to buy honest 100% whole wheat bread, make sure it's called *whole-grain bread*—it's made from the entire wheat berry, as bread should be.[1]

Here is a recipe which you just might get hooked on. It is so strong all across the nutritional score board that it makes a valuable addition to any diet.

[1]Fremes, R. and Z. Sabry, *Nutriscore*. Methuen, New York, 1976, p. 150.

Whole-grain Bread Recipe

5½ c. hard spring whole wheat flour (not whole wheat pastry flour)
2 c. soy flour
1 c. rolled oats, ground
¾ c. wheat bran
1 c. sunflower seeds

4 c. warm water (90° to 115°F.)
2 T yeast granules
2 T honey
1 T soy oil
3 t Vege-Sal

Place grain ingredients (whole wheat flour, soy flour, oat flour, and bran) in a large heatproof mixing bowl and set it in the oven at the lowest temperature for 20 minutes. (Warm flour facilitates the rising of the bread.)

Meanwhile, gradually sprinkle the yeast into the warm water to dissolve it. Stir the honey into the mixture and set it aside while the flour is being warmed. After 10 minutes the yeast should foam up and bubble. Then add the soy oil and Vege-Sal to the liquid. (Or add Vege-Sal to the flours first.)

Pour the liquid into the warmed flour. Stir the mixture vigorously with a metal or wooden spoon, gradually adding the sunflower seeds. The mixture will make a sticky dough. (Do not knead it.)

Oil two large bread pans (1½ quart, 9⅝ × 5½ × 2¾ inches) with unrefined soy oil. Fill the pans half full with the dough. Cover pans lightly with clean tea towels and put them in a warm place with no drafts. Let the dough rise for an hour, or just to the tops of the pans.

Bake the loaves for 40 minutes at 375°. Turn off the heat and leave the loaves in the oven for another for another 20-30 minutes.

Remove from the oven. Let the loaves cool for 20 minutes before loosening them by running a knife around the edges. Invert the pans to remove the loaves and let them cool on a rack.

Makes two large loaves, 15 to 20 slices (servings) each.

Note: If dough does not rise to the tops of the pans, the yeast is too old. Bread can still be baked and eaten, but will be flat.

15 to 20 servings per loaf
Average serving = approx. 8 grams balanced protein
18 to 22% of daily protein need.

Oven Loaves

The loaf category was one of our first experimental areas. We wanted to devise a pleasing meat-loaf substitute and came up with half-a-dozen successes. Try Mock-Meat Loaf, Pizza Meat Loaf, Soy Granule Burger Loaves (and the variant, Potato-Topped Burger Pie), Sesameat Vegetable Loaf, Sunflower Seed Loaf, and our superb Sausage-style Corn Loaf. These loaves are high in protein and other nutrients. Many people like them better than loaves made with meat.

We have our own complementary versions of some old vegetarian standbys like Peanut Carrot Loaf, Bean and Grain Loaf, Cottage Cheese Squares, and Lentil Squares. But we also have quite a few new additions to vegetarian loaf cuisine based on our discovery of the soybean batter-millet flour combination. Soybean batter invites vegetable fillings and stuffings for new kinds of vegetarian fare. Try Three-Bean Pie, a combination of soy batter with the old favorite, Three-Bean Salad. Mock Turkey Loaf has a savory layer of bread stuffing inside. Spring Holiday Roast is a ham-style oval loaf filled with pockets of seasoned chopped greens. Baked Ring Mold is one of our loveliest party creations—a ring mold containing bits of pimiento, parsley, and tiny onions, served with colorful vegetables heaped in the center.

Loaves are convenient to use as your own sandwich slices and "cold cuts" that you can't buy. You can make one or two loaves a week just for sandwiches. They are delicious with wholesome health-food store relishes, mayonnaise, mustard, catsup, and lettuce, sprouts, tomatoes, or other vegetables on whole-grain bread.

Once you have learned our loaf techniques you'll come up with all kinds of recipes of your own.

Mock-Meat Loaf

A small savory loaf of ground nut and seed meats, containing tender vegetables, garnished and flavored with tomato sauce.

½ c. walnut meal
½ c. sunflower seed meal
½ c. rolled oats, ground
½ c. ground soy nuts, packed
1 T nutritional yeast
2 T wheat germ
2 T wheat bran
½ t ground thyme
1 c. grated carrots
1 stalk celery, minced
1 onion, quartered
2 eggs
1 Vegex cube, ground
1 can (8 ozs.) tomato sauce

Stir together the nut meals, ground oats, soy nuts, yeast, wheat germ, bran, and thyme in a mixing bowl. Add the grated carrots and celery.

Put the quartered onion and 2 eggs with the ground Vegex cube into a blender container. Blend until the onion is chopped fine or completely puréed, as you like. Pour the purée into the mixing bowl and stir well, moistening all ingredients thoroughly.

Press the mixture by spoonfuls into a 1-pint loaf pan which has been well oiled with crude soybean oil or liquid lecithin. Bake at 350° for 45 minutes.

After removing from the pan onto a heatproof platter, cover the loaf with half the tomato sauce and return to the oven to keep warm. The sauce will be absorbed somewhat, adding to the flavor of the loaf. Serve with additional sauce.

3 to 4 servings
Average serving = approx. 12 grams balanced protein
28 to 34 % of daily protein need

Pizza Loaf

A granule burger loaf with pizza ingredients: oregano, Parmesan cheese, pizza sauce, and mozzarella cheese, garnished with green pepper rings.

Basic Recipe for Granule Burger*
1 egg, slightly beaten
½ c. milk
¼ c. pizza sauce
½ t leaf oregano, crushed
¼ t pepper (optional)
¼ c. chopped onion
½ c. whole wheat bread crumbs
¼ c. sunflower seeds, ground or ¼ c. sesame seeds, ground
½ c. pizza sauce
½ c. shredded mozzarella cheese
Green pepper rings

Prepare the granule burger. Break up the mass with a fork and add the egg, milk, and pizza sauce, mixing well. Stir in the oregano, pepper, and chopped onion.

Add the bread crumbs and ground seeds. Mix well.

Oil a square (1½-quart) shallow baking dish with unrefined soy oil and lecithin. Pack the loaf mixture into the dish, smoothing the top with the back of a spoon. Bake at 350° for 30 minutes.

Remove the loaf from oven. Loosen it around the edges with a knife. Turn it onto a heatproof platter.

Spread the top of the loaf with ½ c. pizza sauce. Sprinkle with ½ c. shredded mozzarella cheese. Return to oven for 5 minutes, or until the cheese is melted. Garnish with green pepper rings. Let stand for 10 minutes before cutting to serve.

Note: To double this recipe, increase the baking time to 1 hour.

4 to 6 servings
Average serving = approx. 14 grams balanced protein
32 to 39% of daily protein need

Soy Granule Burger Loaves

Three very substantial soy-oat-wheat protein loaves serving two people each, with the texture and appearance of actual meat loaves.

⅓ c. soy granules
⅓ c. whole wheat flour
⅓ c. soy nuts, ground
⅓ c. rolled oats
⅓ c. finely chopped walnuts
¼ c. wheat germ
¼ c. wheat bran
1 onion, chopped
2 T fresh chopped parsley

1 c. hot water
1 Vegex cube, smashed
1 T soy sauce
1 t cereal coffee
½ c. tomato sauce

Mix the dry ingredients together in a bowl. Stir in the chopped onion and parsley.

Separately, dissolve the Vegex particles in the hot water; then add the soy sauce and cereal coffee to the liquid. Pour this liquid mixture into the dry ingredients, mixing thoroughly. Add the tomato sauce, folding it in well. Let the mixture stand for 10 minutes to absorb the liquid.

Separate the mixture into three parts, forming three oval loaves on a cookie sheet lightly oiled with unrefined soy oil.

Bake the loaves at 350° for about 40 minutes, or until a cake tester comes out clean. Serve with additional tomato sauce.

Makes 4 to 6 servings.

Variations: Substitute ¼ c. sunflower or sesame seeds, ground, for chopped walnuts.

Make a *Potato-topped Burger Pie* by using the above recipe for a meat loaf crust in a 9-inch pie pan oiled with unrefined soy oil. Press the loaf mixture into the pie pan, making a ¾-inch rim around the edge and flattening the middle to make a wide well. Bake as directed above, then fill with seasoned mashed potatoes (4 cooked potatoes mashed with a tablespoon of butter and 2 tablespoons of yogurt) and top with shredded cheese. Return the pie to the oven and allow the cheese to melt—just a minute or two—or place it under the broiler for 3 minutes to brown lightly.

Seasoned mashed potatoes may be mixed with chopped cooked kale or colorful cooked mixed vegetables for more variations.

4 to 6 servings
Average serving = approx. 11 grams balanced protein
26 to 31% of daily protein need

Sesameat Vegetable Loaf

A delicious, meaty, filling loaf with a nice solid texture, formed from complementary sesame, soy, and wheat, fortified with eggs and cheese. Vegetable bits add flavor and moisture.

⅓ c. sesame seeds, ground
¼ c. soy nuts, ground
¼ c. soy powder (low fat)
¼ c. raw wheat germ
1 T yeast flakes
¼ t garlic powder
1 t dried parsley flakes
⅛ t ground thyme
½ t marjoram, crushed
1 Vegex cube, ground
½ c. hot water
1 small onion, diced
½ c. grated raw beets
½ c. grated raw carrots
1 stalk diced celery
1 T olive oil
2 eggs
1 c. grated Cheddar or other cheese

In a mixing bowl, stir together the dry ingredients (sesame meal through ground Vegex cube). Add the hot water, mix well, and let stand a few minutes for the moisture to be well absorbed.

Heat the olive oil in a skillet and lightly sauté the grated and diced vegetables. Cover and let steam for 5 minutes over low heat. Fold the vegetables into sesameat mixture.

Beat the eggs and mix them into the batter. Stir in the cheese. Mix well. Put the mass into a loaf pan (9 x 3 x 2 inches) oiled with liquid lecithin or unrefined soy oil. Bake for 50 minutes at 375°.

4 servings
Average serving = approx. 14 grams balanced protein
32 to 39% of daily protein need

Sunflower Seed Loaf

A delicious, nutty, firm-textured loaf with the added crunch of vegetable bits.

½ c. sunflower seeds, ground (¾ c. meal)
6 T sesame seeds, ground
¼ c. pecan meal or wheat germ
½ c. soy nuts, ground
½ t celery seed, ground
1 t dried parsley or handful fresh, minced
¼ c. grated carrot (1 small)
¼ c. finely chopped celery (½ stalk)
1 small onion, minced
1 egg
⅓ c. milk
2 t apple cider vinegar
1 t lemon juice
1 T soy sauce
Cheese Sauce (optional, see recipe below)

Mix all dry ingredients together well in a bowl (sunflower seeds through parsley). Fold in the chopped and grated vegetables.

In a small bowl, beat the egg; then add the milk. Pour this liquid into the dry mixture and stir. Beat in the remaining liquid seasonings with a spoon.

Pack the loaf mix into a 1-quart casserole or loaf pan that has been oiled with liquid lecithin or unrefined soy oil. Bake at 350° for 30 to 35 minutes, or until firm. Serve with cheese sauce.

Makes 3 to 4 servings.

Cheese Sauce

1 T butter or oil
2 T whole wheat pastry flour
1 c. milk
¼ c. grated cheese

Using medium heat, warm the butter or oil in a non-stick saucepan and stir in the flour, mixing it in well. Gradually add the milk, stirring constantly so that the flour is dissolved and the sauce thickens and bubbles, for about a minute. Stir in the cheese so that it melts.

3 to 4 servings
Average serving = approx. 14 grams balanced protein
32 to 39% of daily protein need

Sausage-style Corn Loaf

Hickory-smoked nutritional yeast flavors granule burger with sausage seasonings, cornmeal, corn kernels, and diced onion in a firm-textured loaf.

Basic Recipe for Granule Burger*
1 T hickory smoked yeast
¼ c. minced parsley
½ c. diced onion
½ t sage
¼ t garlic powder
¼ t nutmeg
¼ c. sunflower seeds, ground
¼ c. cornmeal
½ c. tomato sauce
1 c. frozen corn

Prepare the basic recipe for granule burger. Stir the seasonings into the prepared granule burger (yeast through nutmeg).

Add the sunflower seed meal and cornmeal. Stir in the tomato sauce and mix well.

Heat ¼ c. water in a small saucepan. When the water boils add the frozen corn. Cover, lower heat, and let simmer a minute or two. Place half of the cooked corn and the cooking water in a blender container and purée. Add the purée and remaining corn kernels to the granule burger mix. Mix thoroughly so that all ingredients are well dampened.

Pack the mixture into a 1-quart loaf tin (8½ x 4½ x 2¼ inches) oiled with unrefined soy oil. Bake at 350° for 35 to 40 minutes. Let the loaf rest for 5 minutes before removing it. Insert a knife around the edges of the loaf between the loaf and sides of pan. Invert the loaf onto a serving platter.

4 to 6 servings
Average serving = approx. 11 grams balanced protein
26 to 31% of daily protein need

Vegetable Nut-Meat Loaf

Fresh sweet vegetables in this loaf of nut and seed meals make it moist and succulent.

½ c. walnut meal and chopped walnut mixture
½ c. sunflower seed meal
½ c. rolled oats, ground
¾ c. soy nuts, ground
¼ t leaf marjoram
¼ t leaf thyme
1 T yeast flakes
1 t Vege-Sal
1 fresh tomato, chopped
1 c. grated fresh zucchini
1 onion, quartered
2 eggs
1 Vegex cube, broken
Brown Sauce (see recipe below)

Combine the nut meals and ground oats in mixing bowl with the yeast, herbs, and Vege-Sal. Stir in the grated zucchini and chopped tomato.

Put the two eggs and the quartered onion along with the broken Vegex cube in a blender container. Blend until the onion is chopped and the egg is well beaten. (Or mince the onion fine, beat the eggs well, and dissolve the pulverized Vegex cube in a tiny amount of hot water. Then mix all three together.)

Pour the egg mixture into the vegetable-nut mixture and fold all ingredients together until evenly moistened. Spoon the batter into a 1½-pint loaf pan which has been prepared by greasing with crude soybean oil. Bake at 350° for 45 to 50 minutes, or until a cake tester comes out clean and the loaf is nice and firm.

Turn the loaf out onto a serving platter and garnish with some of the brown sauce. Serve in slices with additional sauce.

Makes 3 to 4 servings.

Brown Sauce

1 t vegetarian beef-style soup base mix
½ c. boiling water
2 t cornstarch or 1¼ t arrowroot
Dash Vege-Sal

Combine the cornstarch and soup base mix in a saucepan. Add a table-spoon or so of cold water until both are dissolved. Gradually pour in the boiling water; stir well and bring to a boil, still stirring. Allow the mixture to boil for 1 minute. Add a dash of salt if desired.

3 to 4 servings
Average serving = approx. 12 grams balanced protein
28 to 34% of daily protein need

Peanut-Carrot Loaf

A delicately peanut-flavored soy nut and sesame meal loaf filled with crunchy grated carrots and garnished with a festive cranberry sauce.

⅓ c. peanut butter
¾ c. milk
½ t garlic powder
1 t soy sauce
2 T chopped fresh parsley
1 c. grated carrots
1 small onion, minced
1 c. soy nuts, ground
½ c. sesame seeds, ground
2 T wheat germ
2 T wheat bran
Cranberry Sauce (see recipe below)

In a small bowl, smooth together the peanut butter and milk. Add the garlic powder and soy sauce.

In a larger bowl, place the prepared vegetables, nut meals, wheat germ, and bran, and mix them thoroughly. (If you like the carrots soft instead of crunchy, sauté them briefly before mixing them into the batter.) Blend in the peanut liquid with a spoon until a batter-like mass is formed.

Pack the batter into a small (1½-pint) loaf pan which has been spread with lecithin coating. Bake at 350° for 30 to 40 minutes, or until loaf is as firm as desired. Serve with Cranberry Sauce.

Makes 4 servings.

Cranberry Sauce

2 c. fresh (or frozen) whole cranberries
½ c. apple juice
¼ c. apple juice
⅓–½ c. honey

Put cranberries in a blender container with ½ c. apple juice. Blend until partially puréed. Heat the cranberry mixture with additional ¼ c. apple juice in a saucepan until it comes to a boil. Stir in the honey and let simmer for 5 to 10 minutes, covered. Return to a blender and process until as smooth as desired.

Makes about 1½ cups of sauce.

4 servings
Average serving = approx. 11 grams balanced protein
26 to 31% of daily protein need

Bean and Grain Loaf

Soybeans complemented by millet and bulgar wheat combine with lentils and sesame seeds in this loaf seasoned with onion, parsley, and thyme. Loaf slices are good served with tomato sauce or brown sauce.

2 c. cooked soybeans, drained
1 c. cooked lentils, drained
1 c. cooked millet
1 c. cooked bulgar wheat
¼ c. whole wheat flour
¼ c. sesame seeds, ground
2 T wheat germ
2 T bran
1 T nutritional yeast
½ t ground thyme
1 egg
1 T low-sodium beef-style soup base
2 T soy sauce
1 t Worcestershire sauce
2 onions, chopped (1 cup)
1 T oil
2 T chopped parsley
Tomato Sauce* or Brown Sauce*

Cooked beans and grains should be fairly dry for a firm loaf.

If you have no pre-cooked beans and grains for this recipe, cook them as follows: Use ¾ c. dried soybeans, soaked overnight in 1½ c. of water. Drain, then pressure cook in water just to cover for 40 minutes. Or simmer in a regular pot for 2 hours.

Use ⅓ c. washed dry lentils. Bring ¾ c. of water to a boil, add lentils, and simmer, covered, for 30 to 40 minutes.

For millet, bring ¾ c. water to a boil, add ⅓ c. dry millet, then simmer, covered, for 20 minutes.

For bulgar wheat, follow the above procedure for millet, but simmer for only 15 minutes.

When beans and grains are cooked, mash the well-drained soybeans in a large bowl with a potato masher. Add the well-drained lentils and mash.

Stir in cooked cereals (sprinkled with Vege-Sal, if desired), whole wheat flour, ground sesame seeds, wheat germ, and bran. Add the nutritional yeast and ground thyme.

Beat the egg in a small bowl. Add to it the dried soup base, soy sauce, and Worcestershire sauce. Pour this liquid into the bean and grain mixture.

Sauté the chopped onions in the oil over moderate heat. Add the onions and chopped parsley to the bean and grain mixture. Mix thoroughly. (Omit sautéing the onions if you like crunchy onion chunks in the cooked loaf.)

Oil a 1-quart loaf tin with unrefined soy oil, then flour it with whole wheat flour. This method helps the cooked loaf to slide out easily onto a serving platter.

Pack the loaf mixture into the prepared loaf tin. Bake at 375° for 45 minutes, or until nicely browned and firm. Let the loaf rest for about 10 minutes before loosening it with a knife and turning it out onto a serving platter. (If you refrigerate the prepared loaf before baking, increase baking time to 1 hour.)

To serve, cut the loaf into thick slices. Serve with tomato sauce or brown sauce.

Makes 4 to 6 servings.

4 to 6 servings
Average serving = approx. 13 grams balanced protein
30 to 36% of daily protein need

Cottage Cheese Squares

A firm, meaty cottage cheese and soy nut meal combination cut into individual squares, each topped with a bit of tomato sauce and cheddar cheese.

¾ c. soy nuts, ground
½ c. chopped pecans or walnuts
2 t low-sodium chicken soup seasoning
½ t ground thyme
½ t Vege-Sal
2 eggs
1 c. cottage cheese
1 medium onion, chopped
1 T oil
8 little slices of Cheddar cheese
Tomato Sauce*
3 T wheat germ

Mix together the dry ingredients (soy nuts through Vege-Sal) in a bowl.

Separately, beat the eggs and fold in the cottage cheese. Sauté the onion in the oil and add it to egg mixture. Pour the wet ingredients into the dry ones and mix well.

Prepare a shallow 1½-quart Pyrex rectangular baking dish by oiling it with liquid lecithin and soy oil. Pour the food mixture into the dish, packing it down to about a ¾-inch thickness. Sprinkle about 3 T of wheat germ over the top. Bake at 350° for 20 to 25 minutes.

Cut into 8 squares, put a dab of tomato sauce on each square, then garnish each with a little slice of cheese. Return to the oven for a moment so that cheese melts. To serve, lift out the squares with a wide spatula.

Makes 4 to 6 servings.

4 to 6 servings
Average serving = approx. 15 grams balanced protein
35 to 42% of daily protein need

Lentil Squares with Eggplant Sauce

A low brown loaf balancing lentils with sesame seeds and soy nuts, fortified with wheat germ, egg, and cheese, this is cut into squares and topped with a tomato sauce full of eggplant chunks.

1 c. dried lentils
2½ c. water
1 Vegex cube, ground
¼ c. lentil cooking liquid
¼ c. sesame seeds, ground
½ c. soy nuts, ground
1 c. pecan meal or chopped walnuts, or a combination
2 T wheat germ
2 T wheat bran
1 onion, chopped fine
¾ c. small chunks of Swiss cheese
1 egg, beaten
Eggplant Sauce (see recipe below)

Bring the 2½ c. water to a boil in a saucepan, and slowly add the lentils so that the water does not stop boiling as you add them. Cover and let simmer for 30 minutes. Add the ground Vegex, mixing it in well. Drain the liquid from the lentils and reserve it, partly for the loaf and the rest for the Eggplant Sauce.

Mash the lentils a bit in a mixing bowl, using a potato masher. Add the ¼ c. of the lentil cooking liquid, then stir in the ground sesame seeds, soy nuts, and pecans or walnuts. Mix in the wheat germ and bran.

Put in the chopped onion, cheese, and beaten egg, stirring all together well.

Press the mixture into a shallow square baking dish (8 x 8 x 2 inches) oiled with crude soy oil. Bake at 350° for 25 minutes. Cut into 9 squares to serve. Serve with Eggplant Sauce.

Makes 4 to 6 servings.

Eggplant Sauce

1 large or 2 medium eggplants
1 large onion, chopped
2 T oil
2 cups tomato sauce
Reserved lentil cooking liquid

Pare the eggplant if it is waxed, then cut into ½-inch chunks. Heat the oil in a large skillet and sauté the onion briefly, then add the eggplant and keep stirring over medium heat for 3 minutes. Pour in the tomato sauce and lentil cooking liquid, lower heat and simmer for 15 minutes, or until the eggplant is as soft as you like it. Serve over Lentil Squares.

4 to 6 servings
Average serving = approx. 16 grams balanced protein
37 to 44% of daily protein need

The Lentil Plant

Soy-Millet Loaf

A creamy-colored, small, firm-textured loaf with a delicious mild taste, made from a quick blender batter of ground soaked soybeans and millet flour with nut meals and seasonings.

1 c. soaked soybeans, drained
¾ c. water
1 T oil
½ t onion powder
½ t celery seed
½ t oregano or basil
1 T soy sauce
2 t low-sodium chicken-like seasoning (optional)
½ c. raw millet, ground to fine flour
2 T cashew nuts, ground
2 T sunflower seeds, ground
¼ c. minced onion

Put the first eight ingredients (soybeans through seasoning) in a blender container and purée until perfectly smooth. Pour the mixture into a bowl. Stir in the ground millet, mixing well. Fold in the nut and seed meals and minced onion.

Pour the batter into a small loaf tin (about 1½ pints) which has been oiled with liquid lecithin or crude soy oil. Bake at 350° for about 1 hour, or until the top is crusty and a thin skewer inserted in the middle of the loaf comes out clean.

Makes 3 to 4 servings.

Variation: For *Baked Vegetarian Hash*, omit the onion powder through soy sauce, but add ½ t Vege-Sal and ¼ t poultry seasoning. Stir these prepared vegetables into the batter: 1 medium potato and 1 carrot, grated; 1 stalk celery and 1 small onion, finely chopped; 2 T parsley and 2 T pimiento, chopped. Add 1 T mayonnaise, if desired. Spread the batter in a shallow 8-inch square baking dish oiled with unrefined soy oil and lecithin. Bake at 375° for 45 minutes. Makes 4 servings.

3 to 4 servings
Average serving = approx. 12 grams balanced protein
28 to 34% of daily protein need

Three-Bean Pie

A pie-shaped soy-millet loaf combination filled with the traditional three-bean salad, mushrooms, and onion. It is served in wedges like pieces of pie for a nice change from the rectangular loaf.

1 t oil
½ c. chopped onion (1 medium)
1 c. chopped fresh mushrooms
1 c. soaked soybeans, drained
½ c. water
3 T tomato purée
1 T oil
1 T soy sauce
½ t Vege-Sal
½ c. millet, ground
¼ c. sesame seeds, ground
¼ c. sunflower seeds, ground
½ c. cooked kidney beans
½ c. cooked chick-peas
½ c. cooked green beans, cut in 1-inch pieces

In a small skillet, heat the 1 t oil and sauté the onion in it over moderate heat, stirring, for about 1 minute. Add the mushrooms, stir until they just begin to get tender; cover, shut off the heat, and let steam for a few minutes while you prepare the rest of the recipe.

Put the soaked soybeans in a blender container with the water, tomato purée, oil, soy sauce, and Vege-Sal. Blend until very smooth. Remove to a bowl.

Mix in the ground millet, sesame, and sunflower seeds. Stir in the cooked beans (previously seasoned, if you prefer), and the sautéed vegetables.

Oil a 9-inch pie plate with soybean oil or liquid lecithin. Pour the food mixture into the plate and smooth the top of it. Bake at 350° for 30 to 40 minutes, or until a cake tester comes out clean when inserted in the center of the pie. Cut into 8 segments to serve.

4 servings
Average serving = approx. 13 grams balanced protein
30 to 36% of daily protein need

Mock Turkey Loaf

A soy-batter loaf filled with a savory bread and vegetable stuffing, served in slices with brown gravy and cranberry sauce. For a festive half-round shape, bake the loaf in a well-oiled Pyrex bowl and turn it out onto a round or oval platter, then surround it with holiday fruit or vegetable garnishes.

Batter:

2 c. soaked soybeans, drained
¾ c. milk or water
2 T low-sodium chicken-like seasoning
1 t Vege-sal
½ t garlic powder
2 T oil
1 c. millet, ground to fine flour
⅔ c. pecans, ground
1 medium onion, chopped
1 large stalk celery, chopped
1 T oil

Purée the soybeans with the milk or water in a blender until absolutely smooth. Add the chicken-like seasoning, Vege-Sal, garlic powder, and 2 T oil. Blend until mixed.

Pour the batter into a mixing bowl, removing the residue with a narrow flexible spatula. Stir millet flour and ground pecans into the batter.

Lightly sauté the onion and celery in 1 T oil. Fold the vegetables into the batter.

Stuffing:

½ c. chopped celery
½ c. chopped onion
1 T oil
½ c. grated carrot
¼ c. chopped fresh parsley
1½ c. whole wheat bread cubes (or 1 c. bread cubes plus 1 c. chopped mushrooms)
½ t crushed sage
½ t ground thyme
3 T soy flour
3 T chick-pea flour
⅓ c. water
¼ t Vege-Sal
1½ t soy sauce
⅛ t garlic powder

Lightly sauté the celery and onion in 1 T oil. Remove from the heat. Stir in the grated carrot, parsley, bread cubes (or bread cubes and mushrooms), sage, and thyme.

In a mixing bowl, combine the soy and chick-pea flours with water, Vege-Sal, soy sauce, and garlic powder. Mix well.

Fold the bread and vegetable mixture into flour-water batter and mix well.

Assembly:

Oil a large (9⅝- x 5½- x 2¾-inch) loaf pan with unrefined soy oil and lecithin. Line the bottom of the pan with oiled foil.

Pour half of the soybean batter into the pan. Pile the stuffing in the middle of the batter, leaving a 1-inch border of batter clear of stuffing around the edges. Smooth the remaining batter over the stuffing, filling in the borders.

Bake at 350° for 1 hour, or until the loaf is brown and crusty, and a cake tester comes out clean. Let cool for 10 minutes, then loosen with a knife inserted between the edges of the loaf and pan.

Turn out onto an oval or rectangular platter. Peel off the liner carefully if it sticks to the loaf.

Makes 6 to 8 servings.

Variation: For an attractive loaf with "light meat" and "dark meat," mix the ground pecans (or use ground walnuts) with only a little less than half of the soybean batter. Spread the plain butter on the bottom of the foil-lined oiled loaf pan or metal bowl. Then spread the stuffing mixture, varied by using 2 beaten eggs instead of the soy and chick-pea flours and ⅓ c. water. (Use 1 t poultry seasoning instead of sage and thyme.) Spread the remaining batter mixed with nut meal over the stuffing, then bake as directed.

Brown Gravy

1 c. vegetable cooking water
1 Vegex cube
1 t low-sodium chicken-like seasoning
1 T cornstarch
2 T cold water

In a saucepan, heat the vegetable cooking water with crumbled Vegex cube and 1 t chicken-like seasoning.

Combine cornstarch with 2 T cold water in a small cup, mixing well. Add cornstarch mixture to heated liquid, stirring constantly until mixture boils. Let boil gently for 1 minute.

Serve gravy with Mock Turkey Loaf.

Cranberry Sauce

2 c. fresh (or frozen) whole cranberries
¾ c. apple juice
⅓-½ c. honey

Put cranberries in a blender container with ¾ c. apple juice. Blend until puréed. Heat the cranberry mixture in saucepan until it comes to a boil. Stir in honey and let simmer for 5 to 10 minutes, covered. Serve chilled.

Makes about 1½ c. of sauce.

6 to 8 servings
Average serving = approx. 11 grams balanced protein
26 to 31% of daily protein need

Spring Holiday Roast

An unusual oval-shaped ham-style roast with fillings of savory greens, covered with a honey glaze and served with a creamy mustard sauce.

1 c. soaked soybeans, drained
¾ c. tomato purée
⅓ c. water
1 T oil
½ t Vege-Sal
1 T soy sauce
½ c. millet, ground to flour
⅓ c. pine nuts, ground
¼ c. wheat germ
¼ c. bran
2 T Bakon Yeast
1 small onion, chopped
Celery tops from 1 stalk, chopped
1 package frozen spinach, kale, or mustard greens, mostly defrosted
1 t oil

Put the soaked soybeans, tomato purée, water, 1 T oil, Vege-Sal, and soy sauce in a blender container. Blend until smooth. Remove batter to a bowl, getting out all of it with a flexible spatula.

Stir millet flour and ground pine nuts into the batter. Add wheat germ, bran, and Bakon Yeast. Mix well.

Heat 1 T oil in a small skillet. Sauté the onion and celery. Add spinach, stirring until it is warmed through. (Other greens need longer cooking. Steam them for a few minutes over low heat.)

Oil a 1-quart oval baking dish with unrefined soy oil and liquid lecithin. Pour about one-third of the soybean batter into the bottom of the dish.

With a spoon, take dabs of the vegetable filling and drop them at random over the batter. Pour more batter over the first layer, covering the fillings. Place more dabs of filling over this layer. Repeat until all is used, ending with a layer of batter.

Bake at 350° for 1 hour, or until a cake tester comes out clean from the center of the loaf. Let cool for 10 minutes so that the loaf will be firm when you loosen it with a knife between the edge of the loaf and the dish. Slide a nylon spatula down the side of the loaf to loosen it underneath.

Turn the loaf onto an oval platter. (Have the loaf dish right-side up on the countertop. Place the platter over it, upside down. Using potholders, turn everything over, holding baking dish and platter together. If the loaf is sufficiently loosened, it will come out as a beautiful oval mound onto the platter.)

Glaze the loaf with the honey glaze described below. Surround it with watercress, cooked baby carrots, and slices of yellow squash. Serve with Creamy Mustard Sauce.

Makes 4 to 6 servings.

Honey Glaze

1½ t cider vinegar
2 T honey
½ t prepared (wet) mustard

Combine all ingredients in a cup and mix thoroughly. Spread the glaze over the loaf.

Creamy Mustard Sauce

⅓ c. mayonnaise
⅓ c. yogurt
1½ T prepared mustard

Mix mayonnaise and yogurt thoroughly in a small bowl. Stir in mustard to taste. Serve with ham style roast.

4 to 6 servings
Average serving = approx. 11 grams balanced protein
26 to 31% daily protein need

Baked Ring Mold

An attractively different pimiento, parsley, and tiny onion filled loaf in the shape of a wreath, made from a soybean, chick-pea, and millet batter with sunflower seed meal added for flavor and a substantial texture. This makes a lovely company entrée served with a green vegetable piled in the center. Garnish the ring with parsley and pimiento for your holiday buffet table.

1¼ c. soaked soybeans, drained
⅔ c. soaked chickpeas, drained
2 c. water or vegetable stock (include reserved onion liquid)
1 t Vege-Sal
2 T soy sauce
2 t low-sodium chicken-like seasoning
2 T oil
½ c. raw millet, ground (⅔ c. millet flour)
⅔ c. sunflower seeds, ground (1 c. sunflower meal)
1 bottle (5 ozs.) sweet cocktail onions (reserve vinegar)
⅓ c. chopped fresh parsley
2-3 T chopped pimientos

Put the drained soybeans and chick-peas in a blender container. Measure the vinegar from the cocktail onions in a measuring cup. Add enough water to make 1 c. altogether. Pour this liquid into the blender container. Add another cup of water or vegetable water. Blend until the mixture is absolutely smooth. Add the Vege-Sal, soy sauce, chicken-like seasoning, and oil. Whirl until mixed. Pour the batter into a bowl.

Stir in the millet flour and sunflower seed meal, mixing in well. Fold in chopped parsley, pimientos, and whole cocktail onions.

Have ready a 4-cup ring mold well greased with unrefined soy oil and lecithin. Pour the batter into the mold and bake at 350° for 45 minutes. Put a foil tent over the pan to prevent excessive browning and bake another 20 minutes, or until a cake tester comes out clean from the middle of the ring.

When done, run a knife between loaf and pan until loaf is loosened, and turn out onto a round platter. Garnish the ring with additional pimiento slices and parsley, if desired. To serve, fill the ring with broccoli or another green vegetable.

For sandwich slices, bake this recipe in a loaf pan.

6 to 8 servings
Average serving = approx. 11 grams balanced protein
26 to 31% of daily protein need

Soy Batter Tamale Loaf

A golden square loaf of light texture, combining the proteins of soybeans, millet, and cornmeal. The vegetables inside it provide a variety of crunchy bits and unusual flavors: tomatoes, corn, green peppers, onion, celery, and olives.

1 c. soaked soybeans, drained
¾ c. water or vegetable liquid
1 t Vege-Sal
1 T oil
⅓ c. millet, ground to flour
⅓ c. cornmeal
1 onion, chopped (¾ c.)
1 stalk celery, chopped (½ c.)
½ green pepper, chopped (¾ c.)
1 T oil
1 can (16 ozs.) stewed tomatoes, drained
1¼ c. frozen corn, mostly defrosted; or canned corn, drained
¼ c. sliced Spanish olives
½ c. chopped black olives

Put the soaked soybeans in a blender container with the water (or vegetable liquid), Vege-Sal, and oil. Blend until very smooth and creamy. Pour the batter into a mixing bowl, scraping out the residue with a narrow rubber spatula.

Stir the ground millet and cornmeal into the soybean batter.

Heat the 1 T oil and sauté the chopped onion, celery, and green pepper very briefly—just until heated through. Pour the vegetables into the soy batter.

Stir in the drained tomatoes and the corn. Add the olives. Mix well.

Oil a square (about 10 inches) 2-quart shallow casserole dish with unrefined soy oil and lecithin. Pour the soybean batter into it. Smooth the surface of the batter with a large spoon.

Bake at 350° for 1 hour, or until a cake tester comes out clean from the center of the loaf.

4 to 5 servings
Average serving = approx. 10 grams balanced protein
23 to 28% of daily protein need

Soy-Vegesquares

A complementary soy-sesame combination filled with mushrooms and other vegetable bits, cut into delicate squares and served with creamy sauce.

1 c. soaked soybeans, drained
⅓ c. water
1 t Vege-Sal
⅓ c. sesame seeds, ground
½ c. chopped walnuts
½ c. wheat germ
½ c. chopped fresh parsley
1 T oil
4 stalks of celery, minced
2 medium carrots, grated
1 medium onion, minced
2 c. sliced fresh mushrooms
Creamy Sauce (see recipe below)

Purée the soybeans in a blender container with the water and Vege-Sal. Remove to a bowl, then stir in sesame meal, chopped walnuts, and wheat germ. Fold in the parsley.

Sauté the celery, carrots, and onion in a skillet, using 1 T oil. Add the mushrooms and stir briefly over heat. Pour the vegetables into the soybean mixture. Mix well.

Pack the mixture into a shallow rectangular pan or Pyrex dish (1½-quart) greased with crude soybean oil or liquid lecithin. The mixture will be only about 1 inch thick. Bake at 350° for about 1 hour, or until top is brown and crusty. To serve, cut into 8 squares and lift them out carefully with a spatula. Garnish with Creamy Sauce.

Makes 4 servings.

Creamy Sauce

1 T butter or oil
2 T whole wheat pastry flour
1 c. milk
½ t Vege-Sal

Heat the butter or oil in a small non-stick saucepan over medium heat. Stir in the flour until mixed well with the fat. Gradually add the milk, blending it with the flour mixture, and cook, stirring constantly, until the mixture thickens and bubbles, for 1 minute. Add Vege-Sal to taste.

4 servings
Average serving = approx. 13 grams balanced protein
30 to 36% of daily protein need

Ham-style Loaf

A savory textured loaf made with chopped ham-style granule burger, egg, and milk.

Basic Recipe for Chopped Ham-style Bulgar Wheat Granule Burger*
½ c. finely chopped onion
1 egg, slightly beaten
½ t dry mustard
½ c. evaporated milk
2 T chopped parsley

If desired, substitute ¼ c. pecans, ground, for the nuts in the Bulgar Wheat Granule Burger recipe.

Mix the onion, egg, dry mustard, milk, and chopped parsley into the granule burger mixture.

Oil a small loaf tin (about 1 quart) with unrefined soy oil and lecithin. Pour the granule burger mixture into the tin. Bake at 350° for 30 to 40 minutes, or until the loaf is firm and lightly browned. Let the loaf stand for 10 minutes before turning out onto a serving dish.

4 to 6 servings
Average serving = approx. 12 grams balanced protein
28 to 34% of daily protein need

Savory Ring Loaf

Onion-flavored granule burger mix fortified with sunflower seed meal, milk and eggs, baked in a ring mold, inverted onto a platter, then served sliced with mushroom sauce.

3 c. dry Granule Burger mix*
½ c. sunflower seeds, ground
1½ c. hot water or vegetable liquid
1½ T soy sauce (1 T plus 1½ t)
¼ c. dehydrated onion soup mix
¾ c. hot water
½ c. evaporated milk
3 T catsup
1 T Worcestershire sauce
2 eggs, beaten
Mushroom Sauce (see recipe below)

Put 3 c. dry granule burger mix in a mixing bowl. (Use 1½ times the basic recipe, or 3 c. of convenience mix. To halve ⅓ c., use 3 T. To halve ¼ c. use 2 T.) Stir the ground sunflower seeds into the mix.

Stir the soy sauce into 1½ c. hot water. Pour the liquid into the dry mix, stirring well.

Dissolve the ¼ c. onion soup mix in ¾ c. hot water. Pour it into the granule burger mix, distributing it throughout. Add the evaporated milk, catsup, Worcestershire sauce, and beaten eggs. Mix thoroughly.

Oil a 1-quart ring mold with unrefined soy oil and liquid lecithin. (If you omit the lecithin, some of the loaf will probably stick in the pan.) Pour the granule burger mixture into the pan. Smooth the surface of it with the back of a spoon. Bake at 350° for 30 minutes.

Loosen the ring mold after letting it stand for 10 minutes. Insert a table knife between the loaf and the sides of the pan, running it all the way around. Do it also around the smaller center ring. Place a serving platter over the pan. Invert everything (using potholders to prevent burns) while holding the platter and ring mold together. The ring loaf should drop out onto the platter so that you can lift away the mold pan. Serve slices of the loaf with Mushroom Sauce. (This loaf is attractive filled with peas and encircled on the top with cooked carrot slices.)

Makes 4 to 6 servings.

Mushroom Sauce

1 T oil
2 T whole wheat pastry flour
½ c. reserved liquid from can of sliced mushrooms
¼ c. milk or evaporated milk
Dash Vege-Sal
1 (8 ozs.) can sliced mushrooms

Heat the oil in a saucepan over moderate heat. Stir in flour, mixing thoroughly. Gradually add mushroom liquid, stirring constantly, until mixture bubbles and thickens. Stir in milk, Vege-Sal and sliced mushrooms. Heat through. Serve with ring loaf.

4 to 6 servings
Average serving = approx. 17 grams balanced protein
39 to 47% of daily protein need

The Sunflower

Cheese-Nut Loaf with Mushroom Sauce

Cheese, milk, and egg complement soy, nuts, rice and oats in this mushroom-flavored loaf with sauce.

1 c. coarsely shredded Cheddar cheese
1 c. soy nuts, ground
¾ c. walnut meal
½ c. cooked brown rice
¼ c. rolled oats
1 egg, beaten
½ c. milk
¼-½ c. finely chopped mushrooms
1 medium onion, minced
1 clove garlic, minced
Mushroom Sauce (see recipe below)

Combine all ingredients in a large bowl and mix well. Allow to stand a few minutes for the soy nuts and oats to absorb moisture.

Grease a 1-quart loaf pan or baking dish with liquid lecithin or crude soy oil. Pack the loaf mixture firmly into the loaf pan or dish and bake in a 350° oven for about 50 minutes, or until firm and browned on top.

Let the pan stand for 10 minutes after removing from the oven. Loosen with a knife or spatula and turn out on platter. Cut into 4 portions and serve with Mushroom Sauce.

Makes 4 to 6 servings.

Mushroom Sauce

1½ T oil
1 c. sliced mushrooms
1½ T whole wheat pastry flour
1 c. milk
additional grated cheese (optional)

Heat 1½ tablespoons of oil in a saucepan. Add 1 c. of sliced mushrooms and sauté briefly. Stir in the flour, coating the mushrooms. Gradually add 1 c. milk, stirring until the sauce thickens and bubbles a bit. More grated cheese may be added if desired.

4 to 6 servings
Average serving = approx. 13 grams balanced protein
30 to 36% of daily protein need

Soy Granules and Millet Loaf

Complementary soy and millet bound with eggs make a wholesome delicate loaf with vegetable bits inside.

½ c. millet
1½ c. water
½ c. dry soy granules
Water or cooking water
2 eggs
¼ c. tomato juice
1 T butter or oil
½ c. chopped green pepper
½ c. chopped green onions
½ c. chopped fresh mushrooms
½ t marjoram, crushed
1-2 t Vege-Sal

Cook the millet by bringing 1½ c. water to a boil, stirring in the millet, and allowing it to steam, covered, over low heat for about 30 minutes.

Put ½ c. dry soy granules in a measuring cup and add enough water or vegetable cooking water to make a total of 1 c. Let the mixture soak for about 10 minutes.

Beat the 2 eggs in a bowl and stir in the tomato juice. Mix in the cooked millet and soaked soy granules.

Heat the butter or oil in a skillet and sauté the green peppers and the white parts of the green onions until just barely tender. Stir in the mushrooms briefly to absorb a bit of oil. Pour the vegetables into the millet-soy mixture.

Stir the mixture well, adding the marjoram and Vege-Sal to taste. Pack well into a loaf pan oiled with lecithin or crude soy oil, and bake at 350° for 45 minutes. Serve portions with tomato sauce, if desired.

3 to 4 servings
Average serving = approx. 13 grams balanced protein
30 to 36% of daily protein need

Tamale Loaf

A golden square loaf of light texture, combining the proteins of cornmeal, millet, and soy nuts. The vegetables inside (tomatoes, corn, green peppers, onion, celery and olives) provide a variety of crunchy bits and unusual flavors.

2 T olive oil
1 onion, chopped
⅓ c. chopped celery
1 medium green pepper, chopped
1 c. water plus reserved liquid from tomatoes and corn
½ t paprika
⅓ c. cornmeal
⅓ c. millet, ground to flour
2 c. stewed tomatoes (16 oz. can)
1¼ c. canned corn, drained (12 oz. can) (reserve liquid)
½ c. chopped black olives
¼ c. sliced Spanish olives
⅓ c. chopped pecans
⅓ c. soy nuts, ground
2 eggs, beaten

Sauté the onion, green pepper, and celery in the olive oil, using a large skillet. Add the water and paprika. Bring to a boil, then add the mixture of cornmeal and millet flour gradually, stirring constantly. Lower heat and cook, covered, for 10 minutes.

Stir in the tomatoes, corn, olives, pecans, ground soy nuts, and eggs. Mix well.

Transfer the mixture to a 2-quart shallow casserole oiled with liquid lecithin and crude soy oil. Bake at 350° for 45 minutes. Cut into 4 squares to serve.

4 servings
Average serving = approx. 11 grams balanced protein
26 to 31% of daily protein need

Oven Patties and Individual Forms

Oven patties are ideal foods for the creative cook. Not only can you make simple little patties, like Cashew Patties, Wheat Germ Sunflower Patties, and Soy Grits Cheeseburgers by baking circles of batter on a cookie sheet; you can also make croquettes, cutlets, balls, little loaves, and various filled or stuffed muffin-shaped containers using food batters.

Versatile soybean batter makes lovely croquettes when baked in muffin tins. Serve the meaty muffins inverted, with a sauce garnish. Try Soy-Muffin Croquettes, Country Croquettes, Ham-style Croquettes, and Soy Flakes Timbales. You can bake these in miniature loaf tins, too.

We have some nice easy-to-make cutlet variations: Soy Curd Sunflower Cutlets, Vegenut Cutlets, and Cottage Cheese Cutlets, one of our very best company dishes, with tomato sauce and melted cheese. Our version of Felafels is baked instead of deep-fried. The recipe for Soy Balls with Cheese Sauce is a variation of the felafel idea. Instead of fish sticks and fillets, try our Fish-style Soy Curd Sticks and Soy Curd Fillets, also baked instead of deep-fried. They're delicious with coleslaw.

One of the most appealing ideas for individual oven shapes is a burger-like container or cup filled with savory bread stuffing and vegetable bits, spinach, and cheese, or pizza sauce garnished with strips of cheese. Try Vegetable-stuffed Granule Burger Cups, Stuffed Meat Muffins and Pizza Burgers.

A beautiful and delicious dish can be made with crisp potato patties topped with granule burger, sliced tomato, and melted cheese: Tomato-Burger Hash Browns.

You'll think of many variations of these basic recipes, using different stuffings and different baking tin shapes.

Cashew Patties

An easy baked cashew nut patty made with the complementary proteins of wheat flour and soybean batter, seasoned with onion, and served with a mushroom sauce.

1 c. soaked soybeans, drained
½ can (10½ ozs.) condensed mushroom soup
¼ c. milk
⅓ c. cashew nuts, ground
¼ c. gluten flour (or whole wheat flour)
2 T wheat germ
2 T bran
1 medium onion, chopped
2 t oil
Mushroom Sauce (see recipe below)

Put the soybeans, soup, and milk in a blender container. Blend until the bean particles are very fine. Pour the mixture into a bowl, scraping the residue out with a rubber spatula.

Stir in the ground cashews and gluten flour (or whole wheat flour). Mix in the wheat germ and bran.

Heat the 2 t oil in a small skillet and sauté the onion until it starts to soften; then stir it into the batter.

With a spoon, place 8 patties (about 2½ inches in diameter) on an unoiled non-stick baking sheet. Bake at 350° for 25 minutes.

Makes 4 servings.

Mushroom Sauce

Serve patties with a sauce made by heating a mixture of the remaining condensed mushroom soup and another ¼ c. milk.

4 servings
Average serving = approx. 11 grams balanced protein
26 to 31% of daily protein need

Wheat Germ Sunflower Patties

Patties made of cottage cheese blended with eggs, wheat germ, sunflower seed meal, and herbs, served with eggplant sauce.

1 Vegex cube, crushed
1 T hot water
2 eggs
1 c. cottage cheese
1 onion, minced
½ t thyme
¼ c. chopped fresh parsley
½ c. sunflower seeds, ground
½ c. wheat germ
Eggplant Sauce (optional)
(see page 62)

In a mixing bowl, dissolve the crushed Vegex cube in the hot water. Add the eggs and beat them well. Stir in the cottage cheese, breaking up the curds with a fork and mixing well. Add the minced onion.

Mix in the thyme and parsley, then the ground sunflower seeds and wheat germ. With a spoon, smooth the batter evenly to form a flat surface in the bowl, then divide the surface into quarters by drawing lines with the spoon. Scoop out each large quarter and divide it in half to make 2 patties. You will have 8 patties altogether.

Bake the patties on a lightly oiled cookie sheet at 350° for 20 minutes. Serve with Eggplant Sauce, if desired.

4 servings
Average serving = approx. 15 grams balanced protein
35 to 42% of daily protein need

Soy Grits Cheeseburgers

A quick and easy baked soyburger balanced with wheat and ground sesame or sunflower seeds, topped with melted cheese.

½ c. quick-cooking soy grits or ½ c. soy granules
1 c. water
1 small onion, chopped (divided)
1 garlic clove, chopped
Pinch white pepper
½ t oregano
½ t Vege-Sal
1 egg, beaten, or egg substitute (see below)
2 T wheat germ
2 T bran
1 T chick-pea flour
1 slice whole wheat bread, crumbed
¼ c. sesame or sunflower seeds, ground
6 thin slices of Swiss cheese

Bring the 1 c. water to a boil in a small saucepan. Add the soy grits or granules. Add half of the chopped onion and all of the chopped garlic. Cover, lower heat, and simmer for 5 minutes.

Stir in the pepper, oregano, and Vege-Sal. Remove to a mixing bowl. Add the remaining chopped onion.

Add the dry ingredients (wheat germ, bran, crumbs, chick-pea flour, and ground seeds). Mix well. Stir in beaten egg or egg substitute.

Make 6 patties on a non-stick baking sheet by filling a circular hamburger shaper with a spoon. Bake at 350° for 20 minutes.

Add Swiss cheese slices to the patties. Bake another 2 minutes, or until the cheese is melted.

Egg Substitute

1 T whole wheat pastry flour
1 T chick-pea flour
2 T water
Pinch Vege-Sal

Combine all ingredients in a cup and blend together well with a fork. Add to the recipe in place of one beaten egg. This is a binding substitute.

3 servings
Average serving = approx. 12 grams balanced protein
28 to 34% of daily protein need

Soy Muffin Croquettes

Individual chicken-style croquettes shaped as upside-down muffins and garnished with white sauce. A blender batter of soybeans, seasonings, ground nuts, millet flour, and chopped vegetables, baked in a muffin tin.

1 c. soaked soybeans, drained
¾ c. water
1 T oil
½ t onion powder
½ t basil or poultry seasoning
1 T soy sauce
2 t low-sodium chicken-like seasoning (optional)
¼ c. cashew nuts, ground
½ c. millet, ground to fine flour
¼ c. chopped onion, sautéed
½ green pepper, minced and sautéed
1 c. White Sauce (see recipe below)

Put the first seven ingredients (soybeans through seasoning) in a blender container. Purée for 60 seconds, or until absolutely smooth.

Pour the batter into a bowl and add the ground nuts and millet flour. Stir in the sautéed onion and green pepper.

Spoon the batter into a 6-muffin tin oiled with liquid lecithin or crude soy oil, filling the compartments just barely level with the top of the tin. (The batter expands very little when baked.) Put the remaining small amount of batter into an oiled custard cup of comparable size.

Bake at 350° for 25 to 30 minutes, or until the muffins are slightly crusty. Remove them to a serving platter, narrow end up, and pour about 2 tablespoons of white sauce over each one. Garnish with parsley, if desired.

Makes 3 to 4 servings.

White Sauce

1 T butter or oil
1 T cornstarch or 2 t arrowroot
1 c. milk
½ t Vege-Sal or to taste

Heat the butter or oil in a small non-stick saucepan over medium heat. Blend in the cornstarch or arrowroot. Remove from the heat. Gradually add the milk, mixing until smooth. Return to medium heat, stirring constantly, until the sauce thickens and comes to a boil. Boil for 1 minute. Add the Vege-Sal to taste.

Variations: Add ¼ t garlic powder; substitute ¼ t rosemary and ¼ t thyme for the basil. Substitute ¼ c. wheat germ for the cashew nuts; ½ c.

chopped green onion for the onion; or 3 to 4 chopped mushrooms for the green pepper. Add cheese to the white sauce.

3 to 4 servings
Average serving = approx. 12 grams balanced protein
28 to 34% of daily protein need

The Soybean Plant

Country Croquettes

Crunchy outside, tender inside, these chicken-style soy-millet batter croquettes are made with celery, onion, and grated potato with a whole wheat bread crumb coating. They are served with gravy.

1 c. soaked soybeans, drained
¾ c. water or milk
1 T oil
½ t Vege-Sal
1 T low-sodium chicken-like soup base
½ c. millet, ground fine
1 medium potato, grated
1 stalk celery, finely chopped
1 small onion, chopped
2 t oil
3 slices whole wheat bread, crumbed (1½ c. fresh crumbs)
Country Gravy (see recipe below)

Put the soybeans and liquid in a blender container with the oil, Vege-Sal, and chicken-like seasoning. Purée until the bean particles are fine. Pour the batter into a bowl.

Mix in the ground millet and then the grated potato.

Sauté the celery and onion in 2 t oil over medium heat until they start to become tender. Add the vegetables to the soy batter, mixing them in well.

Divide the batter in the bowl into 8 portions with the tip of your spoon. Scoop out each portion with the spoon, dropping it into the plate filled with whole wheat bread crumbs. Roll each croquette well in the crumbs and set it on an ungreased non-stick baking sheet, forming a peak with your fingers for a cone-shaped croquette. Make 8 of these.

Bake at 350° for 30 minutes. Serve croquettes with Country Gravy.

Makes 4 servings.

Country Gravy

1-2 T butter or oil
2 T whole wheat pastry flour
1 c. milk or vegetable water
½ t Vege-Sal
2 t low sodium chicken-like seasoning

Heat the butter or oil in a small non-stick saucepan over medium heat. Stir in flour until blended with the fat. Gradually add milk, stirring constantly, until the mixture thickens and bubbles for a minute. Stir in Vege-

Sal and chicken-like seasoning, mixing until they are dissolved. Serve gravy over Country Croquettes.

4 servings
Average serving = approx. 11 grams balanced protein
26 to 31% of daily protein need

Ham-style Croquettes or Little Loaves

A tomato-pink soybean and millet flour batter bakes into individual servings with a subtle smoked ham-like flavor from Bakon Yeast and ground pine nuts. Serve these croquettes or small loaves with a white or cheese sauce garnish.

1 t oil
1 stalk celery, minced
1 medium onion, minced
1 c. soaked soybeans, drained
¾ c. tomato purée
⅓ c. water
1 T olive oil
1 T soy sauce
1 T Bakon Yeast
¼ t sage
½ t Vege-Sal
½ c. millet, ground fine
⅓ c. pine nuts, ground
1 T bacon-flavored bits (optional)
White Sauce or Cheese Sauce (see recipes below)

Heat 1 t oil in a small skillet. Add the celery and onion, stirring 2 minutes over moderate heat. Cover, remove from heat, and allow to steam while you prepare the rest of the recipe.

Put the soaked soybeans in a blender container with the tomato purée, water, oil, soy sauce, yeast, sage, and Vege-Sal. Blend until smooth. Pour the mixture into a bowl, extracting it all with a rubber spatula.

Stir the ground millet, pine nuts, and optional bacon bits into the soybean mixture. Fold in the sautéed onions and celery.

Oil an 8-cup muffin tin with soybean oil or liquid lecithin. Distribute the food mixture evenly among the cups, filling not quite to the rim—about ¼ inch from the top. Bake at 350° for 30 minutes.

For little loaves, fill 5 miniature loaf tins (4¾ x 2½ x 1 inches deep, measured across the rim and down the side) just barely to the top. Bake at 350° for 30 minutes.

Turn out the croquettes or loaves on a platter and serve with White Sauce or Cheese Sauce and sprigs of parsley, if desired.

Makes 4 servings.

White Sauce

2 T oil
2 T whole wheat pastry flour
¼ t Vege-Sal
1 c. hot milk

Put the oil, flour, and Vege-Sal in a blender container. Add a little hot milk. Gradually add the rest of the hot milk while blending. Pour the mixture into a saucepan and stir for 2 to 3 minutes over moderate heat until the sauce bubbles.

Cheese Sauce

Add ¼ c. Cheddar cheese cubes into the above sauce while it is still hot and stir until the cheese melts.

4 servings
Average serving = approx. 11 grams balanced protein
26 to 31% of daily protein need

Soy Flakes Timbales

Moist tender half-rounds of protein flakes and nut meals bound with a light egg and milk custard, containing succulent vegetable chunks, these timbales are baked in custard cups.

1 egg
½ c. milk
1 t soy sauce
½ c. cooked soy flakes
½ c. sesame seeds, ground
¼ c. soy nuts, ground
1 c. whole wheat bread cubes
½ c. chopped green onions
½ c. chopped fresh tomatoes
1 T oil

Beat the egg in bowl and add the milk. Stir in the soy sauce. Mix in the cooked soy flakes, seed meal, soy nut meal and bread cubes, allowing the mixture to stand for the moisture to be absorbed.

Heat the oil in a small skillet and sauté onion and tomato in it briefly. Pour the vegetables into the mixture in the bowl and stir well until distributed throughout the other ingredients.

Spoon the mixture into four 4-ounce custard cups oiled with unrefined soy oil or liquid lecithin. Bake at 350° for 30 minutes, or until the timbales are firm. Turn out upside-down on a serving platter.

Makes 4 servings.

Note: To cook soy flakes, bring 2 c. water to a boil, add 1 c. of soy flakes, and simmer for 1 hour, covered.

4 servings
Average serving = approx. 11 grams balanced protein
26 to 31% of daily protein need

Muffin Soy-Meat Loaves

Savory individual soy-meat loaves covered with a creamy brown sauce—a blender batter baked in muffin cups.

1 c. soaked soybeans
½ c. soaked garbanzo beans
¾ c. water
1½ T oil
2 t soy sauce
1 Vegex cube, ground
1 T nutritional yeast
1 t Gravy Master
1 t cereal coffee
¼ t ground thyme
½ c. rolled oats
½ c. sesame seeds, ground (⅔ c. meal)
1 small onion, chopped
1 carrot, grated (about ⅓ c.)
2 heaping T mayonnaise
1 T dried parsley or handful fresh minced parsley

Put the beans, water, oil, soy sauce, and seasonings up to thyme in a blender container. Purée until absolutely smooth. Remove the batter to a bowl. Stir in the rolled oats and ground sesame seeds.

Sauté the chopped onion and grated carrot in a skillet using 1 t oil. Add to the batter. Stir in the mayonnaise and parsley.

Place the batter in a 6-muffin tin which has been oiled with liquid lecithin. Heap the batter on each muffin to form a rounded top, so that all of the mixture fits in the tin. Bake at 350° for 30 to 40 minutes, or until a dry crust has formed and a thin skewer comes out clean when inserted.

Makes 3 to 4 servings.

Serve over wheat-soy noodles with *sauce:*

1 T oil
2 T whole wheat pastry flour
1 Vegex cube, ground
1 c. water
½ t Gravy Master
¼ c. sour cream or yogurt

Using medium heat, warm the oil in a non-stick saucepan and gradually stir in the flour, mixing well. Slowly pour in the water and ground Vegex while stirring so that the flour mixture is dissolved. Keep stirring until the sauce thickens and bubbles a bit. Stir in the Gravy Master. Remove the sauce from heat and mix in the sour cream or yogurt. Pour some sauce over each round muffin loaf.

3 to 4 servings
Average serving = approx. 11 grams balanced protein
26 to 31% of daily protein need

Soy Curd-Sunflower Patties

Soy curd, sesame and sunflower meal combine with wheat, egg, parsley, and onion for an oven patty with excellent flavor, texture, and consistency.

2 T Wheatena
½ c. water
1 c. Soy Curd*
½ c. sunfl ower seeds, ground
¼ c. sesame seeds, ground
¼ c. wheat germ
1 T parsley, minced
1 small onion, minced
1 egg, beaten
1 T soy sauce
1 T catsup

Bring ½ c. water to a boil and stir in the Wheatena. Lower the heat and simmer for 5 minutes, covered.

Mix the soy curd with the seed meals and wheat germ in a mixing bowl. Stir in the cooked Wheatena. Add the parsley and onion.

Beat the egg in a small bowl. Mix in the soy sauce and catsup. Pour the liquid into soy curd mixture, stirring until well blended.

Make 8 patties by spooning the soy curd mixture onto a lightly oiled cookie sheet. Bake at 350° for 20 to 25 minutes.

Makes 4 servings.

Variation: To make 4 *cutlets*, omit Wheatena. Use 8 c. minced celery instead of parsley. Make 4 cutlet shapes about ½ inch thick from the mixture, and roll them in seasoned coating mix.* Bake at 350° on a small cookie sheet, lightly oiled, for 25 minutes.

4 servings
Average serving = approx. 14 grams balanced protein
32 to 39% of daily protein need

Vegenut Cutlets

A simply made baked cutlet of nutmeals and sautéed vegetable bits bound with a soybean batter, served with an easy cheese sauce.

¼ c. walnuts, ground
¼ c. almonds, ground
¼ c. pecans, ground
½ c. sunflower seeds, ground
2 T sesame seeds, ground
2 T wheat germ
½ t garlic powder
½ t paprika
½ t Vege-Sal
¼ t marjoram, crushed
½ c. soaked soybeans, drained
⅓ c. water
1 stalk celery, minced
1 small onion, minced
2 t oil
1 small carrot, grated
Cheese Sauce (see recipe below)

Mix the nut and seed meals and wheat germ together in a bowl. Stir in seasonings (garlic powder through marjoram).

Put the soaked soybeans in a blender container. Add ⅓ c. water and blend until smooth. Pour the batter into the nutmeal mixture. Mix well.

Heat 2 t oil in a small skillet. Sauté the celery and onion briefly. Remove from the heat, then stir in grated carrot. Fold the vegetables into nut and soy mixture.

Make 5 cutlets from the batter by dropping it from a large spoon onto a non-stick baking sheet. Smooth and shape them a bit with a spoon. Bake at 350° for 25 minutes. Serve with Cheese Sauce.

Makes 5 servings.

Cheese Sauce

2 t cornstarch
½ c. water
¼ c. instant powdered milk
¼ c. grated cheese

Mix the cornstarch and water in a small saucepan. Bring to a boil and let bubble for 1 minute. Reduce heat. Stir in powdered milk until it is dissolved. Mix in the grated cheese, stirring until melted. Serve with Vegenut Cutlets.

5 servings
Average serving = approx. 12 grams balanced protein
28 to 34% of daily protein need

Cottage Cheese Cutlets

Large baked ovals of cottage cheese and nutmeals bound with egg, topped with tomato sauce and melted cheese, then served on a bed of brown rice or wheat-soy noodles with more sauce.

2 eggs
1 c. cottage cheese
½ t marjoram, crushed
1 small onion, minced
1 Vegex cube, ground
2 T hot water
2 T wheat germ
2 T wheat bran
½ c. soy nuts, ground
½ c. pecan meal or walnut meal
Tomato Sauce*
5 thin cheese slices
Brown Rice or Wheat-Soy Noodles

Beat the eggs in a mixing bowl. Stir in the cottage cheese, breaking up the curds as you do so. Mix in the marjoram and minced onion.

Dissolve the ground Vegex cube in the hot water in a small cup. Add this liquid to the contents of the bowl.

Stir the wheat germ and bran into the bowl. Then mix in the ground soy nuts and pecan or walnut meal.

Oil a baking sheet with unrefined soy oil. Heap the mixture onto the sheet with a large spoon, making 5 oval patties. Bake at 350° for 20 minutes.

Remove from the oven, then spread each oval with one or two tablespoons of Tomato Sauce. Top each with a thin slice of cheese (mozzarella or Cheddar is good). Return to the oven until the cheese is melted, just a minute or so. Serve on a bed of brown rice or wheat-soy noodles.

5 servings
Average serving = approx. 13 grams balanced protein
30 to 36% of daily protein need

Felafels

A mildly seasoned, balanced vegetable protein version of the Middle Eastern chick-pea balls, including the ground sesame seeds in the balls themselves, which are not deep-fried, but baked instead. Additional sesame seed sauce may be served with the felafels.

2 c. soaked chick-peas
½ c. water
1 clove garlic, cut up
2 T or more fresh parsley
1 t Vege-Sal
½ t dried mustard
½ t tumeric
½ c. sesame seeds, ground
¼ c. wheat germ
¼ yeast flakes
½ c. whole wheat bread crumbs
1 T oil
Sesame Sauce (see recipe below)

Put the soaked chick-peas and the ½ c. of water in a blender container. Add the seasonings (garlic through turmeric). Blend until smooth.

Pour the mixture into a bowl. Stir in the ground sesame seeds and wheat germ. Mix well.

Mix together the yeast flakes and bread crumbs in a flat bowl. Stir in the oil until it is well blended with the dry mixure.

Using a teaspoon, drop hunks of the chick-pea mixture into the bread crumb mixture, rolling them to make 1-inch coated balls.

Place the balls on an ungreased cookie sheet, cover them with foil, and bake at 350° for 15 minutes. Uncover, turn the balls over, and bake uncovered for another 10 minutes.

Serve the balls with Sesame Sauce, if desired, as an entrée. Or put the balls in whole wheat pita bread with sauce and chopped lettuce and tomato.

Makes 6 servings.

Sesame Sauce

⅓ c. toasted sesame seeds
¼ c. water
1 T lemon juice
1 clove garlic
1 t Vege-Sal

Combine all ingredients in a blender container and purée until smooth. Serve with felafels.

6 servings
Average serving = approx. 11 grams balanced protein
26 to 31% of daily protein need

Soy Balls with Cheese Sauce

Little high-protein balls made of a blender batter of soybeans mixed with ground seeds and nuts, served with cheese sauce.

2 c. soaked soybeans
½ c. water
1 onion
¼ t thyme
1 t Vege-Sal
¼ c. sunflower seeds, ground
¼ c. sesame seeds, ground
¼ c. finely chopped walnuts
¼ c. wheat germ
¼ c. yeast flakes
½ c. whole wheat bread crumbs
1 T oil
Cheese Sauce (see recipe below)

Put the soybeans, onion, and water in a blender container with the thyme and Vege-Sal. Blend until smooth. Pour the batter into a bowl. Stir in the ground seeds, chopped walnuts, and wheat germ.

In a flat bowl combine the yeast flakes and bread crumbs, mixing well. Stir in the oil until it is well blended with the dry ingredients.

With a teaspoon, take chunks of the soybean batter and drop them into the bread crumb mixture, forming coated balls about 1 inch in diameter.

Place the balls on an unoiled cookie sheet. Cover with aluminum foil and bake at 350° for 15 minutes. Uncover the sheet, turn the balls and bake for another 10 minutes, without the foil.

Serve with Cheese Sauce.

Makes 6 servings.

Cheese Sauce

1 c. skim milk
2 t arrowroot
2 T cold water
½-¾ c. grated cheese

Heat the milk in a small saucepan. Blend the arrowroot in the cold water and slowly add it to the milk. Let the mixture bubble a minute over medium heat. Stir in the cheese so that it melts. Serve over Soy Balls.

6 servings
Average serving = approx. 13 grams balanced protein
30 to 36% of daily protein need

Fish-style Soy Curd Sticks

These sticks start with a soft dough using the tangy protein of soy curd complemented by wheat and wheat germ, with the texture and balance of bran, oats, and ground soy nuts. They are rolled in a special Seasoned Coating Mix, then baked until firm and served with Tartar Sauce or coleslaw.

½ c. soy nuts, ground
¼ c. gluten flour (or whole wheat)
1 T wheat germ
1 T wheat bran
1 T rolled oats
½ t onion powder
¼ t Vege-Sal
½ t low-sodium chicken soup base
1 t dried parsley
½ c. Soy Curd*
1 t lemon juice
2 T mayonnaise
¼ c. milk or water
¼ c. Seasoned Coating Mix*
Tartar Sauce (see Index) or coleslaw

Mix the dry ingredients (ground soy nuts through rolled oats) together in a bowl. Stir in the seasonings (onion powder through dried parsley).

Add the soy curd, lemon juice, and mayonnaise. Mix. Stir in the milk and blend together thoroughly until a soft dough is formed.

Turn the dough out onto a plate or cutting board and shape it into a rectangle about 7 x 4 x ¾ inches thick. Cut the rectangle into 8 sticks about ¾ inch wide. (If you make the dough in advance and chill it for several hours, it will be easier to shape and cut.)

Roll the sticks in the Seasoned Coating Mix. Bake on a lightly oiled small cookie sheet at 350° for 25 minutes.

Serve with Tartar Sauce or coleslaw.

4 servings
Average serving = approx. 10 grams balanced protein
23 to 28% of daily protein need

Soy Curd Fillets

In these baked fillet shapes rolled in fine cornmeal, soy curd is complemented by egg and cottage cheese, and given body and texture by oats, soy nut meal, wheat germ, and bran. The fillets are served with a special Tartar Sauce made with yogurt and mayonnaise.

½ c. Soy Curd*
¼ c. cottage cheese
1 scrambled egg, chopped fine
½ t Savorex
1 small onion, chopped
1 raw egg
½ t Vege-Sal
½ c. rolled oats
⅓ c. soy nuts, ground
2 T wheat germ
¼ c. wheat bran
½ c. finely ground cornmeal
Tartar Sauce (see recipe below)

In a mixing bowl, combine the soy curd, cottage cheese, chopped scrambled egg, and Savorex. Mix well.

Put the chopped onion, raw egg, and Vege-Sal in a blender container. Blend briefly to beat the egg and crush the onion. Pour this liquid into the soy curd mixture.

Add the dry ingredients (oats through bran) to the soy curd mixture. Stir together until everything is well mixed. Allow the batter to stand a few minutes for the oats and bran to absorb moisture.

Divide the batter into quarters with your spoon, then divide each quarter in half, forming 8 fillet shapes about 3½ x 2½ inches and ½ inch thick. Roll each in the finely ground cornmeal. Place the fillets on a non-stick baking sheet and bake at 350° for 20 minutes. Serve with Tartar Sauce.

Makes 4 servings.

Tartar Sauce

¼ c. yogurt
¼ c. mayonnaise
1 t lemon juice
¼ t dry mustard
1 T chopped olives
1 T chopped pickle
1 T minced green onion
1 T chopped capers
1 T minced fresh parsley

Combine all ingredients in a small bowl and mix well. Makes about ¾ c. of sauce.

4 servings
Average serving = approx. 15 grams balanced protein
35 to 42% of daily protein need

Vegetable-stuffed Granule Burger Cups

Sunflower seed granule burger cups stuffed with seasoned chopped onion, celery, carrot, mushrooms, and bread crumbs, baked and basted with sauce.

Basic Recipe for Granule Burger*
1 T oil
¼ c. minced onion
1 c. finely chopped celery
¼ c. grated carrot
1 c. chopped fresh mushrooms
¼ t paprika
⅛ t rosemary, crumbled
¼ c. fresh whole wheat bread crumbs
2 T soy powder
Dash of Vege-Sal
3 T milk or water
1 c. water or vegetable water
2 t low-sodium beef-style soup base
1 T whole wheat pastry flour
¼ t Vege-Sal
2 t oil

Mix the granule burger, using ¼ c. sunflower seeds (ground) in place of chopped walnuts. Add the liquid from basic recipe and mix well. Let stand until it is firm.

Meanwhile, prepare the stuffing. Heat 1 T oil in a non-stick skillet. Add the onion and celery, stirring until nearly tender. Stir in the carrot and mushrooms. Sprinkle with paprika and crumbled rosemary. Stir thoroughly until the mushrooms start to become tender. Remove from heat.

Add the bread crumbs, soy powder, and the dash of Vege-Sal. Mix in milk.

Oil an 8-inch square shallow baking dish with unrefined soy oil. Divide granule burger mixture into 4 portions, making fat patties from them. Place the patties in baking dish. Shape the patties into cups depressed in the center with high rims to hold the stuffing.

Divide the stuffing evenly into the cups of the patties, leaving a mound of stuffing above each cup. Bake in a 350° oven and for 10 minutes while you prepare sauce.

Mix 1 c. water, soup base, 1 T whole wheat pastry flour, Vege-Sal, and 2 t oil. Heat the mixture in the non-stick skillet used for stuffing. Cook over medium heat, stirring constantly, until the mixture bubbles. Allow it to bubble for 1 minute. Remove from heat.

After 10 minutes of baking, baste the stuffed burgers with 1 T sauce each. Bake for 10 more minutes. Baste once again, with another tablespoon of sauce for each stuffed burger. Bake for 10 more minutes. Use remaining sauce as gravy to serve with stuffed burgers.

4 servings
Average serving = approx. 13 grams balanced protein
30 to 36% of daily protein need

The Sunflower

Spinach-stuffed Muffin Cups

A savory burger-like muffin-cup shell stuffed with a mixture of spinach, bread crumbs, and cheese. Soy, sesame or sunflower seeds, oats and wheat provide complementary proteins, supplemented with cheese in the stuffing.

Burger Cups

⅓ c. sesame seeds or sunflower seeds, ground
¼ c. soy granules
¼ c. soy nuts, ground
¼ c. rolled oats
¼ c. wheat germ
¼ c. bran
2 T chick-pea flour
2 T whole wheat flour
1 small onion, minced
1 t flaked dried parsley (or 1 T fresh, minced)
¼ t garlic powder
1 T nutritional yeast flakes
⅛ t ground thyme
¾ c. hot water
1 Vegex cube
2 T catsup
1 T oil

Mix the dry ingredients together in a bowl (ground seeds through whole wheat flour). Stir in the minced onion. Stir in seasonings (parsley through thyme).

Separately, dissolve the Vegex cube in hot water in a Pyrex cup. Stir in the oil and catsup. Pour the liquid into the dry ingredients, mixing thorougly. Let the mixture stand, absorbing the liquid while you prepare the stuffing.

Stuffing:

½ (10 ozs.) package frozen spinach, thawed
2 T spinach cooking water
½ t soy sauce
1 T whole wheat pastry flour
1 T chick-pea flour
⅓ c. whole wheat bread crumbs
¼ c. grated Swiss or mozzarella cheese

Thaw the half package of spinach (cut in two with a freezer knife) over a bit of simmering water in a steam rack, covered. Do this only long enough to separate it. Some ice crystals may remain.

Mix the spinach cooking water and soy sauce with the flours in a bowl. Add thawed spinach, bread crumbs, and grated cheese. Mix.

Assembly:

Oil a 6-muffin tin with unrefined soy oil. Divide the burger mixture evenly into the 6 parts. With the back of a spoon, pack the mixture along the sides and bottom of each cup, leaving a hollow in the middle. Fill each hollow with the spinach mixture.

Bake at 350° for 30 minutes. If desired, place an aluminum foil sheet lightly over the muffin tin after 15 or 20 minutes of baking time to keep the stuffed muffins from becoming too crisp on top.

When done, run a knife between each muffin and the cup to loosen it all around, lift out the muffin and remove it to a serving platter. Serve the muffins with a mushroom, tomato or white sauce, if desired.

3 servings
Average serving = approx. 12 grams balanced protein
28 to 34% of daily protein need

Pizza Burgers

Big granule burger cups filled with mushroom-tomato sauce and topped with melted cheese strips.

⅓ c. soy granules
⅓ c. rolled oats
⅓ c. soy nuts, ground
⅓ c. whole wheat flour
⅓ c. walnuts, finely chopped
¼ c. wheat germ
¼ c. bran
1 medium onion, minced

1 c. hot water
2 t low-sodium beef-like soup base
1 T soy sauce
1 T oil
1 c. tomato sauce, divided
1 c. chopped mushrooms
2 t oil
Cheese slices

Mix the dry ingredients (soy granules through bran) together in a bowl. Stir in minced onion.

Put hot water in a Pyrex measuring cup with soup base, soy sauce, and oil. Pour the liquid into the dry ingredients, mixing well so that liquid is well distributed. Let stand for 10 minutes for liquid to be thoroughly absorbed.

Mix ½ c. tomato sauce into the burger mix after it has absorbed its own liquid. Mix well. Form 6 large patties, placing them on a lightly oiled baking sheet. Make a well in the center of each burger, leaving a ½-inch raised rim. Bake at 350° for 30 minutes.

In a small non-stick skillet, sauté 1 c. chopped mushrooms in 2 t oil over moderate heat. Add the mushrooms to the remaining ½ c. tomato sauce. Apportion sauce among the burgers, filling the wells.

Crisscross narrow cheese slices like spokes of a wheel over the burgers. Bake another 5 minutes, or until cheese melts.

6 servings
Average serving = approx. 12 grams balanced protein
28 to 34% of daily protein need

Tomato-Burger Hash Browns

Crispy potato patties topped with a chili-seasoned granule burger mixture, garnished with sliced tomatoes, melted cheese and chopped parsley.

Potato Patty Bases:

4 c. grated potatoes, unpeeled
1 medium onion, chopped
½ t Vege-Sal
3 T oil

Mix the potatoes, onions, and Vege-Sal. Heat the oil in a large iron skillet or electric skillet (350°). Place the potato mixture by large spoonfuls on the skillet. Allow them to brown on one side, then turn and brown the other side—about 5 minutes per side.

Makes 16 potato patty bases (2½ to 3 inches in diameter).

Granule Burger Topping:

1 recipe Granule Burger*
1 T oil
1 onion, chopped
1 can (8 ozs.) tomato sauce
½ c. tomato juice
½ t chili powder
½ t Vege-Sal (optional)
⅛ t garlic powder
1 t Worcestershire sauce

Form granule burger into 2-inch balls and place on a steam rack in a pressure cooker over 1 c. of water. Pressure cook for 2 minutes. Let pressure drop naturally. (If you have no pressure cooker, use a regular pot and steam rack over 1 c. of water. Bring the water to a boil, keep covered, and lower heat to steam the balls for 20 minutes.) Chop the balls into several pieces with a knife and set them aside.

Heat 1 T oil in a skillet. Sauté the onion. Add the tomato sauce, tomato juice, and seasonings (chili powder through Worcestershire sauce). Stir in the granule burger chunks. Lower heat and simmer for 5 minutes, covered.

Garnish and Assembly:

2 tomatoes, sliced thinly into 8 pieces each
1 c. grated Cheddar cheese
Parsley

Place potato patty bases on a large non-stick cookie sheet. Spoon burger topping onto each patty until it is all used. Place a slice of tomato on each topped patty, then a tablespoon of grated cheese. Bake at 350° for 10 minutes, or until heated through and cheese is melted. Garnish with chopped parsley, if desired.

Makes 4 to 6 servings.

4 to 6 servings
Average serving = approx. 11 grams balanced protein
26 to 31% of daily protein need

The Sunflower

Granule-Burger Potato Pinwheel Patties

A granule burger layer rolled around a layer of seasoned mashed potatoes, sliced into pinwheel patties lightly browned in the oven.

Basic Recipe for Granule Burger*
2 T minced parsley
¼ c. minced onion
¼ c. tomato sauce
2 c. diced cooked potatoes
1 T butter (optional)
3 T mayonnaise
3 T grated Parmesan cheese
¼ c. finely diced celery
2 T chopped green onion

Prepare granule burger, using ground sunflower seeds instead of chopped walnuts. Mix minced parsley and onion into the granule burger. Stir tomato sauce into the mixture. Let stand to firm up.

Mash cooked potatoes with butter and mayonnaise. Stir in grated cheese, diced celery, and green onion. Mix thoroughly.

Place aluminum foil loosely over a 10- x 15-inch non-stick baking sheet. Spread the granule burger mixture thinly and evenly over the foil on the sheet in an 8- x 14-inch rectangle.

Carefully spread the mashed potato mixture thinly and evenly over the layer of granule burger, except for a 1- x 8-inch strip at the end of the granule burger layer.

Lift the foil at one end to begin rolling up as for a jelly-roll. Peel away the foil from the granule burger as you roll. When the roll is formed, fasten the unspread end of it by pressing it firmly against the body of the granule burger roll.

Chill the roll, wrapped in part of the foil, for at least ½ hour.

Cut the roll in 8 pinwheel slices, 1 inch thick. Place them on the baking sheet very lightly oiled with unrefined soy oil. Bake at 350° for 25 to 30 minutes.

6 to 8 servings
Average serving = approx. 9 grams balanced protein
21 to 25% of daily protein need

Little Lentil Loaves

Tiny individual loaves of lentils, eggs, wheat, nuts, and cheese, garnished with creamy mushroom sauce or tomato sauce.

1 c. dried lentils
2½ c. water
1 Vegex cube, ground
2 eggs
1 onion, minced
2 T chopped parsley
¾ c. grated Cheddar cheese
¾ c. whole wheat bread crumbs
1 c. finely chopped walnuts
¼ c. wheat germ
¼ c. sesame seeds, ground
2 T wheat bran
Creamy Mushroom Sauce* or Tomato Sauce*

Bring the 2½ c. of water to a boil in a saucepan, and slowly add the lentils so that the water does not stop boiling as you add them. Cover and let simmer for 30 minutes. Add the ground Vegex, mixing it in well so that it dissolves. Drain the liquid from the lentils and reserve it for the sauce. You should have 2 cups of lentils, drained.

Partially mash the lentils in a bowl with a potato masher. Add the eggs and beat all together with an egg beater. Stir in the onion and parsley, then the cheese.

Mix in the dry ingredients. Shape the lentil mixture into six small oval loaves, humped on top. Place them on a lightly oiled (with crude soy oil) baking sheet. Bake at 350° for 20 minutes. Serve the loaves with Creamy Mushroom Sauce or with Tomato Sauce made with reserved lentil cooking liquid (see Basic Recipes).

6 servings
Average serving = approx. 11 grams balanced protein
26 to 31% of daily protein need

Sunflower Seed Squares

Easy oven-baked squares of nut and seed meals mixed with blenderized vegetables, egg, and seasonings, served with Cheddar Cheese Sauce and garnished with parsley.

½ c. sunflower seeds, ground
6 T sesame seeds, ground
¼ c. pecan meal or wheat germ
½ c. soy nuts, ground
¼ c. chopped carrot (1 small)
¼ c. chopped celery (½ stalk)
1 small onion, quartered
1 egg
½ t celery seed
1 t dried parsley or 2 T fresh, minced
1 T soy sauce
1 t lemon juice
2 t apple cider vinegar
Cheddar Cheese Sauce (see recipe below)

Combine the ground seeds and nuts in a mixing bowl.

In a blender container, put the chopped vegetables, egg, and all seasonings (celery seed through vinegar). Blend until the vegetables are minced. Pour the blender liquid into dry mixture, mixing well.

Divide the food into quarters, then divide each quarter in half. Flatten the pieces to make 8 squares. Place them on a lightly oiled cookie sheet and bake at 350° for 20 minutes. Serve with Cheddar Cheese Sauce and garnish with parsley.

Makes 4 servings.

Cheddar Cheese Sauce

2 T oil
2 T whole wheat pastry flour
¼ c. tomato juice
¾ c. hot milk
¼ c. Cheddar cheese cubes

Put the oil, flour, and tomato juice in a blender container and mix on low speed. Slowly add the hot milk while blending. Add the cheese; cover and blend on regular speed. Pour the mixture into a saucepan and stir over moderate heat until it bubbles.

4 servings
Average serving = approx. 13 grams balanced protein
30 to 36% of daily protein need

Skillet Burgers

Skillet burgers are probably among the quickest main dishes. The simplest kind are made from mashed cooked beans mixed with complementary ingredients and made into burger shapes browned in a skillet. Try Bean Burgers, Great Northern Bean Cutlets, Quick Felafel Patties, or Lentil Swinger Burgers. If you have cooked soybeans on hand, you can make Golden Eggplant Burgers, High-Protein Macroburgers, Soybean Cottage Cheese Patties, and the various Soybean Cutlets with Nuts and Herbs.

Quickly put together patties can be made with cooked grains mixed with complementary soy granules or ground soy nuts: Bulgar Wheat Burgers, Millet-Soy Patties, Wheat-Soy Patties, and Oat and Soy Patties. Use ground soy nuts and sesame seeds with minced vegetables for quick Vegetarian Hash-Burgers. Sesame Burgers are easy to make with soy nut and seed meals; or use ground sunflower seeds with egg for Sunflower Seed Patties.

Cottage cheese is a reliable protein for quick skillet burgers. Try Cheese-Nut Patties.

Granule burger mix can be used to make hamburger-like sandwiches (Soy Granule Burger Sandwiches) or unusual patties with grated potatoes (Spicy Indian Patties).

Our prize recipes in this catgory are made with soaked soybean batter. They don't require eggs or pre-cooking to hold together. We especially like Soy-Millet Cutlets, a hearty dish for company meals as well as daily family fare. With soaked soybeans on hand, Super Soy Burgers, Salisbury Steak-style Burgers, and Ham-style Skillet Rounds are quick and easy for family dinners. For a delightful change, make Soy Foo Yung using soy batter instead of eggs with Chinese vegetables.

Bean Burgers

A very easy skillet burger made from puréed beans complemented with sesame or sunflower seed meal, fortified with ground soy nuts and a melted cheese topping.

2 c. cooked pinto beans or other tasty beans
½ c. sesame seeds or sunflower seeds, ground
2 T wheat germ
2 T bran
½ c. soy nuts, ground
1 small onion, minced
1 T soy sauce
¼ c. catsup
1 T oil
6-8 thin slices of Cheddar or jack cheese

Force cooked beans through a food mill or purée them in the blender. Put the pulp in the mixing bowl.

Stir in the ground seeds, wheat germ, bran, and ground soy nuts.

Mix in the minced onion, soy sauce, and catsup.

Heat an electric skillet to 350° and spread 1 T oil over the surface. Form 6 large burgers on the skillet by filling a circular hamburger shaper, or make 8 smaller burgers by scooping the mixture with a large spoon.

Brown the burgers, uncovered, about 5 minutes per side. Turn them carefully with a wide spatula.

Place thin slices of cheese on the burgers, and cover the skillet for a few minutes until the cheese is melted.

3 to 4 servings
Average serving = approx. 15 grams balanced protein
35 to 42% of daily protein need

Great Northern Bean Cutlets

A favorite American bean is balanced by millet and fortified by the sesame-soy combination in these good-tasting, firm skillet cutlets garnished with tomato sauce.

⅓ c. millet
⅔ c. water
1 c. canned Great Northern Beans, drained
1 T soy sauce
1 egg, beaten
⅓ c. soy nuts, ground
⅓ c. sesame seeds, ground
1 T wheat germ
1 T bran
1 T oil
Tomato Sauce*

Cook the millet in the ⅔ c. water for 20 minutes.

In a mixing bowl mash the beans thoroughly with a potato masher. Stir in the soy sauce and beaten egg, mixing well. Add cooked millet.

Add the dry ingredients (soy nuts through bran), blending in until no dry spots are left in the mixture.

Spread the 1 T oil over the surface of a pre-heated (350°) electric skillet. Divide the surface of the food mixture into six parts. Scoop out the sections and place them on the skillet, flattening them with a spoon into cutlet shapes.

Brown the cutlets for about 2 minutes per side; cover, lower the heat and cook for another 5 to 10 minutes. Serve with Tomato Sauce.

4 to 6 servings
Average serving = approx. 10 grams balanced protein
23 to 28% of daily protein need

Quick Felafel Patties

Cooked chick-peas puréed with egg, seasoned and mixed with complementary sesame or sunflower seed meal, formed into patties rolled in whole wheat bread crumbs, then browned in oil for pita bread sandwiches. Double the recipe for a quick entrée, allowing more patties per serving. Garnish the entrée servings with Yogurt Sauce.

1 c. cooked chick-peas
1 egg
¼ t dry mustard
¼ t garlic powder
Dash Vege-Sal
2 T minced fresh onion
¼ c. sesame or sunflower seeds, ground
2 T wheat germ
1 T bran
2 T soy nuts, ground
1 T nutritional yeast
½ c. whole wheat bread crumbs (1 slice)
1 T oil
Yogurt Sauce (optional, see recipe below)

Purée the chick-peas in a blender with the egg. Remove the mixture to a bowl, extracting it all with a narrow flexible spatula. Stir in the seasonings and minced onion. Mix in the ground seeds.

Add the wheat germ, bran, ground soy nuts, and yeast. Stir thoroughly.

Put the bread crumbs in a shallow bowl or plate. Divide the batter into 8 portions. Roll each portion in the crumbs, forming a small patty 2¼ to 2½ inches in diameter.

Heat 1 T oil in a non-stick skillet. Brown the patties on each side over medium heat, about 3 minutes per side.

Serve in pita bread pockets with shredded lettuce and mayonnaise, 2 patties per sandwich. Or garnish patties with Yogurt Sauce.

Makes 4 servings.

Yogurt Sauce

¼ c. yogurt
¼ c. mayonnaise
1 t prepared mustard

Mix all ingredients thoroughly in a small bowl. Serve with felafel patties. (Double the recipe if you like more sauce.)

4 servings
Average serving = approx. 12 grams balanced protein
28 to 34% of daily need

Lentil "Swinger" Burgers

Our delicious vegetarian version of the California burger filled with chopped onion, cherry tomatoes, olives, and cheese cubes. We use lentils, millet, and ground soy nuts instead of ground beef.

½ c. dry lentils
½ c. dry millet
2½ c. water
2 eggs
½ t Vege-Sal
1 T Worcestershire sauce
1 T catsup
¼ t ground thyme
¼ t garlic powder
¾ c. soy nuts, ground
2 T wheat germ
2 T wheat bran
1 medium onion, chopped
½ c. chopped cherry tomatoes
¼ c. sliced stuffed olives
½ c. ½-inch cheese cubes
1 T oil

Bring the 2½ c. of water to a boil in a saucepan; add the lentils and millet, cover, and let simmer for 45 minutes, or until all the water has been absorbed. Mash the mixture with a potato masher.

Beat the eggs in a mixing bowl. Add the seasonings (Vege-Sal through garlic powder). Stir in the cooked lentil-millet mixture until everything is evenly moistened.

Pour in the ground soy nuts, wheat germ, and bran, mixing until no dry spots are left. Stir in the chopped vegetables and cheese cubes, mixing well.

Quarter the mixture, then halve each quarter. Make 8 large burgers with your hands. Have the electric skillet heated to 350° (or use an ordinary skillet over moderate heat). Spread the 1 T oil on the skillet. Cook the patties 3 minutes on the first side, covered, with cover vents open. Turn them carefully; cover as before, and cook for another 3 minutes.

4 to 6 servings
Average serving = approx. 14 grams balanced protein
32 to 39% of daily protein need

Golden Eggplant Burgers

Unusual burgers of soybean pulp, oats, wheat germ, and sesame meal, filled with moist and tender eggplant chunks.

2 c. cooked soybeans, drained
1 medium eggplant
1 onion, diced
3-4 cloves garlic, minced
2 T oil

1½ c. rolled oats
¾ c. raw wheat germ
¼ c. sesame seeds, ground
1 t Vege-Sal
½ t-1 t curry powder (optional)
2 T oil for browning

Put the cooked soybeans through a food mill. You should have about 1⅓ c. of pulp. Place it in a large mixing bowl.

Peel and dice the eggplant. Heat the 2 T of oil in a large non-stick skillet and sauté the diced onion, minced garlic, and eggplant over moderate heat until the vegetables start to become tender. Add a few tablespoons of water, cover, lower the heat, and simmer for 15 to 20 minutes, or until the eggplant is very tender.

Meanwhile, mix the rolled oats, wheat germ, ground sesame seeds, Vege-Sal, and curry powder into the soybean pulp. When the eggplant is done, pour it into the soybean mixture. Mix thoroughly to form a pasty dough. The excess moisture will be taken up by the oats and wheat germ.

Make 15 burgers, about 2½ inches in diameter, from the dough.

Have the electric skillet heated to 350°, or use a regular skillet over moderate heat. Cook the burgers on both sides in the oil until golden brown. Cover, then lower heat and let the burgers steam to cook through for another 15 minutes. (You may have to stack some of the burgers if your skillet is small.)

5 servings
Average serving = approx. 10 grams balanced protein
23 to 28% of daily protein need

High-Protein Macroburgers

A serviceable soybean-millet burger fortified with ground oats, wheat germ, and sunflower seed meal, with herbs, spices and chopped vegetables. These macroburgers can provide quick meals from the freezer. They are delicious on whole wheat or wheat-soy bread with your choice of cheese, tomatoes, lettuce, mayonnaise, catsup, or other relishes.

1 c. soybeans
2½ c. water
½ c. millet
2 c. water
¼ c. soy sauce
3 T oil
¾ t dried dillweed, crushed
¾ t dried thyme, crushed
½ t chili powder
¼ t ground cumin (optional)
⅛ t cayenne (optional)
2 cloves garlic, minced, or ¼ t powder
1 c. finely chopped onion (1 large)
½ c. finely chopped celery (1 stalk)
½ c. grated carrot (1 small)
¼ c. finely chopped green pepper
2 t oil
1 T water
½ c. rolled oats, ground
½ c. raw wheat germ
½ c. sunflower seeds, ground
¼ c. wheat bran
2 T oil for browning

Soak the soybeans overnight in 2½ c. water in a covered bowl stored in the refrigerator. Cook them in the soaking water or in the same amount of fresh water for 45 minutes in the pressure cooker.

Bring the 2 c. of water to a boil in a saucepan, add the raw millet, cover, and simmer for 40 minutes. All the water will be absorbed and the millet will be sticky.

In a blender container, put the cooked drained soybeans, soy sauce, oil and seasonings (dillweed through cayenne). Purée until smooth. Remove all the purée to a bowl with a narrow rubber spatula. Mix the cooked millet into the purée.

Heat the 2 t oil in a skillet over moderate heat. Pour the vegetables (except the grated carrot) into the skillet and stir for 1 minute. Add the carrot, stir for another minute, then add a tablespoon of water, cover, and remove from heat to steam briefly.

Separately, mix together the ground oats, wheat germ, sunflower seeds, and bran. Stir these into the soybean mixture.

Fold the sautéed vegetables into the soybean mixture, blending thoroughly. (*Note:* If you are not going to freeze the burgers, the sautéing may be omitted. The vegetables will then be very crisp and crunchy in the burgers. Be sure to put the minced garlic in the blender to purée with the soybeans, or substitute garlic powder.)

Use about ⅓ c. of the mixture for each patty. If desired, use a metal hamburger shaper (3½ inches in diameter). Brown the patties on both sides in the 2 T hot oil using either an electric skillet or a stove-top skillet over moderate heat, for about 3 minutes per side. If desired, cover, lower the heat, and let bake for about 10 minutes for more tender vegetable bits.

To freeze the macroburgers, spoon the mixture into the hamburger shaper as it rests on one half of the waxed side of a rectangle of freezer paper (about 5 x 9 inches). Fold the paper over to cover the burger after removing the shaper. Continue and make about 13 more burgers.

Freeze the burgers in a covered freezer container. Or lay them on a cookie sheet covered with a sheet of aluminum foil. When they are frozen, they may be taken up and put in a plastic freezer bag, and sealed airtight.

Brown the frozen burgers as described above, 3 minutes per side, including the baking over lowered heat in order to warm them through.

Serve the macroburgers on whole wheat or wheat and soy bread or buns, with lettuce, tomato, mayonnaise, catsup, or other relishes as desired.

14 servings
Average serving = approx. 8 grams balanced protein
19 to 22% of daily protein need

Soybean-Cottage Cheese Patties

Soybeans, cottage cheese, eggs, and sunflower seeds combine to make a super-strong protein in these easy and fast patties.

1 c. cooked or canned soybeans
½ c. cottage cheese
2 eggs
1 t instant chicken bouillon
½ t ground thyme
½ t Vege-Sal
1 medium onion, chopped fine
¾ c. soy nuts, ground
¼ c. pecan meal or walnut meal
¼ c. sunflower seeds, ground
2 T wheat germ
2 T bran
1 T oil

Put the soybeans, cottage cheese, eggs, and chicken bouillon in a blender container. Blend until smooth. Pour the mixture into a bowl.

Stir in the ground thyme, Vege-Sal, and chopped onion. Add all the dry ingredients (ground soy nuts through bran) and mix together well.

Flatten the mixture in the bowl with your spoon. Divide the surface of the mixture into quarters, then eighths. Scoop out each segment with the spoon, shape a patty with your hands, and place it on the oiled skillet over moderate heat. Cook about 3 minutes per side. Lower the heat, cover, and let cook another few minutes, until firm.

4 servings
Average serving = approx. 16 grams balanced protein
37 to 44% of daily protein need

Soybean Cutlets with Nuts and Herbs

Savory soybean-millet cutlets with nut meal, vegetable bits, herbs, and a golden wheat germ crust, served with a special vegetable cream sauce.

1 c. cooked drained soybeans
¼ c. milk or water
1 T soy sauce
1 c. cooked millet (⅓ c. raw millet plus ⅔ c. water)
1 large onion, minced
⅓ c. soy nuts, ground
⅓ c. rolled oats, ground
¼ c. almonds, ground
1 t basil, crushed
¼ c. raw wheat germ
1 T oil
Onion-Cheese Sauce (see recipe below)

Put the cooked soybeans through a food mill into a mixing bowl, then stir in milk or water and soy sauce. (Or purée the beans in the blender with the liquid and soy sauce, and scrape it all out into a bowl with a rubber spatula.)

Bring the ⅔ c. water to a boil in a small saucepan. Add the raw millet, cover, and simmer for 20 minutes. All the water will be absorbed. Mix the cooked millet into the soybean purée.

Stir the minced onion into the soybean mixture.

Separately, mix together the ground soy nuts, oats, and almonds. Stir in the crushed basil. Mix this dry combination into the soybean mixture, blending them together well.

Pat the mixture down evenly in the bowl with a spoon, divide it into quarters, then into eighths. Scoop out each segment and form it into cutlet shape with your hands. Each cutlet should be about 3½ x 2 x ¾ inches. Spread the wheat germ on a plate, then roll the cutlets in it until all is used.

Heat the oil at 350° in an electric skillet. Brown the cutlets for 2 minutes on each side, then lower the heat to 225°, cover (vents closed), and bake for 15 minutes. (An ordinary skillet may be used on top of the stove over moderate heat, then covered over low heat.)

Serve the cutlets with Onion-Cheese Sauce.

Makes 4 servings.

Onion-Cheese Sauce

1 large onion, chopped
1 new potato, chopped
1 clove garlic, minced (or ⅛ t garlic powder)
⅓ c. water
¼ t Vege-Sal
1 t low-sodium chicken-style soup base
¼ c. milk
¼ c. grated sharp cheese

Put the vegetables into a saucepan with the water; bring to a boil, cover, and let simmer for 20 minutes. Pour the contents of the pan into a blender container; add the seasonings, milk, and cheese, and blend until smooth. Serve over the cutlets.

Variation: For Cashew-Carrot Cutlets, substitute ¼ c. cashew nuts for almonds; 1 large carrot, grated, for the onion; and 1 t dried dill weed for the basil. Serve with Golden Carrot Cream Sauce.

Golden Carrot Cream Sauce

2 medium carrots, sliced
1 stalk celery, chopped
1 small onion, chopped
1 new potato, chopped
½ c. water
1 t low-sodium chicken-style soup base
¼ t Vege-Sal
½ c. milk

Put the vegetables in a saucepan with ½ c. water. Bring to a boil, cover, lower the heat, and simmer for 20 minutes. Add the soup base, Vege-Sal, and milk. Pour all into a blender container and purée until smooth. If the sauce is sweeter than desired, stir in 1 t lemon juice.

Variation: For Marjoram-Walnut Cutlets, substitute ¼ c. walnuts for almonds; 1 stalk celery and 1 tiny onion, minced, for large onion; and 1 t marjoram for basil. Serve with Celery Cream Sauce.

Celery Cream Sauce

1 large stalk celery, chopped
1 small onion, chopped
1 new potato, chopped
⅓ c. water
¼ t Vege-Sal
1 t low-sodium chicken-style soup base
¼ c. milk or buttermilk

Put the vegetables in a saucepan with ⅓ c. water. Bring to a boil, cover, and simmer for 20 minutes. Pour the contents of the pan into a blender container, add the seasonings and milk, and blend until smooth. Serve over the cutlets.

4 servings
Average serving = approx. 12 grams balanced protein
28 to 34% of daily protein need

Bulgar Wheat Burgers

Delicious savory burgers with a nut-like taste, made of bulgar wheat balanced by soy nuts, fortified with the peanut-sesame combination, filled with chopped mushrooms and onion.

1 c. water and ½ c. parboiled dry bulgar wheat (or 1½ c. cooked bulgar wheat)
1 egg
¼ c. peanut butter
Dash Worcestershire sauce
1 T soy sauce
¾-1 c. raw chopped mushrooms
1 small onion, chopped
1 t oil
½ c. sesame seeds, ground
½ c. soy nuts, ground
¼ t garlic powder
2 T oil
Tomato Sauce*

Bring 1 c. water to a boil; add ½ c. parboiled bulgar wheat. Cover, lower the heat, and simmer for 15 minutes. Or use regular bulgar wheat cooked in the usual way.

Beat the egg in a bowl. Blend in the peanut butter. Add Worcestershire sauce and soy sauce. Pour the liquid into the bulgar wheat.

Mix in the ground seeds, soy nuts, and garlic powder. Fold in the chopped mushrooms. Sauté the onion until soft in 1 t oil. Fold the onion into the bulgar wheat mixture.

Divide the mixture into thirds, then sixths. Form six thick 3-inch patties. Heat the oil in a skillet over moderate heat (or use an electric skillet at 350°). Brown the patties about 5 minutes per side. Cover, lower the heat, and cook for another 5 minutes. Serve with Tomato Sauce.

3 servings
Average serving = approx. 14 grams balanced protein
32 to 39% of daily protein need

Millet-Soy Patties

Cooked millet and ground soy nuts provide the complementary proteins in these good-tasting patties with bits of crunch and a satisfying flavor.

1 c. water and ⅓ c. dry millet (or 1 c. cooked millet)
1 t low-sodium chicken-style soup base
¼ t Vege-Sal
1 c. soy nuts, ground
2 T wheat germ
2 T wheat bran
⅓ c. walnuts, finely chopped
½ t celery seed, ground
1 handful fresh parsley, minced
½ c. water
1 T soy sauce
1 T oil

Bring the 1 c. water to a boil, add the "chicken" broth base, Vege-Sal, and millet; cover and simmer for 45 minutes. (Or use 1 c. of previously cooked millet, and add the seasonings to the additional ½ c. water in the recipe.)

Put the cooked millet in a mixing bowl. Stir in the ground soy nuts, wheat germ, and bran. Add the chopped walnuts, celery seed, and minced parsley.

Mix the ½ c. water and 1 T soy sauce together. Pour the liquid into the millet mixture, stirring until all of it is absorbed.

With your spoon, make lines in the flattened mixture in the bowl to quarter it, then halve each quarter. Form 8 patties from the divisions. Brown them on each side for 2 to 3 minutes in the 1 T oil in a skillet (or in an electric skillet at 350°) over moderate heat.

4 servings
Average serving = approx. 11 grams balanced protein
26 to 31% of daily protein need

Wheat-Soy Patties

A complementary bulgar wheat and soy nuts combination with a hearty wheat and tomato taste with hints of green pepper.

1 c. water and ½ c. bulgar wheat (or 1 c. cooked bulgar wheat)
1 c. soy nuts, ground
2 T wheat germ
2 T wheat bran
1 T soy powder
¼ t garlic powder
1 can (6 ozs.) tomato paste
½ c. water or vegetable water
1 T soy sauce or Vege-Sal to taste
1 medium onion, minced
½ large green pepper, minced
2 t oil
1 T oil

Pressure cook the bulgar wheat in 1 c. water for 20 minutes. (If bulgar wheat is the parboiled kind, simmer for 15 minutes in a regular covered saucepan.)

Combine the 1 c. cooked bulgar wheat with the dry ingredients (ground soy nuts through soy powder) in a mixing bowl. Mix thoroughly.

Separately, mix the tomato paste with ½ c. water. Take 5 tablespoons of this thick tomato sauce and stir them into the bulgar wheat mixture. Season the remaining tomato sauce with the 1 T soy sauce or Vege-Sal to taste, and use it to serve with the patties when they are ready. (Heat the sauce if desired.)

Sauté the minced onion and green pepper in the 2 t oil in a small skillet. Fold the sautéed vegetables into the bulgar wheat mixture. (If you like the vegetables very crisp in the patties, omit the sautéing.)

Turn out the mixture onto a cutting board and divide it into 8 portions. Form into small patties, about 2½ inches in diameter.

Heat the 1 T oil over moderate heat in a skillet (or in an electric skillet at 350°), and brown the patties about 3 minutes on each side. Serve them with the remaining tomato sauce.

4 servings
Average serving = approx. 11 grams balanced protein
26 to 34% of daily protein need

Oat and Soy Patties

Complementary oat and soy form simple-to-make savory eggless patties reminiscent of sausage with a hint of sage, onion, and garlic.

1½ c. rolled oats
½ c. soy granules
1 t sage
1¾ c. water
3 T soy sauce
2 T oil
1 clove garlic, minced
1 small onion, chopped
1 stalk celery, chopped
1 c. soy nuts, ground
¼ c. walnuts, finely chopped
2 T nutritional yeast
Oil for browning

Mix the oats, soy granules, and sage together in a bowl.

Bring the water to a boil in a saucepan. Add the oil, soy sauce, chopped garlic, onion, and celery.

Gradually add the oat-soy mixture to the boiling water. Remove from the heat, stir a bit, and add ground soy nuts, walnuts, and yeast. Mix well. Let stand until all the moisture is absorbed.

Spoon the mixture onto a lightly oiled skillet (or electric skillet) over moderate heat, making patties about 3 inches in diameter. (A hamburger shaper makes nice uniform patties.)

Allow the patties to brown on one side, then turn carefully and finish browning on the second side, about 5 minutes per side.

To serve, lift the patties carefully to a platter with a wide spatula.

6 servings
Average serving = approx. 12 grams balanced protein
28 to 34% of daily protein need

Vegetarian Hash-burgers

Grated potatoes, chopped onion, and celery are combined with the proteins of soy nuts, sesame seeds, and wheat germ to make these tasty skillet-baked hash-burgers.

1 c. soy nuts, ground
½ c. sesame seeds, ground
2 T wheat germ
2 T wheat bran
¼ t garlic powder
1 large potato, grated (about 1 cup)
1 stalk celery, finely chopped
1 small onion, minced
1 T oil
1 T soy sauce
1 T Worcestershire sauce
1 T catsup
½ c. tomato juice
1 T oil
Tomato Sauce* or Yogurt

Combine the dry ingredients (ground soy nuts through garlic powder) in a mixing bowl. Stir in the grated potato, chopped celery, and onion. Add the 1 T oil, sauces, catsup, and tomato juice. Mix well.

Pre-heat an electric skillet to 325°. Spread 1 T oil over the surface of the skillet. Using a circular hamburger shaper, place 6 circular patties on the skillet by filling the form with large spoonsful of the food mixture.

Cover the skillet, leaving the steam vents closed. (These hash-burgers will not puff up.) Let them bake for 10 minutes. Uncover, turn the burgers, then bake, covered as before, 10 more minutes. Lower the heat to 200° and bake for another 5 minutes.

Optional: During the last 5 minutes, place slices of cheese to melt on the hash-burgers.

Serve with Tomato Sauce or Yogurt.

4 to 6 servings
Average serving = approx. 10 grams balanced protein
23 to 28% of daily protein need

Sesame Burgers

Easy skillet burgers from a dry mix of sesame and soy meals with wheat germ and seasonings, bound with egg. Delicious as a supper dish with onion sauce, mushrooms, and parsley, or for burger sandwiches with the traditional relishes.

⅓ c. fresh sesame seeds, ground to meal
¼ c. soy nuts, ground
¼ c. low-fat soy powder
¼ c. raw wheat germ
1 T wheat bran
1 T nutritional yeast
1 t gluten flour or whole wheat flour
1 t dried parsley flakes or 2 T chopped fresh parsley
¼ t garlic powder
⅛ t ground thyme
1 Vegex cube, ground
¼ t celery seed, ground
1 small onion, minced
1 egg
½ c. water or vegetable water
Onion Sauce (optional, see recipe below)
Sautéed mushrooms and parsley

Combine the sesame seed meal, ground soy nuts, soy powder, and wheat germ in a mixing bowl. Add the yeast, bran, gluten flour, and parsley flakes. Mix together well.

Add the dry seasonings (garlic powder through celery seed), mixing in thoroughly. Add the minced onion.

Beat the egg in a separate small bowl, add the liquid to it, and beat together briefly. Stir the liquid mixture into the dry mixture and mix well. Let stand for 10 minutes or so for the liquid to be absorbed.

Use a large spoon to smooth out 6 patties on an oiled electric skillet (heated to 350°). Brown the patties on the first side a few minutes, until they are easily taken up with a spatula. Turn and finish cooking until they are firm. (An ordinary stove-top skillet over moderate heat may also be used.)

Serve for dinner with Onion Sauce, sautéed mushrooms, and a fresh parsley garnish, if desired. Or serve for lunch on bread or buns with chopped lettuce, onion, tomato, mayonnaise, catsup, or whatever relishes you like.

Makes 3 servings.

Onion Sauce

1 T butter or oil
1 large onion, chopped
1 T whole wheat pastry flour
1 c. milk
½ t Vege-Sal or more, to taste

Heat the butter or oil in a small saucepan over medium heat. Sauté the onion, stirring until it starts to become translucent. Mix in the flour so that it is well distributed among the onion pieces. Gradually add the milk, stirring constantly, until the sauce thickens and bubbles for one minute. Add Vege-Sal to taste.

3 servings
Average serving = approx. 14 grams balanced protein
32 to 39% of daily protein need

Sunflower Seed Patties

Ground sunflower seeds combine with egg, ground soy nuts, and wheat germ for the protein in these patties with vegetable bits. The herb seasoning may remind you of sausage.

1 c. sunflower seeds, ground
⅓ c. soy nuts, ground
2 T wheat germ
2 T wheat bran
½ t Vege-Sal
¼ t basil, crushed
1 egg, beaten
¼ c. tomato juice
2 t oil
1 stalk celery, chopped fine
1 small onion, minced
½ small green pepper, chopped
1 medium carrot, grated
1 T oil

Combine the dry ingredients (sunflower seed meal through basil) in a mixing bowl. Stir in the beaten egg and tomato juice, moistening the dry ingredients uniformly.

Heat the 2 t oil in a small skillet. Sauté the chopped celery, onion, and green pepper, stirring for about 2 minutes. Add the carrot, stir briefly, cover, and let steam for 5 minutes over reduced heat. Pour the vegetables into the sunflower seed mixture; combine well.

Divide the mixture into thirds, then sixths. Form 6 patties, shaping them with your hands. Heat the oil in the electric skillet (325°) or in a stove-top skillet, using moderate heat. Cook the patties for 2 to 3 minutes per side, then cover, lower the heat, and let cook for another 5 to 8 minutes.

3 servings
Average serving = approx. 14 grams balanced protein
32 to 39% of daily protein need

Cheese-Nut Patties

Small double-cheese patties with oats and nuts fortified with eggs, baked on the electric skillet, spread with mushroom sauce and garnished with parsley.

2 eggs
½ c. cottage cheese
1 onion, minced
½ t marjoram, crushed
½ c. raw rolled oats
½ c. walnuts, finely chopped
½ c. grated cheese
1 T oil
Mushroom Sauce (see recipe below)
Parsley

Beat the eggs in a mixing bowl. Stir in the cottage cheese, mashing the curds.

Add the minced onion and marjoram. Stir in the rolled oats. Add the chopped walnuts and grated cheese. Mix all together well.

Heat the oil in an electric skillet at 325°. Form the batter into 9 small patties by dropping it onto the skillet with a spoon. Allow the patties to brown well on the first side before turning carefully with a spatula to brown on the other.

Place the patties on a serving platter and spread them with Mushroom Sauce. Garnish with parsley.

Makes 3 servings.

Mushroom Sauce

1 c. chopped fresh mushrooms
1 t oil
¼ c. mayonnaise
¼ c. milk

Heat the oil in a small skillet and sauté the mushrooms in it. Separately, blend the mayonnaise with the milk; add the liquid to the mushrooms, and heat briefly. Serve over Cheese-Nut Patties.

3 servings
Average serving = approx. 15 grams balanced protein
35 to 42% of daily protein need

Soy Granule Burger Sandwiches

In a vegetable protein version of hamburger sandwiches, the flavor of these tender textured soy granule burgers is especially well complemented by the traditional hamburger sauces and relishes.

Basic Recipe for One Pound of Soy Granule Burger,* or 2 cups of Convenience Mix
2 T oil
1 c. water
1 t soy sauce
6-12 wheat-soy bread slices or 6 hamburger buns
Mayonnaise
Catsup
Sliced onions
Pickles
Cheese slices, if desired

Prepare Basic Recipe of Soy Granule Burger Mix. When the mass is firm, divide it into 6 pie-shaped portions. Roll each one into a ball with your hands, and flatten it into a ½-inch thick burger shape. Or press the ball into a hamburger shaper to have uniform patties.

Heat the oil in a very large non-stick skillet or in an electric skillet, using medium heat. Brown the burgers nicely about 2 minutes on each side, turning carefully with a wide spatula.

Pour in the 1 c. water mixed with soy sauce. Cover, lower heat, and let simmer for 20 minutes. (If using an electric skillet, close the vents on the cover.) The water will be absorbed and the burgers will become moist. If cheeseburgers are desired, place slices of cheese on the burgers to melt a few minutes before the cooking time is over, keeping them covered.

Spread the bread or buns with mayonnaise. Place the burgers on each bun or on slices of the bread. Add the onions, pickles, catsup, or other relishes, as desired. Top with additional bread slices if you are using bread, or have the sandwiches open face.

6 servings
Average serving = approx. 10 grams balanced protein
23 to 28% of daily protein need

Spicy Indian Patties

Our vegetarian version of meat patties from an authentic Indian recipe. A blend of wheat, soy, and oats with potato, onion, coriander, cumin, and allspice.

⅓ c. soy granules
⅓ c. soy nuts, ground
⅓ c. oats, coarsely ground
¼ c. whole wheat flour
¼ c. wheat germ
¼ c. bran
¼ c. sunflower seeds, ground or sesame seeds, ground
1 t freshly ground coriander
1 t ground cumin
½ t allspice
1 large potato, finely grated
1 large onion, finely chopped
2 c. hot water, divided
1 Vegex cube
2 T soy sauce, divided
1 c. whole wheat bread crumbs
2 T oil

Combine the dry ingredients (soy granules through ground seeds), mixing together well in a bowl. Mix in the ground coriander, cumin, and allspice. Stir in the grated potato and onion.

Dissolve the Vegex cube in 1 c. hot water, then add 1 T soy sauce. Pour this liquid into the dry mixture, blending with a spoon until all dry ingredients are evenly moistened. Let the batter stand for 10 minutes or so, until the moisture is absorbed and the dough becomes stiffer.

Make 10 oval patties (3 x 2 inches, about ½ inch thick) by scooping up the dough with a large spoon. Roll them in the bread crumbs until coated.

Heat 2 T oil in the electric skillet (350°) or regular skillet on medium heat. Brown the patties well on each side, turning once, about 5 minutes per side.

Combine 1 T soy sauce with another 1 c. hot water. Pour half this mixture into the skillet, cover, reduce heat to 200° (or low) and cook for 10 minutes (vents closed). Uncover, turn patties over, pour in the remaining ½ c. liquid, increase the heat to 225°, cover (vents *open* this time), and cook for 10 minutes more.

5 servings
Average serving = approx. 13 grams balanced protein
30 to 36% of daily protein need

Soy-Millet Cutlets

Firm-textured, substantial skillet-baked cutlets—formed from a blender batter of soaked soybeans mixed with millet flour and pecan meal—with tomato sauce and melted mozzarella cheese.

1 c. soaked soybeans, drained
¾ c. water
1 T catsup
1 T oil
¼ t garlic powder
½ t thyme
½ t sage
½ t Vege-Sal (optional)
¼ t low-sodium chicken-style soup base
½ c. millet, ground to fine flour
½ c. pecan meal (or walnut meal)
¼ c. wheat germ
1 medium onion, minced
1 handful fresh parsley, minced
1 c. Tomato Sauce
8 thin slices of mozzarella cheese

Put the soaked soybeans in a blender container with the ¾ c. water, catsup, oil, and dry seasonings (garlic powder through soup base). Blend until absolutely smooth and liquidy. Pour the batter into a mixing bowl.

Add millet flour, pecan or walnut meal, and wheat germ to the blender batter. Mix thoroughly. Stir in the minced onion and parsley.

Divide the surface of the batter in the bowl into 4 equal portions with the end of a spoon. Divide each portion in half.

Have an electric skillet lightly oiled and heated to 325°. With a large spoon, scoop out each of the 8 batter portions and place it on the skillet in oval form. Cover (vents open) and bake for 10 minutes. Uncover, turn the cutlets, and bake as before for another 10 minutes. Lower the heat to 200° and allow the cutlets to bake for another 8 minutes.

Put about 1 T of tomato sauce on each cutlet, then top with the slices of mozzarella cheese. Replace the cover and let the cheese melt for about 2 minutes. Serve with the remaining tomato sauce.

4 servings
Average serving = approx. 13 grams balanced protein
30 to 36% of daily protein need

Super Soy Burgers

Made from a blender batter of soybeans and garbanzo beans balanced with sesame and oats, this is a perfect vegetarian hamburger—excellent in taste, color, and texture. It is especially good with catsup, melted cheese, pickles, onions, and other traditional relishes. Or use it with tomato sauce for a dinner entrée.

½ c. soaked soybeans, drained
½ c. soaked garbanzos, drained
½ c. water
1 T oil
1 small onion, quartered
1 t soy sauce
1 Vegex cube, crushed
1 t Postum
½ t Gravy Master
½ c. sesame seeds, ground
1 T wheat germ
1 T bran
¼ c. raw rolled oats
1 T oil

Put the beans, water, 1 T oil, onion, and seasonings (soy sauce through Gravy Master) in a blender container. Blend until the bean particles are very fine. Pour contents of blender into a small mixing bowl.

Mix the ground sesame seeds, wheat germ, bran, and oats into the batter. Stir thoroughly and allow to stand for 10 minutes for bran and oats to absorb moisture.

Preheat an electric skillet to 325°. Spread 1 T oil over its surface. Place circular hamburger shaper on the skillet and fill with a fifth of the batter, smoothing it with the back of a spoon. Lift the shaper off, leaving the neat round burger. Continue until 5 burgers are shaped.

Cover the skillet and let the burgers cook for 10 minutes, until nicely browned on the bottom. (Make sure the steam vents are *open* on the cover. If they are closed, the batter will puff up too much, resulting in misshapen burgers.) Turn the burgers over with a spatula and cook for 10 minutes more, covered as before. Lower the heat to 200° and allow to bake an additional 10 minutes.

Variation: Use all soaked soybeans (total of 1 c.) instead of half garbanzo beans.

5 servings
Average serving = approx. 12 grams balanced protein
28 to 34% of daily protein need

Salisbury Steak-style Burgers

Big, crusty-brown meaty ovals smothered in a thick onion sauce, these "steaks" are formed from a batter of puréed soybeans and garbanzo beans combined with oats and sesame meal, baked in an electric skillet like thick pancakes.

1 c. soaked soybeans, drained
½ c. soaked garbanzo beans, drained
¾ c. water
1½ T oil
2 t soy sauce
1 Vegex cube, ground
1 T nutritional yeast
1½ t. cereal coffee
1 t. Gravy Master
½ t. ground thyme
½ c. rolled oats
½ c. sesame seeds, ground
1 T oil
Onion Sauce (see recipe below)

Put all ingredients in a blender container except the oats, sesame meal, and the last tablespoon of oil. Blend until the bean particles are of fine consistency. Pour the batter into a bowl and stir in the sesame meal and oats. Allow the mixture to stand for about 10 minutes for the oats to absorb moisture.

Have the electric skillet heated to 325°. Spread a tablespoon of oil on its surface. With a large spoon, divide the surface of the batter in the bowl into 6 equal pie-shaped portions. Scoop out each portion with the spoon and spread it onto the skillet in a large oval shape, slightly flattened and about ¾ inch thick. Cover the skillet (steam vents open) and bake for 10 minutes. Turn the "steaks" with a pancake turner and bake for another 10 minutes, covered as before. Turn the heat down to "warm" and allow to bake for 10 minutes more.

Spoon Onion Sauce over the "steaks" on a serving platter. Garnish with parsley, if desired.

Makes 4 to 6 servings.

Onion Sauce

1 large onion, peeled
1 T oil
2 T whole wheat pastry flour
1 Vegex cube
½ t. Gravy Master
1 c. water

Slice the onion into rings. Sauté it in a skillet in the oil, stirring until it is just barely tender. Stir in the flour and mix well with the onion and oil residue. Pour in the water and Vegex cube, stirring until the flour is well mixed in, the sauce thickens and bubbles a bit, and the Vegex cube is dissolved. Stir in the Gravy Master.

4 to 6 servings
Average serving = approx. 10 grams balanced protein
23 to 28% of daily protein need

The Chickpea or Garbanzo Plant

Ham-style Skillet Rounds

A soy-millet batter skillet cutlet with an appealing tomato-pink color and a subtle hickory-smoked flavor from Bakon yeast and pine nuts.

1 c. soaked soybeans, drained
¾ c. tomato purée
¼ c. water
1 T oil
1 T soy sauce
2 t cider vinegar
1 T honey
½ t Vege-Sal
½ t prepared mustard
1 T Bakon yeast
½ c. millet, ground to fine flour
⅓ c. pine nuts, ground (or almonds)
¼ c. wheat germ
1 medium onion, minced
1 T oil

Put the soaked soybeans in a blender container with the tomato purée, ¼ c. water, 1 T oil, soy sauce, cider vinegar, honey, Vege-Sal, mustard, and Bakon yeast. Blend until smooth. Remove the batter to a mixing bowl, extracting it all with a flexible spatula.

Stir in millet flour, ground nuts, wheat germ, and minced onion. Mix well.

Heat 1 T oil in electric skillet at 325°, spreading it all over the surface.

Make 6 rounds on the skillet by filling a metal hamburger shaper with the batter.

Cover the skillet (vents open) and bake for 10 minutes. Uncover, turn the rounds with a wide spatula, and bake (vents open) for another 10 minutes. Lower the heat to 200° and bake for another 10 minutes.

3 servings
Average serving = approx. 11 grams balanced protein
26 to 34% of daily protein need

Soy Foo Yung

A delicious eggless version of Egg Foo Yung made with a light and savory soy-millet batter filled with bean sprouts, celery, onion, and mushrooms. These Chinese vegetable patties are served with brown rice and Foo Yung Sauce.

1 c. soaked soybeans, drained
1 c. water
1 T oil
½ t Vege-Sal
¼ t garlic powder
1 T nutritional yeast
⅓ c. millet, ground to fine flour
2 T cashew nuts, ground
1 T oil
1 small onion, chopped
1 stalk celery, sliced
½ sweet red pepper, chopped
2 c. fresh mung bean sprouts
4 large fresh mushrooms, sliced
2 T oil, divided
Foo Yung Sauce (see recipe below)

Put the soaked soybeans in a blender container with the water. Add the oil, Vege-Sal, and garlic powder. Blend until smooth. Add the yeast, ground millet, and ground cashew nuts. Blend briefly until homogenized. Remove batter to a mixing bowl.

In a medium skillet, heat 1 T oil. Add onion, celery, and sweet red pepper, stirring for ½ minute. Add bean sprouts and mushrooms, stirring for another ½ minute. Lightly sprinkle the vegetables with Vege-Sal, if desired. Pour vegetables into the soy batter. Stir to mix them in.

Heat an electric skillet to 350°. Add 1 T oil, spreading it with a spatula. When the oil is heated, spoon the vegetable batter onto the skillet in 4 portions, making 4-inch patties. Bake covered (vents open) for 10 minutes.

Meanwhile, use a regular skillet over moderate heat for 3 more patties, having the lid off-balance to let steam escape. (Or wait until the first batch of patties has set, remove them to a baking sheet, and bake 20 minutes at 350°. Use the electric skillet for the remaining 3 patties and finish them in the oven also.)

If you have used 2 skillets, simply put all the patties into the electric skillet after they have cooked 10 minutes per side. Lower the heat to 200° and bake for another 10 minutes, vents closed.

Serve patties with Foo Yung Sauce and brown rice.

Makes 2 to 3 servings. For larger quantities, use the skillet-to-oven method described above, placing patties lightly browned on one side in the skillet, unbrowned side down on an oiled baking sheet. Bake them for 20 minutes in a 350° oven.

Foo Yung Sauce

1 c. hot water
1 Vegex cube
2 t soy sauce
1 T cornstarch
2 T water

In a saucepan, dissolve the Vegex cube in 1 c. hot water. Add 2 t soy sauce. In a cup, dissolve 1 T cornstarch in 2 T water. Pour the cornstarch solution into the Vegex mixture. Boil for 1 minute.

2 to 3 servings
Average serving = approx. 14 grams balanced protein
32 to 39% of daily protein need

Vegetarian Sausages

Savory sausage-like fingers made of ground soy nuts, sesame seeds, walnuts, herbs, and spices.

1 c. soy nuts, ground
⅓ c. sesame seeds, ground
⅓ c. rolled oats, ground
½ c. ground and chopped walnuts
1 egg
1 medium onion
2 T soy sauce
1 T low-sodium beef-like soup base
½ t Gravy Master (optional)
¼ t garlic powder
¼ t marjoram
¼ t ground thyme
½ t sage
½ t paprika
¼ t celery seed
1 T olive oil
½ c. water
2 t soy sauce

Place all the ground nuts, seeds, and oats in a mixing bowl.

Put the egg and coarsely chopped onion, then soy sauce, soup base, Gravy Master, herbs and seasonings (garlic powder through celery seed) in a blender container. Liquify, then pour into the dry ingredients and mix well.

Spoon some of the mixture on a sheet of waxed paper, squeeze it out to a long roll about ¾ inch thick, and cut it into 3-inch long pieces.

Shape the ends of the pieces like sausages by rolling with your hands. Continue until all of the mixture is used. You should have about 16 such sausages.

Sauté the sausages in 1 T olive oil in a large non-stick skillet over low heat—soy browns very easily. Turn the sausages often.

When the sausages are browned, pour in a mixture of ½ c. water and 2 t soy sauce; bring to a boil, cover, lower the heat, and simmer until the water is absorbed, about 10 minutes. Turn the sausages once or twice during the simmering.

8 servings
Average serving = approx. 6 grams balanced protein
14 to 17% of daily protein need

Pies and Crust Items

The egg custard pie is a familiar vegetarian dish with many variations using different cheeses, mushrooms, onions, and various vegetables. But it is also usually too high in animal fat and cholesterol to depend on for daily protein. Substituting soy-millet batter for the egg custard makes a delicious healthful change in these filled pie crust main dishes. Examples are Zucchini Pie, Herb Tomato Pie Provençale, Mushroom Pie, Sherry Burger Pie and, in miniature, Mixed Vegetable Tarts.

Soyloaf cubes mixed with cheese or vegetables and sauce make nice pie fillings for main dishes. Try Cheese and Loaf Cube Pie, Puff Crust Pie, Parisian Pot Pies, and Chicken-style Pot Pie.

Pizzas are one of the most popular main-dish crust items. Try our Delectable Vegetarian Pizza, using sesame sausage rounds as an option for filling. We also have a pie with a burger-like base filled with tomato sauce and cheese—Vegemeat Crust Pizza. (A variation, filled with mashed potatoes, is Vegemeat Crust Shepherd Pie.) Tomato Cheese Pie is a pizza-like variation with a soy granule crust and an egg and cheese custard over sliced tomatoes. Using granule burger you can also make Vegetarian Chili Pizzas. Vege-Sausage Egg Pizza is a pizza variation without tomato sauce using vegetable protein sausage links.

Some turnover-style filled crust items to eat out of hand are Vegetarian Calzones, Vegetarian Pasties, Vegetarian Samosas, and Chili Turnovers, which use granule burger or soyloaf cubes with vegetables for fillings.

High-protein Biscuit Dough, Basic Crust for main-dish pies, Whole Wheat and Soy Yeast Pizza Dough and a Whole Wheat Oil Pie Crust to be used in the recipes precede them in this section and are followed by an asterisk* when referred to in the recipes.

Basic Biscuit Dough

1 c. whole wheat pastry flour
¼ c. soy powder
1 t baking powder
¼ t Vege-Sal
2 T peanut oil
½ c. milk or water

Combine the dry ingredients (flour through Vege-Sal). Stir in the oil and cut into small lumps with a pastry blender. Stir in the milk or water and mix well. Gather the dough into a ball.

Roll out ½ inch thick on a lightly floured board. Cut into biscuits or use as directed in your recipe. For biscuits, bake at 400° for 15 minutes on a lightly oiled cookie sheet.

Basic Crust

¼ c. soy nuts, ground
¼ c. low-fat soy powder
½ c. whole wheat pastry flour
½ c. rolled oats, ground
1 t baking powder
1 egg or 2 t egg replacer with ¼ c. water
¼ c. peanut oil
¼ c. milk or water

Combine the dry ingredients (ground soy nuts through baking powder) in a large bowl. Mix well.

Beat the egg or egg replacer in a small bowl. Stir in the peanut oil and milk or water.

Pour the liquid mixture into the dry ingredients and stir until smooth. Gather the dough into a ball. Knead it 15 times right in the mixing bowl. (If dough is too sticky, add a bit more flour. This happens if the egg is large.)

Place the ball of dough between two sheets of waxed paper and roll it out to a 12-inch round. Peel off the top layer of waxed paper and place the pizza pan or pie tin over the rolled out dough. Slide your hand under the remaining piece of waxed paper and invert the dough into the pan. Carefully peel off the waxed paper and shape the dough to the pan.

To prebake before filling, bake at 400° for 10 minutes. Otherwise follow the directions in your recipe.

Makes one 12-inch pizza crust or one 9-inch quiche or soy-pie crust with a high fluted edge.

Note: Egg replacer is a commercial leavening powder found in health food stores.

Whole Wheat and Soy Yeast Pizza Dough

1 c. warm water (110°-115° F.)
1 T dry yeast granules
1 t honey
1 T oil
1 t Vege-Sal
1½ c. whole wheat flour
½ c. soy powder
½ c. whole wheat flour

Combine the yeast granules and warm water in a bowl. Add the honey, oil, and Vege-Sal. Let stand for 5 minutes, or until the yeast becomes frothy. Stir in the 1½ c. of whole wheat flour and the soy powder.

Beat the dough until smooth and elastic. Gather up the dough and knead it on a board floured with another ½ c. whole wheat flour. Knead until the dough is smooth, 5 to 10 minutes, incorporating all the flour on the board.

Cut the dough in half. Set one half aside and roll the other half into a ball. Roll the dough ball out with a rolling pin until it is the size of the pizza pan. Pull and stretch the dough to fit into the pan (oiled with unrefined soy oil). Turn up the edges of the dough to form a rim.

Repeat with the other ball of dough.

Bake the crust for 10 minutes at 400° on the lower rack of the oven so that the bottom of the crust gets crisp. Fill the crust with seasoned sauce and bake for another 10 minutes. Add cheese and return to the oven until the cheese is melted, about 5 minutes.

Makes 2 whole wheat and soy pizza crusts.

Variations: For a pressed bran crust, increase the warm water by ⅓ c. Add ⅓ c. bran and 2 T nutritional yeast to dry ingredients. After kneading, just spread half the dough into the oiled pizza pan, pressing it outward from the center. Repeat with the other half of the dough.

For a whole wheat, oat, and soy crust, substitute ½ c. oat flour for ½ c. whole wheat flour.

Whole Wheat Oil Pie Crust

1 c. whole wheat pastry flour
½ t Vege-Sal
¼ c. oil
3 T cold water

Mix the whole wheat pastry flour and Vege-Sal together in a Pyrex measuring cup. Add the cold water to the oil and beat the liquids together with a fork.

Gradually add the liquid to the dry ingredients in the pie pan, mixing with the fork. When the ingredients are well blended, press the crust evenly with your fingers over the entire inner surface of the pie pan. Prick the bottom of the crust with the fork in a few places.

Bake at 375° for 20 minutes.

Makes one 9-inch pie crust.

Variations: For a bran pie crust, substitute ¼ c. bran for ¼ c. flour. For a whole wheat and soy crust, substitute ¼ c. soy powder for ¼ c. flour.

For a rolled-out crust, put flour, Vege-Sal and 1 T wheat germ into a bowl. Mix the oil and cold water in a measuring cup, adding an additional tablespoon of oil. Stir liquid all at once into the flour and mix until all flour is dampened. Shape flour mixture into a ball and roll it out between two sheets of waxed paper with a rolling pin. Peel off the top layer of waxed paper and invert crust into a pie tin. Shape to fit the tin.

Zucchini Pie

A very big supper pie made with high-protein wheat, soy, and oat crust filled with a soy-millet custard laced with green onion and grated zucchini.

1 recipe Basic Crust (see page 141)
1½ c. soaked soybeans, drained
2½ c. water
2 T tomato paste or catsup
1 T oil
1 T soy sauce
1 t Vege-Sal
1 T honey
1 T lecithin granules
¼ c. soy milk powder (a low-fat soy powder)
¼ t turmeric
⅝ c. millet, ground
¼ c. cashew nuts, ground
1½ t oil
¾ c. chopped green onions
3 c. coarsely grated zucchini
Vege-Sal

Roll out the basic crust dough between two layers of waxed paper to a ⅛-inch thickness. Fit the dough into a 10-inch pie tin. Crimp up the excess dough, making a fluted edge.

Put the soaked soybeans in a blender container with 2½ c. water. Add the tomato paste through turmeric. Blend until the batter is absolutely smooth. Pour the batter into a mixing bowl, removing every bit of it from the blender container with a flexible spatula.

Stir the ground millet and cashew nuts into the soy batter.

Heat 1½ t oil in a skillet and sauté the green onions, stirring for 1 minute over moderate heat. Add the grated zucchini and stir for 2 minutes more. Sprinkle the vegetables with Vege-Sal. Fold them into the soy batter.

Pour the soy batter into the pie crust. Bake the pie at 350° for 1 hour, or until a cake tester comes out clean from the center of the pie.

Makes 8 to 10 servings.

8 to 10 servings
Average serving = approx. 11 grams balanced protein
26 to 31% of daily protein need

Herb Tomato Pie Provençal

An elegant supper pie with a high-protein crust, layers of yeast cheese or cream cheese, parsleyed brown rice, soy custard filled with chopped tomatoes, green onions, and herbs, and a ring of tomato slices on top.

1 recipe Basic Crust*
½ c.-¾ c. Vegetable Protein "Cheese" Spread* or softened dairy cream cheese
1 c. cooked brown rice
¼ c. chopped parsley
1 c. soaked soybeans, drained
¾ c. milk or water
1 t Vege-Sal
½ c. millet, ground to flour
¼ c. cashew nuts, ground
1 T olive oil
1 large onion, chopped
3-4 cloves of garlic, minced
2 T chopped parsley
3 T chopped green onions or chives
½ t leaf basil, crushed
½ t leaf tarragon, crushed
1 can (1 lb.) whole tomatoes
1 large fresh tomato
2 T Parmesan cheese
2 T whole wheat bread crumbs

Roll the basic crust dough out between two sheets of waxed paper. Fit the dough into a 9-inch pie pan, making a high fluted edge about 1 inch above the rim of the pie tin.

Spread the yeast cheese or cream cheese on the bottom of the pie crust. Spread the cooked rice mixed with ¼ c. chopped parsley over the cheese layer.

In a blender container, purée the soybeans with water or milk and Vege-Sal. Remove the batter to a bowl. Stir in the ground millet and cashew nuts.

Sauté the onion and garlic briefly in olive oil. Stir them into the soy batter. Stir in the chopped parsley, chives, basil, and tarragon.

Pour half of the soy batter mixture into the pie pan over the rice and cheese layer.

Drain the canned whole tomatoes. (Save the liquid for soup or sauce.) Chop the tomatoes coarsely and spread them over the batter in the pie. Pour the remaining soy batter into the crust over the layer of chopped tomatoes.

Slice the fresh tomato thinly and lay a circle of tomato slices around the outer edge of the pie. Brush a little oil on each tomato slice.

Bake the pie at 350° for 1 hour. After 20 minutes, cover the pie loosely with a piece of aluminum foil to prevent excessive browning and drying out of the tomatoes. Ten minutes before the pie is done, remove the foil shield. Mix the Parmesan cheese and whole wheat bread crumbs together. Sprinkle them over the tomato slices.

6 to 8 servings
Average serving = approx. 13 grams balanced protein
30 to 36% of daily protein need

The Rice Plant

Mushroom Pie

A high-protein pie crust spread with yeast cheese or dairy cheese, topped with a soy-millet custard filled with sliced mushrooms.

1 recipe Basic Crust*
¾ c. Vegetable Protein "Cheese" Spread* or grated dairy cheese
1 c. cooked soybeans, drained
1 c. water
1 t Vege-Sal
2 t oil
½ c. millet, ground to fine flour
2 T cashew nuts, ground
2 c. sliced fresh mushrooms
2 t oil
1 medium onion, chopped (1 cup)

Roll out the ball of basic crust dough between two pieces of waxed paper to ⅛-inch thickness. Fit the dough into a 9-inch pie tin, crimping up the excess dough to form a high fluted edge.

Spread the yeast cheese or dairy cheese on the bottom of the crust.

Put the soybeans, water, Vege-Sal and 2 t oil into a blender container, and purée until the batter is absolutely smooth. Remove the batter to a mixing bowl, extracting it all with a flexible spatula.

Mix the ground millet and ground cashew nuts into the soybean batter. Stir in the sliced mushrooms, folding them in to distribute the batter between them.

Heat 2 t oil in a small skillet. Sauté the onions briefly. Fold the onions into the batter.

Pour the batter into the prepared pie shell and smooth it with a spatula.

Bake the pie at 350° for 1 hour, or until a cake tester comes out clean when inserted in the center of the pie.

6 to 8 servings
Average serving = approx. 13 grams balanced protein
30 to 36% of daily protein need

Sherry Burger Pie

A high-protein pie crust filled with granule burger and onion topped with soy custard.

1 recipe Bulgar Wheat Granule Burger,* cooked
1 c. hot water or vegetable water
2 t low-sodium beef-style soup base
¼ t Vege-Sal
2 t Worcestershire sauce
1 c. sliced onions
1 clove garlic, minced
1 T oil
¾ c. soaked soybeans
1 c. evaporated milk or vegetable cooking water
¼ c. millet, ground to fine flour
3 T sherry
½-1 t Vege-Sal
1 recipe Basic Crust*
2 T chopped fresh parsley

Mix the hot water, soup base, Vege-Sal, and Worcestershire sauce together. Pour into the chunked cooked granule burger. Let stand until the liquid is absorbed.

Sauté the onions and garlic in 1 T oil until barely tender. Mix them into the granule burger.

Put the soaked soybeans and evaporated milk or vegetable water into a blender container. Blend until absolutely smooth. Pour in the millet flour, sherry, and Vege-Sal. Blend until mixed.

Roll out basic crust and fit it into a 10-inch pie tin, making a high rim with excess dough.

Place the granule burger mix in the bottom of the pie shell, covering it evenly. Sprinkle parsley over the granule burger. Pour the soybean mixture over granule burger.

Bake at 350° for 45 minutes.

6 to 8 servings
Average serving = approx. 13 grams balanced protein
30 to 36% of daily protein need

Mixed Vegetable Tarts

Small pies made with high-protein crusts and soy-millet custard filled with diced mixed vegetables—carrots, celery, green beans, peas, and onions.

4 c. diced mixed vegetables (carrots, celery, green beans, peas, onion) or 4 c. frozen mixed vegetables
2 T oil
2 T water
2 c. soaked soybeans, drained
1½ c. milk or water
2 T oil
1 t onion powder
2 T soy sauce
½ c. millet, ground to fine flour
½ c. cashew nuts, ground
2 recipes Basic Crust

In a skillet sauté the diced vegetables in 2 T oil over moderate heat, stirring constantly. Add 2 T water, lower heat, cover, and let steam for 2 to 3 minutes, or until they are just tender-crisp.

Put the soaked soybeans, milk or water, onion powder, 2 T oil, and soy sauce in a blender container. Blend until the batter is absolutely smooth. Pour the batter into a mixing bowl, removing the last traces with a rubber spatula.

Stir in the ground millet and cashew nuts, mixing thoroughly. Mix in the vegetables.

Roll out each ball of basic crust dough to ⅛-inch thickness between two sheets of waxed paper. Make 3 tart crusts from each recipe. Cut 7-inch circles from the dough and fit them into tart pans (3¼ inches in diameter at bottom, 5¼ inches from rim to rim, and 1 inch deep), crimping the dough up to form high fluted edges.

Fill the tarts with the soy-vegetable mixture, dividing it evenly among the six. Bake at 350° for 40 minutes, or until a cake tester comes out clean and the tarts are lightly browned.

6 servings
Average serving = approx. 13 grams balanced protein
30 to 36% of daily protein need

Deviled Spread and Spinach Pie

The basic high-protein crust spread with a layer of soy sandwich loaf, a layer of yeast cheese or dairy cheese, and a topping of savory soy-millet custard filled with spinach.

1 recipe Basic Crust*
1 c. Deviled Sandwich Spread*
½ c. Vegetable Protein "Cheese" Spread* or ½ c. grated dairy cheese
1 c. soaked soybeans, drained
¾ c. water or milk
1 t Vege-Sal
2 t oil
½ c. millet, ground
¼ c. cashew nuts, ground
1 package (10 ozs.) frozen chopped spinach, mostly thawed, or 1 lb. fresh spinach, lightly cooked and chopped (1-1¼ c.)

Roll out the ball of basic crust dough between two pieces of waxed paper to ⅛-inch thickness. Fit the dough into a 9-inch pie tin, crimping up the excess dough to form a high fluted edge.

Spread and pat the deviled sandwich spread about ½ inch thick in the bottom of the crust. Spread the yeast cheese or dairy cheese over it.

Put the soaked soybeans, water, Vege-Sal, and oil into a blender container. Blend until the mixture is absolutely smooth. Remove the batter to a bowl, then stir in the ground millet and ground cashew nuts, mixing thoroughly. Stir in the chopped spinach.

Pour the spinach-soy batter into the prepared crust, distributing it evenly. Bake the pie at 350° for 1 hour. (After 20 minutes or so, cover the pie loosely with foil so that the crust does not become too brown.)

6 to 8 servings
Average serving = approx. 13 grams balanced protein
30 to 36% of daily protein need

Cheese and Loaf Cube Pie

An unusual pie with the high-protein basic crust and a lattice topping of dough strips. The filling is made of cubes of soy-meat, cheese, eggs and green pepper bits.

1 recipe Basic Crust*
1 c. soy-loaf* (any style) cut into ½-inch cubes
1 c. ½-inch cubes of jack cheese
½ green pepper, chopped fine
2 eggs, beaten

Roll out basic crust dough between two sheets of waxed paper, making it ⅛ inch thick. Fit part of the crust into an 8-inch pie tin. (Cut the remaining crust dough into long strips for a lattice strip topping and set them aside.) Bake the crust for 10 minutes at 350°.

Put the loaf cubes, cheese, cubes and chopped green pepper in the partially baked pie shell. Pour the beaten eggs over all. Crisscross ½-inch-wide strips of dough over the filling. Bake at 350° for 30 minutes.

4 servings
Average serving = approx. 15 grams balanced protein
35 to 42% of daily protein need

Puff Crust Pie

A puffy flour and egg crust encircles a savory filling of diced ham-style soy loaf, sliced mushrooms, tomato slivers, and cheese.

Crust:

½ c. whole wheat pastry flour
2 T soy powder
½ c. water
¼ c. oil
2 eggs
¼ c. Swiss cheese cubes

Sift the flour and soy powder together into a small bowl.

Combine the oil and water in a small saucepan. Bring to a boil and pour in the flour all at once, stirring vigorously until the mixture forms a ball in middle of the pan. Let cool for 5 minutes.

Stir in the eggs one at a time with a wooden spoon, beating well to insure puffiness of the crust. Mix in the cheese cubes.

Spoon this puff-paste in a wreath around the sides of a 9-inch pie tin oiled with unrefined soy oil, leaving the center open. Bake at 400° for 20 minutes.

Filling and Assembly:

1 onion, diced
1 T oil
1½ c. sliced fresh mushrooms
2 T whole wheat pastry flour
2 t low-sodium chicken-like soup base
½ t Vege-Sal
1 c. hot water
1½ c. Ham-style or chicken-style Soyloaf* cubes (ham-style or chicken-style)
1 tomato, quartered and slivered
1 T chopped parsley
¼ c. shredded Swiss or Cheddar cheese

In a skillet, sauté the onion in the oil until tender. Add the mushrooms and sauté briefly. Stir in the flour and mix well.

Put the chicken-like seasoning and Vege-Sal into 1 c. hot water, then pour the water mixture into the mushrooms and onions, stirring until the sauce is thickened. Carefully fold in the soy loaf pieces. Add the tomato slivers to the skillet.

Remove the puff-crust from the oven and lower the heat to 350°. Pour the soy loaf and mushroom filling into the center of the pie tin, add shredded cheese, and bake an additional 20 minutes at 350°. Sprinkle with parsley before serving.

4 servings
Average serving = approx. 12 grams balanced protein
28 to 34% of daily protein need

Parisian Pot Pies

Individual pie crusts filled with cubed soyloaf or granule burger, chopped carrots, celery, onion, mushrooms, string beans, and a creamy brown sauce.

2 recipes Basic Biscuit Dough*
4 c. Beef-style Soyloaf* (cut in ½-inch cubes), or 1 recipe cooked cubed Granule Burger*
2 T oil
4 medium carrots, pared
4 stalks celery, thinly sliced
2 medium onions, coarsely chopped
1½ c. frozen chopped string beans (or raw, thinly sliced, French cut; or pre-cooked)
6 large mushrooms, sliced
2 c. water
2 T soy sauce
1 T low-sodium beef-style soup base
2 T cornstarch
⅔ c. mayonnaise (regular or eggless)

Divide one recipe of basic biscuit dough into 6 portions. Lightly oil the bottoms of 6 small (5-inch) 1¾ c. baking dishes with unrefined soy oil. Stretch and pat a portion of the dough into the bottom of each dish. Bake at 400° for 10 minutes.

Slice the carrots in thin diagonal slices. Halve the larger slices. Heat the 2 T oil in a very large non-stick skillet. Stir in the sliced carrots, celery, onion, and raw or frozen chopped string beans. Stir-fry over moderate heat for 2 minutes. Add the sliced mushrooms.

Mix the 2 c. water with soy sauce, soup base, and cornstarch. Pour the liquid into the skillet with the vegetables. Bring to a boil, cover, lower heat and let simmer for 5 to 10 minutes, or just until the vegetables are tender-crisp. (Stir in the cooked string beans, if you are using them, after the vegetables in the skillet have reached the tender-crisp stage.)

Mix in the mayonnaise, then the cubed soyloaf or granule burger.

Apportion the vegetable and soyloaf filling among the 6 crust-filled baking dishes.

Divide the remaining biscuit crust recipe into 6 pieces. Flatten out the pieces with your fingers (or roll them out with a rolling pin) and shape them over the filling around the edge of each baking dish, leaving the center open.

Bake at 400° for 15 minutes.

6 servings
Average serving = approx. 11 grams balanced protein
26 to 31% of daily protein need

Wheat

Chicken-style Pot Pie

Mixed vegetables and mushrooms with soyloaf cubes in a creamy sauce, baked in a casserole dish under a wheat and soy biscuit crust.

3 c. diced Dark Chicken-style Soyloaf*
1 T oil
1 medium onion, diced
4 c. frozen mixed vegetables
1 can (4 ozs.) mushroom pieces, drained (reserve juice for sauce); or 1 c. sliced fresh mushrooms
1½ c. vegetable cooking water
1 T chicken-style soup base
½ t Vege-Sal
2 T cornstarch
1 T oil (optional)
2 T whole wheat pastry flour
½ c. evaporated skim milk
1 recipe Basic Biscuit Dough*

Prepare half the Basic Recipe for Dark Chicken-style Soyloaf. Chill before dicing so that the cubes will be firm.

Sauté the diced onion in the oil in a large skillet over moderate heat. Stir in the frozen mixed vegetables. Stir until no frost remains. Add the mushrooms. Lower the heat, cover, and let steam for 5 minutes.

Mix together the vegetable water, soup base, Vege-Sal, cornstarch, oil (optional), and whole wheat pastry flour. Stir into the vegetables. Raise the heat, bring to a boil, and let bubble a minute. Stir in the evaporated milk.

Add the diced soyloaf to the skillet, stirring the pieces into the sauce and under the vegetables. Pour the mixture into a shallow 10-inch-square casserole dish (about 2-quart capacity).

Roll out the biscuit dough to a square shape approximately the size of the casserole. Place the dough over the vegetable mixture. Pinch the dough against the sides of the dish, making a fluted edge. Cut four steam slits in the center of the crust.

Bake at 375° for 20 minutes.

Makes 4 to 6 servings.

Variations: Use 4 c. fresh mixed vegetables, steamed, instead of frozen. Or use 3 c. of cooked, drained, seasoned soybeans (or other beans) instead of the diced soyloaf. Or apportion the vegetable mixture among individual baking dishes and fit pieces of crust over each one. (You may need to make another half-recipe of biscuit crust for 6 servings.)

4 to 6 servings
Average serving = approx. 10 grams balanced protein
23 to 28% of daily protein need

Delectable Vegetarian Pizza

A different kind of pizza with a specially formulated high-protein crust (wheat, soy, and oats); a filling of tomato sauce, grated carrot, green onions, and mushrooms; and little sesame sausage patties under the cheese topping.

Crust for Two Pizzas:

½ c. soy nuts, ground
½ c. low-fat soy powder
1 c. whole wheat pastry flour
1 c. rolled oats, ground
2 t baking powder
2 eggs or 4 t egg replacer beaten with ½ c. water
½ c. peanut oil
½ c. milk

Combine the dry ingredients (ground soy nuts through baking powder) in a large bowl. Mix well.

Beat the eggs or egg replacer in a small bowl. Stir in the peanut oil and milk.

Pour the liquid mixture into the dry ingredients and stir until smooth, then gather the dough into a ball. Knead it 15 times right in the mixing bowl.

Divide the dough in half, rolling each half into a ball. Press each ball flat between two sheets of waxed paper as far as it will stretch. Roll very thin with a rolling pin, turning over and alternately rolling each side until the crust is as large as a 12-inch pizza pan.

Peel off one sheet of waxed paper. Invert an oiled pizza pan over the crust on the other sheet of paper. Slip your hand under the paper, pressing the dough against the pan, and turn everything over so that the crust falls neatly into the pan.

Carefully peel off the waxed paper. Pinch up the edges of the dough around the rim of the pie. Bake the two crusts at 400° for 10 minutes. Lower the heat to 350° and remove the crusts for filling.

Sesame Sausage:

⅓ c. sesame seeds, ground
¼ c. soy nuts, ground
¼ c. wheat germ
¼ c. low-fat soy powder
1 t gluten flour (or whole wheat)
1 T nutritional yeast flakes
1 t dried parsley flakes
¼ t garlic powder
¼ t ground thyme
¼ t nutmeg
½ t paprika
1 small onion, minced
½ t oregano
¼ t marjoram

¼ t sage
¼ t savory
¼ t caraway seeds
½ c. hot water
1 Vegex cube, smashed
1 egg or 2 T chick-pea flour mixed with 2 T water

Thoroughly combine the dry ingredients (ground sesame seeds through yeast flakes) in a bowl. Mix in parsley flakes through paprika. Stir in the minced onion.

Combine the remaining herbs and seasonings (oregano through caraway seeds) in a small seed grinder or blender and pulverize them. Add them to the dry mix, stirring in well.

Dissolve the Vegex cube in ½ c. hot water. Pour this liquid into the dry ingredients, mixing well. Mix in the beaten egg or chick-pea flour substitute. Let the sesame sausage mix stand for about 10 minutes, or until all the liquid is well absorbed.

Tomato Sauce:

1 can (16 ozs.) tomatoes, drained
1 can (6 ozs.) tomato paste
1 medium onion, quartered
½ c. fresh parsley
1 T olive oil
2 T soy sauce
½ t Italian herbs or oregano
½ t garlic powder

Put all ingredients in a blender container and purée until smooth. Use only about ½ c. for one 12-inch pizza.

Filling for Each Pizza:

½ c. (about) of above sauce
¼-⅓ c. grated carrot
⅓ c. thinly sliced mushrooms
1 large green onion, minced
¼ t oregano, crushed
1 c. grated cheese

Assembly:

Spread the sauce for each pie (½ c.) evenly over the partially baked crusts. (If desired, brush crusts with a bit of olive oil first.) Sprinkle on the ground oregano, grated carrot, mushrooms, and green onion. (If you like the vegetables very soft, sauté them first. If put on the pie raw, they may be slightly crispy even after baking.)

Put little rounds of sesame sausage mixture over the pies by sliding them off a teaspoon and smashing them down with the back of the spoon. Bake the pies for 15 minutes at 350°, or until sesame sausages and crusts begin to brown.

Remove the pies from the oven, spread on a little more tomato sauce, if desired, and sprinkle with grated cheese. Return the pies to the oven and bake for another 5 minutes, or until the cheese is melted.

Makes 8 servings.

Variations: Use one of the recipes for Pizza Dough made with yeast among the Basic Crust Recipes beginning this section.

8 servings
Average serving = approx. 15 grams balanced protein
35 to 42% of daily protein need

The Sesame Plant

Vegemeat Crust Shepherd Pie

The protein (soy-sesame-oat) is in the savory burger-like crust of this mashed potato-topped pie.

Crust:

½ c. ground soy nuts, packed
¼ c. low-fat soy powder
⅓ c. sesame seeds, ground
⅓ c. rolled oats
¼ c. finely chopped walnuts
1 T nutritional yeast flakes
½ t ground thyme
¼ t garlic powder
1 medium onion, chopped
2 t oil
3 large mushrooms, finely chopped
¼ c. parsley, minced
1 Vegex cube
2 T hot water
1 T catsup
1 T soy sauce
½ t Gravy Master (optional)
1 egg or 2 T whole wheat pastry flour plus 2 T water

Mix the dry ingredients (ground soy nuts through chopped walnuts) together in a bowl. Stir in the yeast flakes, thyme, and garlic powder.

Heat 2 t oil in a small skillet and sauté the onion briefly. Add the onion, chopped mushrooms, and parsley to the dry ingredients.

In a small bowl, dissolve the Vegex cube in 2 T hot water. Add the catsup, soy sauce, and Gravy Master. Break the egg into the bowl (or mix the whole wheat flour and water into it) and beat all the liquid ingredients together with a fork. Pour the liquid combination into the dry ingredients and mix well until everything is evenly moistened.

Oil a 9-inch pie tin with unrefined soy oil. Pack the vegemeat into the tin as a thick pie crust. Bake at 350° for 15 minutes.

Potato Filling:

3 medium potatoes
¼ c. milk
2 T butter (optional)
½ c. cheese cubes
2 T parsley, minced

Cook the unpeeled potatoes (scrubbed and quartered) in the pressure cooker for 10 minutes over 1 c. water. Mash the potatoes with a potato masher, adding the milk and butter. Stir in the cheese cubes and parsley.

Assembly:

Pile the potato mixture into the vegemeat crust (after baking it 15 minutes). Smooth the top of the potato layer with the back of a spoon. Return the pie to the oven and bake for 10 minutes.

6 to 8 servings
Average serving = approx. 11 grams balanced protein
26 to 31% of daily protein need

The Sesame Plant

Vegemeat Crust Pizza

A savory burger-like crust filled with pizza sauce, mushrooms, onions, green pepper, sliced olives, and melted cheese.

Crust:

Follow directions for the crust in Vegemeat Crust Shepherd Pie on page 160.

Filling and Assembly:

½ can (6 ozs.) tomato paste (about ¼ c.)
¼ c. water
2 T Parmesan cheese
1 small onion, chopped
1 clove garlic, crushed, minced
½ c. chopped green pepper
2 t oil
½ c. sliced mushrooms
¼ c. sliced stuffed olives
½ c. grated Cheddar cheese or mozzarella cheese

Mix the tomato paste and water thoroughly in a small bowl. Add the Parmesan cheese.

Sauté the onion, garlic, and green pepper in 2 t oil until they start to become tender. Add the mushrooms, stir briefly, cover, and let steam over very low heat until everything is tender. Stir the vegetables into tomato mixture. Add the sliced olives.

Pour the tomato sauce filling into the baked crust and smooth it out evenly. Bake for 10 minutes at 350°.

Remove the pie from the oven, sprinkle it with grated cheese, and bake for another 5 minutes, or until the cheese is melted.

6 servings
Average serving = approx. 11 grams balanced protein
26 to 31% of daily protein need

Tomato Cheese Pie

An easy pat-in crust made of soy granules and whole wheat flour, filled with egg and cheese custard over seasoned sliced tomatoes.

½ c. soy granules
1 c. hot water
Dash Vege-Sal
½ c. whole wheat pastry flour
1 can (1 lb.) whole tomatoes
¾ c. reserved tomato liquid
1 T cornstarch
1 T minced fresh onion
½ t Vege-Sal
½ t basil, crushed
2 eggs, beaten
¾ c. milk
1 c. shredded Cheddar cheese

Soak the soy granules in hot water with Vege-Sal until they are puffy and much of the water has been absorbed. Stir in the whole wheat flour and mix well.

Oil a 9-inch pie tin with unrefined soy oil. Press the soy granule mixture into the bottom and around the sides of the tin like a crust, smoothing it with the back of a spoon. Make a high rim about ½ inch higher than the rim of the pie tin. Bake the crust at 350° for 15 minutes.

Drain the tomatoes and reserve ¾ c. tomato liquid in a saucepan. Slice the tomatoes onto a plate and drain them further. (Save excess tomato liquid for soup or other cooking.)

Dissolve the cornstarch in the tomato liquid in the saucepan. Stir in the minced onion, Vege-Sal, and basil. Heat, stirring constantly, until the liquid bubbles, 1 minute.

Place the sliced tomatoes on the bottom of the pie shell. Pour the thickened tomato liquid over them.

Add the milk and cheese to the beaten eggs. Pour the mixture over the tomato layer in the pie. Bake at 350° for 40 minutes. Allow the pie to cool for 10 minutes before cutting.

Makes 4 to 5 servings

Variation: Instead of canned tomatoes, use very ripe sliced fresh tomatoes to cover the bottom of the pie crust, and substitute ¾ c. tomato juice for the reserved tomato liquid. Omit Vege-Sal, if desired.

4 to 5 servings
Average serving = approx. 12 grams balanced protein
28 to 34% of daily protein need

Chili Pizzas

High-protein wheat, soy, and oat crusts are covered with chili-seasoned chunked granule burger in tomato sauce with chopped onion, green pepper, and melted cheese topping.

1 recipe Granule Burger*
1 can (8 ozs.) tomato sauce
1 T oil
1 medium onion, chopped
1 green pepper, chopped
1 can (8 ozs.) tomato sauce
1 can (6 ozs.) tomato paste
½ c. water
2 t - 2 T chili powder (to taste)
2 t Worcestershire sauce
2 recipes Basic Crust*
2 c. coarsely grated mozzarella cheese

Chunk the granule burger in a metal bowl and cook over 1 inch of water on a metal rack in the pressure cooker for 5 minutes. Let the pressure drop naturally. Remove and cool. Stir in 1 can of tomato sauce.

In a very large (12-inch) non-stick skillet, sauté the chopped onion and green pepper in oil over moderate heat until tender.

Pour in the second can of tomato sauce, tomato paste, and water. Mix well. Stir in the chili powder and Worcestershire sauce. Simmer for 10 to 15 minutes. Stir in the cooked granule burger mixture.

Roll out each recipe of Basic Crust and fit it on a 12-inch pizza pan. (Roll between layers of waxed paper or freezer paper as directed in the Basic Recipe.) Bake the two crusts at 350° for 10 minutes.

Remove the pizza pans from the oven and spread half of the chili mixture on each pizza crust. Return them to the oven and bake for 15 minutes more.

Remove the pizzas from oven. Sprinkle 1 c. of grated cheese on each pizza. Return them to the oven for a few minutes, until the cheese is melted.

8 servings
Average serving = approx. 14 grams balanced protein
32 to 39% of daily protein need

Vege-Sausage Egg Pizza

A high-rimmed crust filled with egg custard and cheese over slices of soy-grain sausage, chopped green pepper, and onion.

1 recipe Basic Crust*
1 recipe Soy-Grain Sausage*
(2 c. sliced "links")
½ c. chopped green pepper
1 small onion, chopped
2 c. shredded Swiss cheese
4 eggs
1 c. milk
¼ t Vege-Sal
¼ t oregano

Fit the crust into a 12-inch pizza pan, making a high rim with the excess dough. Bake the crust at 350° for 10 minutes. Remove from the oven.

Spread the soy-grain sausage slices evenly over the crust. Sprinkle the chopped green pepper and onion evenly over all.

Spread the shredded cheese over everything. Have the eggs and milk beaten in a blender with Vege-Sal and oregano. Pour the egg mixture over the filling in the crust.

Bake at 350° for 25 minutes.

4 to 6 servings
Average serving = approx. 18 grams balanced protein
42 to 50% of daily protein need

Vegetarian Calzone

Our meatless version of Italian stuffed pies made from a high-protein wheat-soy-oat crust filled with granule burger, tomatoes, cheese and olives.

2 recipes Basic Crust*
½ recipe of Granule Burger*
1 can (1 lb.) stewed tomatoes, drained and chopped
6 slices muenster or mozzarella cheese, chopped (about ¾ c.)
¼ c. grated Parmesan cheese
2 T chopped stuffed olives
2 T bacon flavored bits (optional)
1 t leaf oregano, crumbled

Divide the Basic Crust into 12 portions. Form each into a ball and roll it out to a 6-inch circle.

Cook the crumbled Granule Burger in a metal bowl on the steam rack of the pressure cooker for 5 minutes over ½ c. water. (Or steam 20 minutes in a regular pot with the same utensils.)

Combine the cooked crumbled granule burger in a bowl with chopped drained tomatoes, chopped cheese, Parmesan cheese, olives, bacon-flavored bits, and oregano. Apportion this filling among the 12 circles of dough—about ¼ c. filling on one half of each circle. Fold each circle in half, covering the filling. Pinch together the edges of the resulting half-circle.

Brush the tops of the pies with oil. Bake them at 375° for 20 minutes on a lightly oiled cookie sheet.

6 servings
Average serving = approx. 12 grams balanced protein
28 to 34% of daily protein need

Vegetarian Pasties

A meatless version of Cornish pasties, granul burger replacing beef in individual pies. The high-protein crust folds over a moist and savory filling of granule burger, diced potatoes, turnips, onion, and parsley.

1 recipe of Granule Burger*
1 t garlic powder
2 medium potatoes, diced
2 medium white turnips, diced
1 medium onion, diced
2 T oil
2 recipes Basic Crust*
1¾ c. hot water
2 Vegex cubes
¼ c. water
2 T cornstarch
2 T Worcestershire sauce
¼ c. chopped parsley

Add 1 t garlic powder to dry granule burger mix before adding the liquid for the basic recipe.

Cook the granule burger in a metal bowl in the pressure cooker. First break up the mass into irregular chunks with a spoon, then place the bowl on the pressure cooker rack with ½ c. water in the cooker. Close the cooker, bring it up to pressure, and cook for 5 minutes. Allow the cooker to cool naturally.

Heat 2 T oil in a skillet. Add the cubed vegetables, stirring over moderate heat for several minutes. Stir in ¼ c. water, cover, and let the vegetables steam on very low heat for 10 minutes.

Roll out each ball of basic crust to a 12- to 14-inch circle. Cut each circle into 4 portions. (An easy way is to roll the dough between two sheets of waxed paper with a pastry cloth underneath the whole thing. When the dough has been rolled out, remove the top sheet of paper, then cut the circle into quarters right through the waxed paper to facilitate the removal of the paper and to keep the dough pieces whole. An alternate way is to cut each ball of basic crust recipe into quarters. Roll each quarter into a small ball. Make 8 circles of dough, 7 inches in diameter, by rolling out the smaller balls between two sheets of waxed paper or plastic food storage bags.)

Dissolve the 2 Vegex cubes in the 1¾ c. hot water. Raise the heat under the vegetables in the skillet and pour in the water. Stir in the ¼ c. water mixed with 2 T cornstarch. Stir until the sauce bubbles and thickens, about 1 minute. Mix in the Worcestershire sauce. Add the cooked granule burger, mixing in well. Stir in chopped parsley.

Divide the filling among the 8 portions of dough. Fold the dough over the filling, pinch the edges together, peel off the waxed paper, and place the filled pasties on a non-stick baking sheet. Cut a few slits for steam vents in the tops of the pasties. Bake at 350° for 30 minutes.

Makes 8 servings.

8 servings
Average serving = approx. 10 grams balanced protein
23 to 28% of daily protein need

Vegetarian Samosas

A special pastry made with whole wheat, soy, and yogurt encloses a savory spiced filling of diced soyloaf with chopped potatoes, onion, green pepper, peas, and tomatoes.

Pastry:

1¾ c. whole wheat pastry flour
¼ c. soy flour
1 t Vege-Sal
3 T oil
8 heaping T yogurt (about 1¼ cups)

Put the flours and Vege-Sal in a mixing bowl. Blend them together well. Stir in the oil. Mix in the yogurt by the spoonful, blending with a fork until the mixture holds together.

Take walnut-sized lumps of dough and slide them across a lightly floured board under the pressure of the heel of your hand. Put the flattened dough pieces together. Wrap the dough airtight and let it rest in the refrigerator for 2 hours or more.

Filling:

2 T oil
1½ c. small diced potatoes
1 large onion, peeled and minced
1 large green pepper, chopped
2 c. frozen peas
2½ c. canned crushed tomatoes
1 T lemon juice
3½ c. diced Beef-style Soyloaf*
½ t powdered ginger
1 t turmeric
1½ t Vege-Sal
½ t chili powder
⅛ t pepper
¼ t caraway seed
¼ t ground coriander
⅛ t ground cloves
⅛ t ground cinnamon

Heat the oil in a large (12-inch) non-stick skillet over moderate heat. Stir in the potatoes. Sauté for 2 minutes. Stir in the onion and green pepper, then frozen peas. Stir-fry for another 2 minutes. Pour in ¼ c. water, bring to a boil, cover, lower heat, and steam for 10 minutes.

Stir in the tomatoes, lemon juice, and all seasonings. Bring to a boil. Stir in soyloaf. Cover, lower heat, and simmer 5 minutes. Refrigerate the filling if you are making it ahead of time.

Assembly:

Divide the dough into 10 golf ball-size pieces. Pat each ball into a circle. Place it between 2 sheets of freezer wrap. Roll hard with a rolling pin to make a 10-inch circle, very thin. Remove the top paper and cut the circle in half.

Place a very generous ¼ c. of filling on one side of each half-circle, leaving a ½-inch border. Spread the filling out evenly with a knife. Fold the other side of the dough over to cover the filling. Fold and pinch together the edges to seal them.

Heat an electric skillet to 400°. Add ¼ inch of oil. When the oil is hot enough to make a drop of water dance, add the turnovers, a few at a time, and cook just under 2 minutes per side, or until golden. Or bake the turnovers on a lightly oiled non-stick cookie sheet at 400° for 15 minutes, or until golden brown, turning them once.

10 servings
Average serving = approx. 10 grams balanced protein
23 to 28% of daily protein need

Chili Turnovers

Circles of cornmeal dough folded over granule burger chili with kidney beans and cheese.

Crust:

¾ c. stoneground cornmeal
¾ c. boiling water
1 c. whole wheat pastry flour
¼ c. soy flour
¾ t Vege-Sal
2 T oil

Put the cornmeal into a bowl. Pour the boiling water into it and mix until all is moistened. Add the remaining ingredients and mix until a dough ball is formed.

Cut the dough ball in half. Cut each half into thirds. Divide all pieces in half again.

Roll each piece of dough between plastic food storage bags, making 6-inch rounds.

Filling:

1 recipe Bulgar Wheat Granule Burger,* cooked
2 cans (8 ozs.) tomato sauce
1-1½ c. cooked kidney beans
¼ t garlic powder
¾ t chili powder (or more, to taste)
1 c. grated cheese

Mix all ingredients together, except the cheese.

Put a heaping ¼ c. measure of filling on one side of each rolled out piece of dough. Place a heaping tablespoon of cheese on the filling. Fold dough over and seal edges.

Bake at 350° for 30 minutes on a lightly oiled baking sheet. (Heat any remaining filling in a small baking dish and serve separately.)

Makes 6 servings.

Variation: For *Chili Cups*, press the rolled out dough rounds into the cups of a 12-section muffin tin oiled with unrefined soy oil and lecithin. Make little stand-up rims by folding over the excess dough. Fill crust cups with granule burger filling. Bake at 400° for 20 minutes. Divide grated cheese among the cups. Bake another 5 minutes. Let chili cups stand outside the oven a few minutes before removing them from the tin.

6 servings
Average serving = approx. 12 grams balanced protein
28 to 34% of daily protein need

Crepes and Thin Pancakes

Filled crepes are often offered as a vegetarian main dish. They are very thin egg and white flour pancakes rolled around a filling of vegetables and sauce. Non-vegetarian versions contain chunks of chicken or beef. For more healthful crepes we use whole-grain flours. They are not so thin this way but are nourishing and hearty. If you don't want to use eggs in the pancakes we have a number of eggless versions preceding the main recipes in this section, or in some of the recipes themselves. Try Soy-Millet Eggless Crepes. For whole-grain crepes made with egg, try Vegetable-filled Crepes.

Instead of meat we use chopped granule burger or soyloaf cubes for fillings along with vegetables. We replace heavy cream with thickened light milk sauces and a bit of cheese. Examples are Mushroom Crepes with Chopped Chicken-style Loaf, Soyloaf a la King Crepes (in muffin cups), Double Soyloaf Crepes with Mushrooms, and Soyloaf and Artichoke Crepes. Using tomato sauce we have Granule Burger Cannelloni, Eggplant Sesameat Crepes, Lasagna Crepes Stacks, and Crepes Creole. Some variations of cornmeal tortillas make Enchilada Casserole or Vegetarian Enchiladas, Vegetarian Tacos, Sesame Enchiladas, and Cornmeal Crepes with Soybean Filling.

Soy curd makes an interesting filling combined with vegetables in Zucchini and Onion Crepes Stack, Pancakes Florentine, and Oriental Crepes, and without vegetables in Soy Curd Blintzes. Soy-millet batter with vegetables fills Farm Vegetable Crepes.

Small Whole Wheat Crepes

½ c. whole wheat flour
2 T soy powder
½ c. skim milk
⅓ c. water
1 egg
1 T oil
¼ t Vege-Sal

Place the ingredients together in a blender container. Blend until smooth. Remove the batter to a bowl and refrigerate for an hour or more before using, if desired, so that flour absorbs liquid. The batter may be used immediately also, if you wish.

Heat a 6- or 7-inch non-stick skillet over moderate heat. When a few beads of water dropped on the skillet sizzle, it is ready. Use 3 T of this batter for each crepe.

Pour the batter into the pan while raising the pan from the heat in order to tilt and spread the batter all over the bottom of the pan. Return the pan to the heat and allow the crepe to cook until the edges start to pull away from the sides of the pan and puffs form in the middle. Turn the crepe with a wide nylon or plastic spatula and cook briefly on the other side. Slip the crepe onto a plate for stacking.

Repeat until 8 small crepes have been made.

Makes 8 six-inch crepes.

Large Recipe Basic Whole Wheat and Soy Crepes

3 eggs
1 c. whole wheat pastry flour
¼ c. soy flour
⅛ t Vege-Sal
1 c. milk
1 c. water
2 T oil

Mix together all ingredients in a blender container. Blend until smooth. Put the container in the refrigerator, covered, for an hour or more before using, to allow the flour to absorb liquid.

Heat an 8-inch non-stick skillet over moderate heat. The pan is ready when a few drops of water sizzle when dropped into it.

Pour a scant ¼ c. batter into the pan, raising the pan from the heat to tilt and spread the batter all over the bottom. Return pan to heat and let crepe cook until the edges start to pull away from the sides of the pan and the crepe puffs up in places. Turn the crepe with a wide nylon spatula and cook for a few seconds longer on the other side. Slip crepe off the skillet onto a plate.

Repeat until all batter is used. Stack the crepes as they are made. Refrigerate them, covered, up to 24 hours before using. Or freeze them tightly wrapped in stacks of 6 or 7 with waxed paper between them.

Makes 14 eight-inch crepes, or 12 ten-inch crepes.

Eggless Wheat and Soy Crepes

¼ c. soaked soybeans, drained
1 c. water
2 t cashew nuts
1 t oil
½ t Vege-Sal
½ c. whole wheat pastry flour

Place the soybeans, water, cashew nuts, Vege-Sal, and oil in a blender container. Purée until absolutely smooth. Add ½ c. whole wheat pastry flour to blender and mix until smooth.

Refrigerate the batter for ½ hour so that liquid is well absorbed by the flour.

Preheat a 7-inch non-stick skillet over moderate heat. When a drop of water sizzles and bounces on the pan, it is ready. Remove the pan from the heat. Scoop up a scant ¼ c. of batter (a ¼ c. measure with a pouring lip and handle makes a good scoop) and pour it into the bottom of the pan. Roll the pan around until the batter covers the bottom as much as possible. With a nylon spatula, even out the batter, spreading it onto the areas that were not covered at first.

Return the pan to the heat and bake the crepe for 2 minutes. When the crepe is ready, the batter should be dry on top, and the edges will curl up away from the pan. The bottom will be slightly brown, and the crepe will move easily when a wide spatula is inserted underneath to turn it. Turn it and let it bake very briefly on the unbaked side. Slide the crepe off the pan onto a plate. Stack the crepes as they are made.

These crepes must be baked after filling to ensure that the soy batter is adequately cooked.

Makes 7 six-inch crepes.

Doubled, makes 14 six-inch crepes.

Soy-Millet Eggless Crepes

1 c. soaked soybeans, drained
1 c. water
1 T oil
½ t Vege-Sal
¼ t garlic powder
1 T yeast
⅓ c. millet, ground
2 T cashew nuts, ground

Put the soybeans, water, oil, Vege-Sal, and garlic powder in a blender container. Blend until smooth. Add yeast, ground millet, and ground cashew nuts. Blend until homogenized. Remove to a bowl, scraping remainder of batter from blender container with rubber spatula.

Heat a 7-inch non-stick skillet on medium heat. Pour a scant ¼ c. of batter on the skillet surface, holding pan up away from heat. Use a nylon spatula to spread the batter gently to a uniform thickness on the bottom of the pan. Return pan to heat and cook exactly one minute.

Use a nylon spatula to loosen the edges of the crepe all the way around its circumference. (If edges do not come up easily, let the crepe cook a bit longer, until edges are dry.) Then gradually loosen the crepe under its center until it lifts easily to turn it on the other side. Cook a few seconds on this side, then remove to a plate. Cook remaining 8 or 9 crepes this way and stack them on the plate.

Fill crepes, place on lightly oiled heatproof plates and bake at 350° for 25 minutes.

Makes 9 to 10 six and one half-inch crepes. (These crepes must be baked to be sure the soy is well cooked. They are more fragile than egg crepes, so should be assembled on individual serving platters to eliminate lifting for serving.)

Vegetable-filled Crepes

Wheat and soy crepes enclose a chopped vegetable filling in a creamy sauce fortified with ground soy nuts and sesame meal, baked with a sliced mushroom sauce topping.

Crepes:

¼ c. whole wheat pastry flour
2 T low-fat soy powder
⅓ c. whole or skim milk
2 eggs, beaten
2 egg whites, beaten (reserve yolks for sauce)

Mix flours together and gradually add to the beaten eggs combined with milk. Beat the batter with a fork until it is smooth.

Heat a 6½- or 7-inch non-stick skillet over medium heat. Pour 2 T batter in the pan. Lift the pan from the heat and rotate it to spread the batter to the edges. Return pan to heat. When the top of the crepe is dry, turn it to brown briefly on the other side with a nylon spatula. Slip the crepe onto a flat plate. Continue baking and stacking the crepes.

Makes 10 crepes.

Filling:

1 c. whole or skim milk
1 c. evaporated milk
2 egg yolks
¼ c. white wine
½ t Vege-Sal
3 c. chopped cooked vegetables (broccoli, carrots, cauliflower)
½ c. toasted sesame seeds, ground
½ c. soy nuts, ground
1 c. sautéed mushrooms

Combine the milks, egg yolks, wine, and Vege-Sal in a large saucepan, beating with a wire whisk to blend. Cook over low heat, stirring constantly, until the sauce has become thick enough to coat a spoon. Pour 1 c. of sauce into a small bowl and reserve it for topping the filled crepes.

Stir the chopped vegetables into the sauce in the pan. Mix in the sesame seed meal and soy nut meal. Reserve sautéed mushrooms for topping the filled crepes.

Assembly:

Spoon a generous ½ c. filling in a line on the center of each crepe. Fold and roll the crepes, placing them seam side down in individual shallow baking dishes, lightly oiled, or one large baking dish. Cover the crepes with sautéed mushrooms and the reserved sauce.

Bake at 350° for 15 to 20 minutes.

5 servings
Average serving = approx. 15 grams balanced protein
35 to 42% of daily protein need

The Soybean Plant

Double Soyloaf Crepes With Mushrooms

Crepes filled with diced chicken-style and ham-style soyloaf, mushrooms and a creamy sauce with minced onion, celery and carrot.

Crepes:
12 small (6-inch) crepes or thin pancakes.

Sauce:
2 T oil
¼ c. chopped green onion
½ c. minced celery
1 large carrot, minced
¼ c. whole wheat pastry flour
2 c. hot water or vegetable water
1 T low-sodium chicken-like soup base
1 t Vege-Sal
2 T sherry
½ c. evaporated skim milk

Sauté the green onions, celery, and carrot in the oil in a saucepan until soft, a few minutes. Stir in flour and cook for 1 minute.

Mix the hot water, soup base, and Vege-Sal. Gradually mix this liquid into the vegetables and cook, stirring constantly, until the sauce thickens and bubbles.

Stir in the sherry. Lower the heat and simmer for a few minutes, covered. (The alcohol from the sherry evaporates away, leaving the distinctive flavor.) Stir in the ½ c. evaporated skim milk.

Filling and Assembly:
2 c. diced Chicken-style loaf*
1 c. diced Ham-style loaf*
2 c. fresh mushroom chunks
1 or 2 T oil
¼ c. chopped fresh parsley
½ t leaf thyme, crumbled
½ c. evaporated skim milk

Combine the diced loaf cubes in a bowl.

Sauté the mushroom chunks in oil until they start to become tender. Stir them into the soyloaf chunks.

Mix in the parsley and thyme.

Stir in about 1½ c. of the above sauce. (Reserve the rest of the sauce for topping the filled crepes.)

Place about ¼ c. of filling on each crepe, then roll it and place it in a large rectangular baking dish oiled with unrefined soy oil. Repeat with all the crepes.

Stir the additional ½ c. evaporated skim milk into the reserved sauce. Pour the sauce over the filled crepes.

Bake at 375° for 20 minutes.

6 servings
Average serving = approx. 11 grams balanced protein
26 to 31% of daily protein need

Wheat

Soyloaf á la King Cups

Crepe cups in muffin tins filled with diced chicken-style soyloaf in mushroom sauce with peas, chopped onion and sweet red and green pepper.

12 small 6- or 7-inch crepes (see page 173)
3 c. diced Chicken-style Soyloaf*
1 T oil
½-⅔ c. diced onion
½ c. finely chopped sweet red pepper
½ c. finely chopped green pepper
1 c. frozen peas (or fresh, cooked)
1 c. sliced fresh mushrooms
1 can (10¾ ozs.) condensed mushroom soup
1 c. evaporated skim milk

Make the crepes. You may have to double a recipe and have leftover crepes to freeze for another meal. (Eggless crepes do not freeze well. Use them within a day or two.)

Sauté the onion and diced peppers in 1 T oil in a medium-size non-stick skillet over moderate heat. Add the peas, stirring until no ice crystals remain. Stir in the mushrooms and keep stirring until they start to soften. Lower the heat. Add the mushroom soup and evaporated milk. Stir until well mixed. Remove from the heat. Add the soyloaf cubes and distribute them well.

Oil two 6-well muffin tins with unrefined soy oil and liquid lecithin. Place one crepe (browned side up) in each well, fitting the center of the crepe down at the bottom of the cup and pressing it gently to fit around the bottom and sides.

Fill each crepe cup with a generous ⅓ c. of the soyloaf filling. Sprinkle with paprika. Bake at 350° for about 15 to 20 minutes, or until the edges of the crepes start to brown lightly and the filling is heated through.

Makes 4 to 6 servings.

Variation: Instead of condensed mushroom soup and evaporated milk, use mushroom sauce in Basic Recipes.

4 to 6 servings
Average serving = approx. 11 grams balanced protein
26 to 31% of daily protein need

Soyloaf and Artichoke Crepes

Rolled whole wheat crepes enclose a filling of diced soyloaf, chopped artichokes (or broccoli), mushrooms and seasoned sauce, are topped with more sauce and melted cheese, and garnished with parsley and lemon slices.

Basic Recipe for 8 small whole wheat crepes*
2 c. diced firm Chicken-style Soyloaf*
1 package (9 ozs.) frozen artichoke hearts (1½ c. cooked), or 1½ c. cooked broccoli pieces
1 medium onion, chopped (½ c.)
2 T butter or oil
1 c. chopped fresh mushrooms
1 T lemon juice
3 T whole wheat pastry flour
Pinch ground nutmeg
1½ c. hot water or vegetable water
2 T low-sodium chicken-style soup base
¾ t Vege-Sal
⅓ c. evaporated milk
¼ c. grated Swiss cheese
Parsley and lemon slices (optional)

Make the crepes according to basic recipe. Set aside.

Cook artichoke hearts according to package directions. Take ¾ c. of them and cut each piece into smaller pieces. (Use remaining ones for garnish.) In a large bowl, mix diced soyloaf and chopped artichoke hearts.

Heat the butter or oil in a saucepan. Sauté the chopped onion. Add the mushrooms and lemon juice. Sauté, stirring often. Mix in the flour and nutmeg. Gradually stir in 1½ c. hot water mixed with the soup base and Vege-Sal. Cook, stirring constantly, until the sauce thickens and bubbles.

Add ⅓ c. evaporated milk to sauce, stirring it in well. Pour 1⅓ c. of this sauce into the soyloaf and artichoke mixture. Add the remaining artichokes to the leftover sauce for garnishing the crepes.

Place ⅓ c. soyloaf filling on each crepe. Roll and place the crepes in an oiled rectangular baking dish or in individual baking dishes.

Spoon reserved sauce with artichokes over crepes. Sprinkle with grated cheese. Bake at 350° for 15 minutes (25 minutes if they have been prepared in advance and refrigerated). Garnish with parsley and lemon slices, if desired.

4 servings
Average serving = approx. 11 grams balanced protein
26 to 31% of daily protein need

Mushroom Crepes

Crepes filled with sautéed mushrooms and chicken-style soyloaf chunks in a creamy cheese sauce.

Crepes:

Use one of the Basic Recipes in the front of this section to make 12 small (6-inch) crepes or thin pancakes.

Sauce:

1 c. hot water
1 t low-sodium chicken-style soup base
½ t Vege-Sal
¼ c. whole wheat pastry flour
3 T oil
2 c. evaporated milk, divided
¼ c. fresh minced parsley
½ t dried tarragon, crushed
½ c. grated cheese

Put the water, soup base, Vege-Sal, flour, and oil in a blender container. Blend until smooth. Pour into a non-stick saucepan and heat, stirring, until sauce bubbles and thickens. Stir in 1½ c. evaporated milk, parsley, tarragon, and cheese. Mix until smooth. (Reserve ½ c. evaporated milk.) Set sauce aside.

Filling and Assembly:

1 lb. fresh mushrooms, sliced (about 6 cups)
2 T oil
2 c. chopped Chicken-style Soyloaf*

Heat 2 T oil in a very large (12-inch) non-stick skillet, using moderate heat. Sauté the mushrooms until they start to become tender. Stir in the chopped soyloaf. Pour in two-thirds of the above sauce. Mix well. (Reserve remaining sauce for topping.)

Fill each of 12 small crepes with a generous ⅓ c. of filling. Fold over the ends of the crepes in a loose roll and place the rolls in lightly oiled baking dishes. (If any filling remains, garnish the filled crepes with it.)

Stir the reserved evaporated milk into the reserved sauce. Pour it over the filled crepes. Bake at 350° for 20 minutes.

6 servings
Average serving = approx. 12 grams balanced protein
28 to 34% of daily protein need

Granule Burger Cannelloni

Italian-style crepes filled with a savory granule burger and spinach mixture, resting in tomato sauce, covered with a rich cream sauce, sprinkled with Parmesan cheese and baked until lightly browned.

Basic Recipe for One Pound of Soy Granule Burger,* or 2 cups of Convenience Mix*
2 T oil (olive suggested)
1 c. chopped onion
2 cloves garlic, minced
2 c. cooked chopped spinach
½ c. chopped carrots
1½ t oregano, crumbled
½ t basil
2 eggs, beaten
½ c. grated Parmesan cheese
2 c. spaghetti sauce
12 Cannelloni Wrappers (see recipe below)
Cannelloni Sauce (see recipe below)

Prepare the Soy Granule Burger. When firm, form 6 small loaves from the mass, and place them in a steam rack over ½ c. water in a pressure cooker. Cover, bring up to pressure, and cook for 5 minutes. Cool cooker under cold running water. Allow loaves to cool slightly while you prepare the vegetables.

In a large skillet, sauté the onion, carrots, and garlic in the oil until soft, about 5 minutes. Stir in the spinach, then the cooked granule burger, which you have cut into chunks. Remove from the heat. Add the crumbled herbs, beaten eggs, and ¼ c. Parmesan cheese. Stir all together.

Spread the spaghetti sauce on the bottom of a large shallow baking dish (about 10 x 12 inches) or lasagna pan, the sides of which you have lightly oiled. Spoon about ¼ c. of the filling in a line onto each cannelloni wrapper. Roll up and place in a single layer in the sauce over the rolls and sprinkle with the remaining ¼ c. of Parmesan cheese. Bake at 350° for 20 minutes, or until heated through and lightly browned on top.

Cannelloni Wrappers

3 eggs
¼ c. low-fat soy powder
½ c. whole wheat flour
1 c. milk or skim milk

Beat eggs in a small bowl, then beat in skim milk. Separately, combine the flours until they are well mixed together. Gradually add them to the eggs, stirring all the while. Beat until batter is smooth, preferably with a wire whisk.

Heat a small non-stick skillet or crepe pan over medium heat. Pour 2½ to 3 tablespoons of batter into the skillet. Rotate the skillet until batter spreads over the bottom of skillet. Cook until the top is dry. Turn and cook briefly on other side. Remove to flat plate. Repeat with 11 more crepes.

Cannelloni Sauce

3 T butter or oil
3 T whole wheat pastry flour
1½ c. whole or skim milk
Dash Vege-Sal
Dash ground nutmeg

Heat the butter or oil in small saucepan. Stir in the flour, dash Vege-Sal, and nutmeg. Gradually stir in the milk. Cook, stirring constantly, until the sauce thickens and bubbles, 1 minute. Pour the sauce over the cannelloni.

6 servings
Average serving = approx. 18 grams balanced protein
41 to 51% of daily protein need

Eggplant Sesameat Crepes

High-protein wheat-soy-millet rolled pancakes filled with diced eggplant, onion, green pepper, tomato and chopped sesame sausage, topped with cheese sauce.

Wheat-Soy-Millet Pancakes:

⅓ c. soy flour
⅓ c. water
½ c. whole wheat pastry flour
⅓ c. millet flour
1¼ c. water or milk
½ t Vege-Sal
2 T oil

Place all ingredients in a blender container. Blend until smooth. Use a small non-stick skillet (6 to 7 inches in diameter) and a scant ¼ c. of batter to make each pancake.

Makes 12 small pancakes.

Filling and Assembly:

1 small eggplant, peeled and diced (about 3½ c.)
2 onions, diced (1 c.)
2 medium green peppers, chopped (1 c.)
1 T oil
1 c. chopped drained tomatoes, canned or fresh
2 T tomato paste
½ t garlic powder
2 t oregano, crushed
1 t Vege-Sal
2 c. chopped Sesameat Sausage*
Cheese Sauce (see recipe below)

Heat the oil in a very large skillet (12 inches) over moderate heat. Sauté the eggplant, onion, and green pepper until the pieces start to become tender. Stir in the tomatoes and distribute them throughout. Cover, lower the heat, and simmer for 3 minutes.

Stir in the tomato paste, garlic powder, oregano, and Vege-Sal. Cover and simmer for 5 minutes.

Stir in the chopped sesame sausage.

Use a generous ⅓ c. of this filling for each pancake. Place it in a thick line down the center of the pancake and fold the ends over in a loose roll. Put the roll in a shallow rectangular baking dish (2 quarts) oiled with unrefined soy oil. Fit 5 more rolls in the dish.

Use another 2-quart dish for the remaining 6 rolls.

Top the rolls with Cheese Sauce, half for each dish. Bake at 350° for 20 minutes.

Makes 6 servings.

Cheese Sauce

2 T whole wheat pastry flour
2 T oil
1 c. milk
Dash of Vege-Sal
¼ c. grated cheese

Place all ingredients in a blender container and blend until smooth. Pour the mixture into a non-stick saucepan over moderate heat and stir constantly until sauce bubbles and thickens. Serve over Eggplant Crepes.

6 servings
Average serving = approx. 11 grams balanced protein
26 to 31% of daily protein need

Lasagna Crepes Stacks

Two large crepes stacks with Italian tomato-sauced granule burger and cottage cheese (or soy curd) fillings alternately layered between the crepes. Grated mozzarella cheese is sprinkled between the layers and over the tomato sauce topping.

1 large recipe Basic Whole Wheat and Soy Crepes*
1 recipe Bulgar Wheat Granule Burger,* cooked
2 recipes Italian-style Tomato Sauce*
2 cups cottage cheese or seasoned Soy Curd*
Italian herb seasoning or oregano, crushed
2 cups grated mozzarella cheese

Prepare the crepes and set them aside. (You should have 14 crepes, about 8 inches in diameter.)

Mix 1 c. Italian-style tomato sauce with the cooked bulgar wheat granule burger.

Lightly oil two 8-inch square baking dishes, or one 8- x 16-inch rectangular dish.

Place one crepe on each dish, or two side-by-side in the long dish. Spread each crepe with one-sixth of the granule burger mix. Spread 2 or 3 tablespoons of tomato sauce over the granule burger on each crepe. Sprinkle 2 tablespoons of grated cheese over the burger. Cover the filling with another crepe.

Spread this crepe with ⅓ c. cottage cheese (or seasoned soy curd), a light sprinkle of crushed herbs, 2 T tomato sauce, and 2 T grated cheese. Top with another crepe.

(You will be making two crepe stacks simultaneously. Each stack contains 7 crepes, with 3 layers of granule burger and 3 layers of cottage cheese or soy curd, alternated.)

Now spread another one-sixth of the granule burger mix, more tomato sauce, and more grated cheese. Top with another crepe. Continue with another layer of cottage cheese or soy curd, another crepe, another layer of granule burger, a final layer of cottage cheese or soy curd, and a final crepe. Spread each top crepe with ¼ cup tomato sauce and ¼ c. grated cheese.

Bake at 350° for 30 minutes.

6 to 8 servings
Average serving = approx. 14 grams balanced protein
32 to 39% of daily protein need

Crepes Creole

Crepes or thin pancakes filled with chopped granule burger and rice with diced green pepper, onion, celery, and herbs, topped with grated cheese.
Crepe:

Use 8 small crepes or thin pancakes, 6 inches in diameter, made from one of the Basic Recipes in the front of this section.

Filling and Assembly:

½ medium green pepper, chopped
1 medium onion, chopped
1 stalk celery, chopped
1 T oil
1 c. tomato sauce
1 small bay leaf, crumbled
¼ t ground thyme
¼ t rosemary, crushed
Dash of pepper (optional)
2 c. chopped cooked Granule Burger* (½ Basic Recipe)
1 c. cooked brown rice
½ c. grated cheese

Heat the oil in a skillet and sauté the chopped onion, green pepper, and celery. Add the tomato sauce and herbs. Bring to a boil, cover, lower heat, and simmer until vegetables are tender. Add cooked granule burger and rice. Stir until mixed.

Fill 8 crepes with about ½ c. filling each. Fold over the ends and place them in a lightly oiled casserole or individual heatproof plates. Sprinkle with grated cheese.

Bake at 350° for 15 to 20 minutes, or until heated through. (Bake 20 to 25 minutes if using pancakes made with soaked soybeans.)

4 servings
Average serving = approx. 10 grams balanced protein
23 to 28% of daily protein need

Enchilada Casserole

High-protein homemade tortillas wrapped around a filling of Granule Burger chunks with bits of onion, green pepper, tomatoes, and kidney beans.

Basic Recipe for One Pound of Soy Granule Burger,* or 2 cups of Convenience Mix*
1 c. chopped onions
2 small green peppers, or 1 large, chopped
2 T oil
1 can (1 pound, 12 oz.) whole tomatoes and liquid
1 can (6 ozs.) tomato paste
½ c. cooking water
2 t chili powder
Vege-Sal to taste (approximately 1 t)
2 c. cooked kidney beans
12 tortillas or fortified cornmeal tortillas*
½ c.-1 c. shredded Cheddar cheese
1 medium tomato, chopped
1 c. shredded lettuce
Pitted ripe olives
1 ripe avocado, peeled and diced (optional)

Prepare the Basic Mix for Soy Granule Burger. When the mass is firm, form 6 small loaves from it and place them in a steam rack over ½ c. water in a pressure cooker. Cover, bring up to pressure, and cook for 5 minutes. Cool cooker under cold running water. Allow loaves to cool until you can handle them. Cut them into ¾-inch chunks.

Sauté the onions and green peppers in oil until soft, using a large skillet. Stir in the tomatoes and their liquid, the tomato paste, cooking liquid, chili powder, and Vege-Sal. Mix together well. Add the granule burger chunks and kidney beans. Let simmer for 5 minutes.

Spoon 1 c. of the liquid from the sauce in the bottom of a lightly greased shallow 6-cup baking dish. Put about ¼ c. of the sauce mixture in a line on the middle of each tortilla. Roll them up and place them in the sauce in the baking dish. Spoon any remaining sauce over the rolls. Sprinkle with the cheese and chopped tomatoes.

Bake at 350° for 20 minutes, or until the enchiladas are hot and the cheese is melted. Garnish with shredded lettuce, olives, and avocado, if desired.

6 servings
Average serving = approx. 14 grams balanced protein
32 to 39% of daily protein need

Vegetarian Enchiladas

Crepes made with cornmeal enclose a filling of cheese, kidney beans, and millet with tomato sauce, bits of celery, green pepper, mushrooms, and onions.

Tortilla Crepes:

3 eggs
⅔ c. milk
⅓ c. tomato juice
2 T oil
½ t Vege-Sal
½ t basil
⅓ c. whole wheat pastry flour
⅓ c. cornmeal
⅓ c. soy powder

Beat the eggs briefly in the blender. Slowly add the milk, tomato juice, oil, Vege-Sal, basil, whole wheat pastry flour, cornmeal, and soy powder. Blend to a smooth batter.

Using a ¼ c. measuring cup, pour the batter onto a heated 6-inch nonstick skillet, tipping the pan from side to side so that the batter flows evenly over the bottom. Allow the crepe to toast over medium heat until it is brown underneath and dry on top—a minute or so. Turn the crepe with a plastic or wooden spatula so that it browns briefly on the other side. As you make each crepe, stack them and keep warm.

Makes 12 crepes.

Filling and Assembly:

1 stalk celery, finely chopped
½ small green pepper, chopped
4 large mushrooms, chopped
1 medium onion, chopped
1 T oil
1 c. cooked kidney beans
1 c. cooked millet
¼ c. sliced stuffed olives
1 can (8 ozs.) tomato sauce, divided
1 c. grated jack cheese

Sauté the chopped raw vegetables in 1 T oil, first doing the celery, onion, and green pepper since they take longer to soften. When they begin to soften, stir in the mushrooms and cover, cooking over low heat until all are tender.

Put the cooked beans through a food mill or mash them with a potato masher. Add the mashed beans and the millet to the vegetables in the skillet and stir thoroughly.

Mix the olives into the skillet, then about ½ c. of the tomato sauce. Stir in the cheese.

Place ¼ c. of the mixture down the center of each tortilla crepe and roll it, then place in a baking dish that has been lightly oiled with unrefined soy oil. Pour the remaining tomato sauce over the completed enchiladas and bake them at 350° for 15 to 20 minutes, or long enough to heat through. (Baking may be omitted if tortilla crepes have been kept warm and filling has been well heated.)

6 servings
Average serving = approx. 13 grams balanced protein
30 to 36% of daily protein need

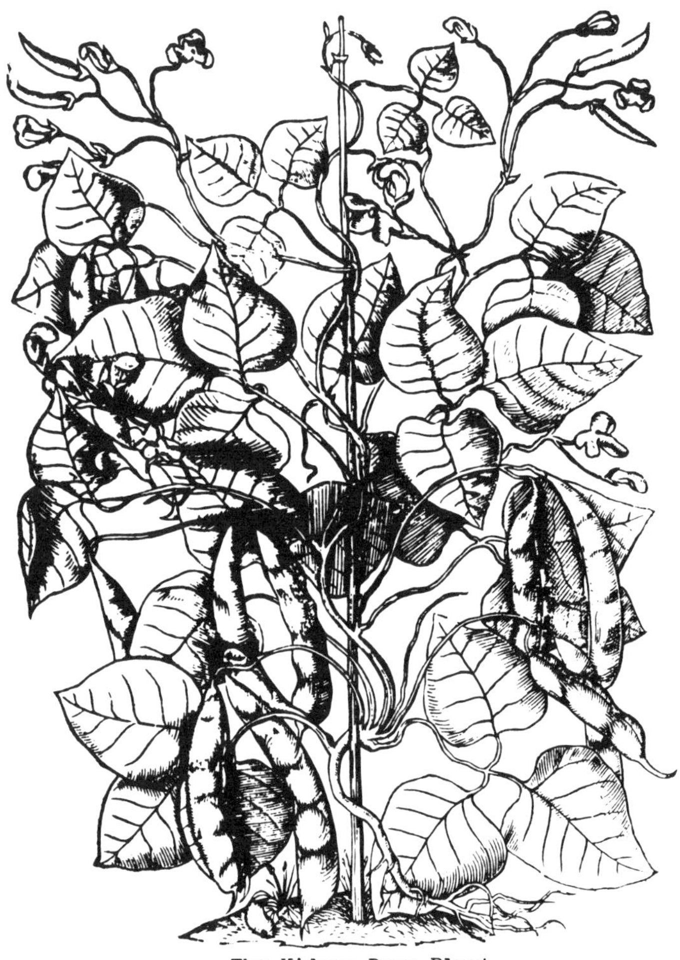

The Kidney Bean Plant

Vegetarian Tacos With Beans

Folded cornmeal tortillas filled with chunked granule burger, pinto beans, tomato sauce, chopped green pepper and onion, grated cheese or soy curd, and shredded lettuce.

Tortillas:

Make basic recipe for Fortified Cornmeal Tortillas*. Use 8 of these for this recipe.

Filling and Assembly:

2 T oil
½ c. chopped green pepper
½ c. chopped onion
1 clove garlic, minced
1 can (8 ozs.) tomato sauce
1½ c. cooked seasoned pinto beans
2 c. chopped cooked Granule Burger*
1 t Vege-Sal
½ t to 2 t chili powder
⅛ t cayenne pepper (optional)
1 c. grated cheese or Soy Curd*
Shredded lettuce

Heat the oil in a skillet. Sauté the green pepper, onion, and garlic until tender. Pour in tomato sauce, seasoned pinto beans, cooked granule burger, and seasonings. Stir to mix well. Heat to bubbling, cover, lower heat, and simmer for 5 minutes.

Fold the tortillas in half, fill with about ⅓ c. filling, then put in 2 T grated cheese or soy curd. Place in an oiled heatproof platter and warm them in a moderate oven for about 10 minutes, if desired. (Heating may be omitted.) Serve with shredded lettuce.

4 servings
Average serving = approx. 12 grams balanced protein
28 to 34% of daily protein need

Sesame Enchiladas

Rolled tortillas are filled with seasoned pinto beans, sesame seed meal, and cream cheese or soy curd, then topped with tomato sauce, diced green pepper, onion, tomato and grated cheese.

Fortified Cornmeal Tortillas:

¾ c. stone ground cornmeal
1 c. whole wheat flour
¼ c. natural soy flour
1 t Vege-Sal
2 T oil
1 c. boiling water

Combine the cornmeal, flours, and salt in a bowl. Stir in oil and boiling water, mixing well to make a soft dough.

Divide the dough in half, then in thirds. Shape the dough into 12 balls. Roll out each ball between 2 sandwich-size plastic bags to form a 5-inch circle. (Or squeeze the balls between plastic bags in a tortilla press.) Bake the tortillas on a hot, lightly greased griddle or ungreased non-stick skillet until lightly browned on one side, then turn and bake on the other side.

Makes 12 tortillas, 5 inches in diameter.

Filling and Assembly:

1½ c. cooked pinto beans, partly mashed
½ c. bean liquid
1 c. tomato sauce
¼ t chili powder (or more)
¼ t garlic powder
1 t dried parsley flakes, or 1 T fresh, minced
¼ t ground thyme
1 T nutritional yeast
1 Vegex cube, ground
1 small onion, minced
⅓ c. fresh sesame seeds, ground
¼ c. soy nuts, ground
¼ c. low-fat soy powder
¼ c. raw wheat germ
8 oz. cream cheese, Neufchatal cheese, or 1½ c. Soy Curd*
2 t oil
½ c. chopped green pepper
½ c. chopped onion
1 c. tomato sauce
1 medium tomato, chopped
½ c. grated cheese (or more, if desired)

Combine partly mashed beans, bean liquid, and tomato sauce. Separately, mix seasonings (chili powder through Vegex cube), onion and ground seeds, nuts, soy powder, and wheat germ. Add the dry mixture to the beans, stirring until well absorbed.

Spread the bean mixture down the middle of each tortilla. Place a long chunk of cream cheese or 2 T soy curd on top of filling before rolling each tortilla and placing it in an arrangement of 2 rows in a large oiled shallow baking dish.

Sauté the chopped green pepper and onion in 2 t oil. Pour the tomato sauce over the rolled tortillas, then sprinkle the sautéed vegetables, chopped tomato, and grated cheese over the sauce.

Bake at 350° for 20 to 25 minutes, or until tortillas are heated through and cheese is melted.

6 servings
Average serving = approx. 11 grams balanced protein
26 to 31% of daily protein need

Cornmeal Crepes With Soybean Filling

Small crepes made with cornmeal are filled with mashed baked soybeans, tomatoes, and chopped onion, then topped with a tomato sauce and melted cheese.

Crepes:

⅓ c. whole wheat pastry flour
¼ c. cornmeal
½ t Vege-Sal
¾ c. milk
1 egg
1 T oil

Put all ingredients in a blender container. Blend until smooth. Let the batter rest in the refrigerator, covered, for about ½ hour, so that the flour and cornmeal can absorb liquid.

Use a scant ¼ c. of batter to make each crepe on a small (7-inch) non-stick skillet. Stack the crepes as you make them and keep them warm in a low oven.

Makes 8 crepes, 6 inches in diameter.

Filling and Assembly:

1½ c. Favorite Baked Soybeans (see page 240) or seasoned cooked soybeans
1 can (1 lb.) tomatoes
1 medium onion, chopped
1 T oil
½ t oregano, crumbled
Reserved tomato liquid
2 T whole wheat pastry flour
1 c. grated cheese

Partly mash the soybeans with a potato masher in a mixing bowl. Drain the tomatoes and reserve the liquid. Chop the tomatoes and mix them into the soybeans.

In a non-stick skillet, sauté the onion in the oil. Pour the soybean mixture into the skillet, then add the crumbled oregano. Mix everything thoroughly. Heat to bubbling.

Fill each cornmeal crepe with about ⅓ c. of this filling. Roll and place them in a lightly oiled heatproof platter.

Mix the reserved tomato liquid in a saucepan with 2 T whole wheat pastry flour. Heat, stirring, until sauce thickens and bubbles. Pour sauce over filled cornmeal crepes. Top with grated cheese. Broil until cheese melts.

4 servings
Average serving = approx. 12 grams balanced protein
28 to 34% of daily protein need

Zucchini and Onion Crepes Stack with Soy Curd

Crepes are stacked like the layers of a cake, with a filling of sautéed zucchini, onions, and soy curd spread between each one. The stack is baked with a creamy cheese sauce topping.

Crepes:

Make one Large Recipe of Basic Whole Wheat and Soy Crepes. Use a scant ¼ c. of batter for each. Use only 12 of these crepes (8 inches) for this recipe. (Freeze the remainder to use with other accumulated crepes for a future main dish.) Or use eggless thin pancakes, if you prefer.

Filling:

¼ c. oil, divided
4 large onions, chopped (4 c.)
6 zucchini (2 lbs.), shredded (5 c.); reserve a few slices for garnish
2 T chopped parsley
1½ t leaf oregano, crumbled
2 t Vege-Sal
3 c. seasoned Soy Curd*

Heat 2 T oil in a very large (12-inch) non-stick skillet and sauté the onion until tender, stirring often, about 10 minutes. Remove the onions to a bowl.

Heat the remaining oil in the same skillet. Add the zucchini and sauté over moderate heat, stirring often, until the zucchini is tender.

Stir in the onion, then the parsley, oregano, and Vege-Sal. Mix thoroughly. Fold in the seasoned soy curd (salted to taste), allowing it to absorb the vegetable juices.

Sauce and Assembly:

1 T oil
1 T whole wheat pastry flour
1 c. milk
Vege-Sal to taste
¼ c. grated Parmesan cheese

Heat the oil in a non-stick saucepan and stir in the pastry flour until they are well mixed. Gradually add the milk, stirring constantly, until the mixture thickens and bubbles 1 minute. Stir in Vege-Sal to taste. Stir in the Parmesan cheese. Set the sauce aside until the crepes stack is assembled.

Oil a 10-inch pie plate with unrefined soy oil. Place one crepe in the plate. Spread it with a generous ½ c. of the filling. Continue stacking and filling, ending with a plain crepe on top.

Arrange a few reserved zucchini slices on top of the crepes stack. Pour the sauce over the stack, letting it run down the sides. Sprinkle with additional Parmesan cheese, if desired.

Bake at 350° for 30 minutes.

6 servings
Average serving = approx. 12 grams balanced protein
28 to 34% of daily protein need

Wheat

Pancakes Florentine

Non-dairy wheat and soy thin pancakes with spinach and soy curd filling, topped with a nutritional yeast "cheese" sauce.

Eggless Wheat-Soy Pancakes

⅓ c. soaked soybeans, drained
⅔ c. water
½ c. whole wheat flour
¼ t Vege-Sal
½ c. soy milk or ½ c. water + 1 T soy powder

Put all the ingredients in a blender container and blend until absolutely smooth.

Use a 7-inch non-stick skillet over medium heat, and ¼ c. of batter for each pancake. Lift the pan from the heat to pour batter into it and tilt it to spread the batter around the bottom. After returning pan to heat, use a nylon spatula to even out the thicker areas of the pancake, spreading the batter wherever the pan is uncoated.

Cook for 2 minutes on the first side, until the edges of the pancake begin to curl away from the pan and the center is dry. The bottom of the pancake should be brown and lift up easily when a spatula is inserted to turn it. Turn and cook another ½ minute on the other side. Slip the pancake from the pan onto a plate. Stack them as they are cooked. (These pancakes must be baked to cook through.)

Makes 8 to 10 pancakes.

Filling and Assembly:

1 large onion, chopped
1 T oil
2 packages (10 ozs. each) frozen spinach, lightly cooked, drained and chopped
2 c. Soy Curd*
2 T soy sauce
½ t nutmeg
1 c. yeast "cheese" spread

Sauté the chopped onion in oil until tender. Add the spinach, soy curd, soy sauce, and nutmeg. Stir until blended. Stir in the yeast "cheese" in chunks. Fill each pancake with a generous ½ c. of filling. Fold over the ends and place them on lightly oiled individual heatproof plates (2 per serving). Bake at 350° for 25 minutes. Serve with yeast "cheese" sauce.

Makes 4 to 5 servings.

Yeast "Cheese" Sauce

3 T yeast flakes
1 T whole wheat pastry flour
1½ t cornstarch
¼ t Vege-Sal
1 c. cold water or vegetable water
1 T soy oil

Combine the yeast flakes, flour, cornstarch, and Vege-Sal in a non-stick saucepan. Add the cold water gradually, stirring until blended and dry ingredients are dissolved. Stir in oil. Heat, stirring constantly, until sauce thickens and bubbles 1 minute.

4 to 5 servings
Average serving = approx. 12 grams balanced protein
28 to 34% of daily protein need

Oriental Crepes

Crepes or thin pancakes filled with soy curd, bean sprouts, onion, green pepper, celery, and mushrooms, with a soy sauce topping.

Crepes:
Use 12 crepes or thin pancakes (8 inches in diameter) made from the Basic Recipes in the front of this section.

Sauce:

2 c. soy curd liquid*
1 T soy sauce
2 T cornstarch
¼ c. water
1 Vegex cube
1 T low-sodium beef-like soup base

Mix the soy curd liquid and soy sauce in a saucepan. Dissolve the cornstarch in ¼ c. water. Pour it into the saucepan. Add the Vegex cube and soup base. Bring to a boil and let bubble for 1 minute.

Filling and Assembly:

1 large onion, diced (1½ c.)
½ green pepper, diced (½ c.)
2 stalks celery, diced (1¼ c.)
1-2 T oil
1 can (4 ozs.) mushrooms, or 1 c. fresh, chopped
1 can (1 lb.) bean sprouts, or 2 c. steamed fresh sprouts
1 T soy sauce
Dash of Vege-Sal
2 c. Seasoned Soy Curd*

Sauté the onion, green pepper, and celery in the oil in a large (12-inch) skillet. Add the drained mushrooms (if fresh are used, stir them until tender) and drained bean sprouts. Stir in 1 T soy sauce and Vege-Sal to taste. Mix in ½ c. of the above sauce, then the soy curd.

Fill each of the 12 crepes or pancakes with a generous ½ c. of this filling. Fold them in a loose roll and place them on oiled individual heatproof baking dishes, 2 per serving. Pour some of the sauce over them.

Bake at 350° for 30 minutes. Serve with remaining sauce.

6 servings
Average serving = approx. 13 grams balanced protein
30 to 36% of daily protein need

Soy Curd Blintzes with Yogurt

Soy curd substitutes for cottage cheese in these pocket-folded eggless wheat and soy pancakes topped with yogurt.

Eggless Wheat and Soy Pancakes:

1¼ c. liquid from making soy curd
⅓ c. soy flour
¾ c. whole wheat pastry flour
2 T oil
½ t Vege-Sal

Put all ingredients in a blender container and blend until smooth. Use a scant ¼ c. batter for each pancake. Make them in a small (6- to 7-inch) non-stick skillet.

Makes 12 pancakes, 6 inches in diameter.

Soy Curd Filling:

2 c. seasoned soy curd*
½ t Vege-Sal
1½ c. yogurt, divided
1 medium onion, chopped (¾ c.)
1 T oil
¼ c. minced parsley

Combine the seasoned cooked soy curd in a mixing bowl with Vege-Sal and ¼ c. of the yogurt. Reserve the remaining yogurt for topping.

Sauté the onion in oil until tender but not brown. Mix the onion with the soy curd. Stir in the minced parsley. Mix thoroughly.

Assembly:

Lay a pancake flat, browned side up, on a plate. Put 2 heaping tablespoons of soy curd filling in the center of the pancake, then shape it like an oblong with your fingers. Fold the sides of the pancakes over the shorter sides of the oblong, then overlap the remaining ends, like an envelope. The pancake will stick together. Make 12 filled pancakes in the same manner.

Heat 2 T oil in a skillet over medium heat. Place the filled pancakes, seam side down, in the skillet and brown a few minutes. Turn, then brown the other side. (If necessary, brown half the pancakes at a time.)

Serve with additional yogurt and a sprinkle of paprika.

6 servings
Average serving = approx. 13 grams balanced protein
30 to 36% of daily protein need

Farm Vegetable Crepes

Crispy baked oat-wheat-soy pancakes filled with chopped green pepper, onion, tomato, corn, and peas in a soy-millet custard batter, topped with yogurt or cream sauce.

Oat-Wheat-Soy Pancakes:

⅓ c. soy flour
⅓ c. water
½ c. whole wheat pastry flour
⅓ c. oats, ground
1 c. water or milk
½ t Vege-Sal
2 T oil

Place all ingredients in a blender container. Blend until smooth. Use a small (6- to 7-inch) non-stick skillet and a scant ¼ c. batter for each pancake.

Makes 12 small pancakes, 6 inches in diameter.

Filling and Assembly:

1 green pepper, chopped (½ c.)
1 large onion, chopped (1¼ c.)
1 T oil for sautéeing
1 c. frozen corn
1 c. frozen peas
1 large tomato, chopped (⅔ c.)
½ t basil, crumbled
½ t Vege-Sal
1 c. soaked soybeans, drained
¾ c. water
½ t Vege-Sal
½ c. millet flour
Yogurt or Cream Sauce (see page 112)

Sauté the onion and green pepper in a skillet using 1 T oil over moderate heat. Stir in the frozen corn and peas, stirring until no frost remains. Stir in the tomato. Season with basil and Vege-Sal. Pour the vegetables into a mixing bowl.

Put the drained soaked soybeans in blender container with ¾ c. water and ½ t Vege-Sal. Blend until smooth. Add millet flour and blend until mixed. Pour the batter into the mixing bowl with vegetables. (Remove all batter from blender container with a flexible spatula.) Mix thoroughly, so that vegetables are coated with batter.

Use ⅓ c. filling for each pancake. Fill pancake and fold over each side, making a loose roll. Place filled pancakes in a large baking dish lightly oiled with unrefined soy oil, or in individual baking dishes. Bake at 350° for 30 minutes.

Serve with Yogurt or Cream Sauce topping.

6 servings
Average serving = approx. 12 grams balanced protein
28 to 34% of daily protein need

The Oat Plant

Chopped Chicken-style Crepes

High-protein wheat-millet-soy rolled thin pancakes filled with chopped chicken-style bulgar wheat granule burger, diced onion, and celery, topped with cheese sauce.

Wheat-Millet-Soy Thin Pancakes:

⅓ c. soy flour
⅓ c. water
½ c. whole wheat pastry flour
⅓ c. millet flour
1¼ c. milk or water
½ t Vege-Sal
2 T oil

Place the soy flour in a blender container with ⅓ c. water. Blend until smooth. Add the remaining ingredients and blend again until smooth. Use a small non-stick skillet (6 to 7 inches in diameter) and a scant ¼ c. of batter for each pancake.

Makes 12 small (6-inch) pancakes.

Filling and Assembly:

Basic Recipe for Chopped Chicken-style Granule Burger,* cooked
1 c. diced onion
1 c. thinly sliced celery
1 T oil
1½ c. Cheese Sauce (see recipe below)

Prepare chopped chicken-style granule burger.

Sauté the celery and onion in oil in a non-stick skillet over moderate heat. Stir in the cooked granule burger. Blend in 1½ cups of the Cheese Sauce.

Spoon ⅓ c. of the granule burger mixture onto each thin pancake. Roll and place in shallow rectangular baking dish (2 quarts) oiled with unrefined soy oil.

Pour the remaining sauce over filled pancakes lined up in the dish. Bake at 350° for 20 minutes.

Makes 6 servings.

Cheese Sauce

⅓ c. whole wheat pastry flour
2 T oil
⅓ c. instant skim milk powder
3 c. vegetable cooking water
2 T chicken-style soup base
1 t Vege-Sal
1 t poultry seasoning
⅔ c. grated cheese

Put all the ingredients, except the cheese, in a blender container. Blend until smooth. Pour into a non-stick saucepan. Stir constantly over moderate heat until bubbling. Remove from heat and stir in the cheese.

6 servings
Average serving = approx. 11 grams balanced protein
26 to 31% of daily protein need

Deviled Spread and Cheese Rolls

Crepes spread with soft savory soyloaf and grated cheese, rolled and baked with more grated cheese for topping.

1 to 1½ c. Deviled Spread*
8 Basic Whole Wheat Crepes
(see page 173)
1 c. grated Swiss cheese
Additional cheese for topping

Spread each crepe with a thick layer of Deviled Spread (2 to 3 T). Sprinkle about 2 T grated Swiss cheese over the filling, then roll, in jelly-roll fashion.

Place rolled filled crepes in oiled baking dish. Sprinkle with another ¼ c. grated cheese and heat in oven until cheese is melted and crepes are heated through, about 15 minutes at 350°.

4 servings
Average serving = approx. 12 grams balanced protein
28 to 34% of daily protein need

Casseroles and Oven Dishes

A good dish to put together ahead of time so that you can be free before dinner while it is baking, a casserole is generally a mixture (or layered assembly) of vegetables, a protein element, and a grain or bean component. It is baked in the oven to heat everything through and mingle the flavors.

With soy nut meat substitutes you can come up with Garbanzo Bean Casserole with Soy Nut Balls, Moussaka Supreme, Eggplant Provençal, or Soy Nut Balls and Vegetable Casserole. Sesame-soy nut sausages combined with beans gives a tasty Vegetarian Cassoulet.

Some cooked lentils with cottage cheese go into our Layered Eggplant Dish. A variation is Layered Eggplant With Soy Curd. Use baby dried lima beans and millet with cottage cheese for Layered Lima-Millet Casserole.

Versatile soy granule burger makes many satisfying casseroles possible. Chopped and chunked, it can make Burger-Vegetable Casserole, Millet and Burger Casserole, Shepherd Pie, Tamale Pie, and Chili Tortilla Casserole. Chopped bulgar wheat granule burger can result in a Chopped Chicken-style Granule Burger Dish, Bulgar Wheat and Soy Hash, or Double Corn, Cheese and Granule Burger Casserole. A really tasty granule burger dish is Baked Ham-style Hash. Shaping granule burger into miniature sausages or balls gives you an ingredient for Vegetarian Indiana Bean Bake, Barbecued Granule Meatballs, Lima Beans and Rice, or Granule Burger Oven Pot with Vegetables.

Molded soy curd batter makes a nice Mock Chicken Divan, or a variation, Mock Chicken Supreme. For just plain but delicious soybeans, try Baked Soybeans or its variation with complementary millet.

Garbanzo Bean Casserole with Soy Nut Balls

Sausage-seasoned soy nut balls are tucked among pieces of leek, carrot slices, chopped cabbage, garbanzo beans, and tomatoes in this flavorful casserole dish.

Soy Nut "Sausage" Balls:

1 c. soy nuts, ground
¼ c. sesame seeds, ground
¼ c. rolled oats, ground
1 T nutritional yeast
1 T Bakon yeast
¼ t garlic powder
½ t ground thyme
½ t paprika
½ t sage
½ t oregano, crushed
¼ t marjoram, crushed
1 t dried parsley, or 1 T fresh parsley, minced
¼ t caraway seeds, ground
¼ c. tomato juice
2 Vegex cubes, crushed
2 eggs
½ c. grated cheese
1 small onion, minced

Combine the ground soy nuts, sesame seeds, and oats in a mixing bowl. Stir in the yeast and seasonings (through ground caraway seeds).

In a separate small bowl, dissolve the crushed Vegex cubes in tomato juice. Add the eggs to the liquid and beat with a fork. Pour the liquid mixture into the dry ingredients and stir to distribute.

Fold in the grated cheese and minced onion.

Divide the batter into 1-inch portions and roll into balls. Set aside.

Vegetables and Assembly:

1 leek, chopped, or 1 c. chopped green onions
4 cloves garlic, minced
2 T olive oil
4 carrots, sliced
2 c. chopped cabbage
2 cans (1 lb. each) garbanzo beans and liquid, or 4 c. cooked seasoned garbanzo beans and 1 c. liquid
1 can (2 lbs.) tomatoes and liquid
1 t leaf thyme, crumbled

Sauté the leek or onion and garlic in olive oil. Stir in the carrots and cook for 3 minutes. Stir in the cabbage and cook for 2 more minutes.

Add the garbanzo beans and liquid, tomatoes and liquid, and thyme. Pour the vegetables into a large (4-quart) casserole dish. Insert the soy nut balls between vegetables. Cover dish and bake at 325° for 1 hour.

6 to 8 servings
Average serving = approx. 11 grams balanced protein
26 to 34% of daily protein need

The Chickpea or Garbanzo Plant

Moussaka Supreme

Layers of tender eggplant slices and soy nut meat chunks in tomato sauce, topped by a creamy cheese sauce with a nicely browned crust.

Soy Nut Meat:

1 c. soy nuts, ground
¼ c. wheat germ
⅓ c. rolled oats
¼ c. sesame seeds, ground
2 T bran
1 T yeast flakes
¼ t garlic powder
⅓ c. grated Swiss cheese
¼ of a 3 oz. pkg. of cream cheese
1 egg
2 t soy sauce
1 T catsup
1 Vegex cube, crushed and dissolved in 1 T hot water
½ t Kitchen Bouquet (optional)
1 T olive oil

Combine the dry ingredients (ground soy nuts through garlic powder) in a medium bowl. Add the grated cheese, mixing it in until well distributed.

In a separate bowl blend the cream cheese, egg, soy sauce, catsup, dissolved Vegex cube and Kitchen Bouquet. Stir this liquid mixture into the bowl of dry ingredients, mixing well. Let stand until fairly dry. (If too wet, add some tablespoons of bran to absorb the moisture. Volume of liquid varies with size of egg.)

Turn out the mass onto waxed paper, flatten with your hands, and cut into small squares or rectangles about 1 to 1½ inch on a side and ½ inch thick.

Heat 1 T olive oil in a large non-stick skillet and briefly brown the squares on both sides. Remove from the skillet and set aside.

Vegetables:

1 eggplant (1 lb.)
1 medium onion
1 clove garlic
1 T olive oil
1 can (8 ozs.) tomato sauce
⅛ t ground cinnamon

Peel the eggplant and slice it crosswise into ¼-inch-thick rounds. Place them in a steam rack over 1 inch of water in a deep pot and steam about 5 minutes, or until the eggplant is just beginning to be tender.

Chop the onion and garlic and sauté until soft in the oil, using the skillet in which the soy nut meat was done. Pour in the tomato sauce and add the cinnamon. Stir, then replace the soy nut meat in the skillet. Cover and remove from the heat.

Cheese Sauce:

1 T butter or oil
2 T whole wheat pastry flour
⅛ t ground nutmeg
¾ c. skim or whole milk
1 t low-sodium chicken-style soup base
1 egg, beaten
½ c. cottage cheese
¼ c. grated cheese

Heat the butter or oil in a non-stick saucepan. Stir in the flour and nutmeg and mix. Pour in the milk gradually, stirring to mix. Add the chicken-style seasoning. Cook over medium heat, stirring, until the mixture thickens and bubbles 1 minute.

Pour half of the hot mixture into the beaten egg in a small bowl, then beat it back into the hot mixture in the saucepan. Cook, stirring, 1 minute. Remove from heat. Stir in cheeses.

Assembly:

Put a layer of eggplant slices in the bottom of a 2-quart (10-inch square x 2-inch deep) casserole, lightly oiled. Pour in the soy nut meat mixture with sauce. Cover the mixture with the remaining eggplant slices. Top with the rich cheese sauce. Bake at 350° for 45 minutes.

4 to 6 servings
Average serving = approx. 14 grams balanced protein
32 to 39% of daily protein need

Eggplant Provençal

A casserole of tomatoes, eggplant, and zucchini rounds with tender soy nut burgers sandwiched between them.

Soy Nut Burgers:

1 c. soy nuts, ground fine
¼ c. walnuts, chopped fine
⅓ c. rolled oats
1 T nutritional yeast
¼ t garlic powder
½ (3 oz.) pkg. cream cheese
1 egg
2 t soy sauce
1 Vegex cube, crushed and dissolved in 1 T hot water
1 T catsup
½ t Kitchen Bouquet (optional)
1 T olive oil

Mix first 5 ingredients together in a bowl. Separately, soften the cream cheese with a fork and beat the egg with it in a small bowl. Add the other liquid ingredients (soy sauce through Kitchen Bouquet). Stir well until blended. Pour the liquid mixture into the dry ingredients, folding in until all is thoroughly mixed.

When the mass is dry and firm, turn it out onto a sheet of waxed paper. Cover with another sheet of waxed paper and use a rolling pin to flatten the mass to a thickness of about ½ inch.

Using a biscuit or cookie cutter, cut 3-inch circles from the dough and put together the dough remnants to make more. You should have 6 patties. Brown them on both sides in 1 T olive oil in a large non-stick skillet over medium heat. Remove the burgers and set aside. Use the skillet for the sauce below.

Vegetables:

1 small eggplant, pared and sliced crosswise in ½-inch-thick rounds
1 large or 2 small zucchini, cut into ½-inch-thick circles

Use a steam rack over 1 inch of water in a deep pot to steam the vegetables for 5 minutes or less, until just barely tender. Bring the water to a boil, then simmer on low heat, covered.

Sauce:

1 can (16 ozs.) tomatoes plus liquid
2 t low-sodium beef-style soup base
1 t Italian herbs
¼ t garlic powder
½ t Vege-Sal

Place the tomatoes over medium heat in the skillet and break them up with your spatula. Add the seasonings and mix well. Simmer briefly.

Assembly:

Put a layer of eggplant on the bottom of an oiled casserole dish. Place the soy nut burgers over the eggplant. Pour the liquid from the sauce over all. Combine the remaining eggplant, zucchini, and tomatoes and arrange them on top of the soy nut burgers. Cover the casserole and bake at 350° for 30 minutes.

4 to 6 servings
Average serving = approx. 12 grams balanced protein
28 to 34% of daily protein need

Soy-Nut Balls and Vegetable Casserole

Easy to do for a large gathering, this recipe combines soy-nut balls with a fancy frozen vegetable combination like broccoli, cauliflower, and carrots in a creamy sauce.

2 recipes for Soy-Nut Meatballs*
2 T oil
2 c. vegetable broth or cooking water, seasoned
2 packages (20 ozs. each) frozen vegetable combination
2 T cornstarch
¼ c. cold water
½ pint light cream or buttermilk

Brown the soy-nut balls in oil in a large deep pot, using moderate heat. Add 2 c. of broth, bring to a boil, cover, lower heat and simmer 15 minutes. Remove balls with a large slotted spoon and set aside.

Bring the liquid to a boil again, then add the frozen vegetables. Bring again to a boil, lower heat, and simmer vegetables, covered, according to the time specified in package directions.

Mix cornstarch with ¼ c. cold water until it dissolves. Stir into the vegetables, raise the heat, and stir until broth thickens and bubbles.

Add soy-nut balls to vegetables, mixing them in. Simmer briefly until balls are heated through. Add cream or buttermilk and blend in well with a large spoon.

8 to 10 servings
Average serving = approx. 12 grams balanced protein
28 to 34% of daily protein need

Vegetarian Cassoulet

Beans baked in tomato sauce with vegetarian sausages made of sesame and sunflower meals seasoned with herbs and spices. Seed sausages complement the beans for more substantial protein.

2 c. (1 lb.) dried Great Northern beans
Water
3 medium onions, diced
2-4 cloves garlic, minced
2 T oil
2 T minced parsley
2 bay leaves
1½ t thyme
Vegetarian Sausages (see recipe below)
1 can (15 ozs.) tomato sauce

Wash beans and soak them overnight in twice their volume of water. (Or bring to a boil in a saucepan, boil 2 minutes, cover, remove from heat and let stand 1 hour.)

In pressure cooker or large pot, sauté the onions and garlic in the oil. Add the beans, soaking liquid, parsley, bay leaf, and thyme. (Water should just cover beans.) Pressure cook for 10 minutes, or bring to a boil, cover and simmer 2 hours in a regular pot.

Vegetarian Sausages

½ c. sunflower seeds, ground
⅓ c. sesame seeds, ground
1 c. soy nuts, ground
⅓ c. rolled oats, ground
¼ t marjoram
¼ t ground thyme
½ t sage
½ t paprika
¼ t garlic powder
1 egg
1 onion, chopped
1 T soy sauce
½ t Gravy Master (optional)
1 Vegex cube, crushed
1-2 T oil

Put the ground seeds, nuts, and oats in a bowl. Stir in the herbs and seasonings (marjoram through garlic powder).

Put egg, chopped onion, soy sauce, Gravy Master, and Vegex cube in a blender container. Liquefy, then pour into the dry ingredients and mix well. You will get a medium-firm dough.

Make ¾-inch-thick rolls out of pieces of the dough, rolling them in waxed paper with your hands. Cut the rolls into 1½-inch segments and shape like little links tapered at the ends.

Brown the little links carefully on all sides in oil over medium heat in a large non-stick skillet. (Browning may be omitted, if desired.)

Mix the tomato sauce with the cooked beans. Layer beans, then vegetarian sausages, alternately in an oiled 2-quart casserole and bake, covered, at 350° for 1 hour.

8 to 10 servings
Average serving = approx. 11 grams balanced protein
26 to 34% of daily protein need

The Sunflower

Layered Eggplant Dish

Eggplant slices, mozzarella cheese, lentils with brown rice, cottage cheese mixed with soy nut and sesame seed meals, and tomato sauce are layered in this casserole.

⅓ c. raw brown rice
⅓ c. dry lentils
1⅓ c. water or vegetable cooking water
2 Vegex cubes, crushed
¼ t mace
¼ t rosemary, crushed
½ t dried mint leaves, crushed
¼ t garlic powder
¼ t onion powder
2 T chopped fresh parsley

1 medium eggplant
¼ c. whole wheat flour
¼ c. oil, divided (optional)
1½ c. pizza sauce or tomato sauce
8 slices of mozzarella or Swiss cheese
1 egg
1 c. cottage cheese
½ c. soy nuts, ground
¼ c. sesame seeds, ground, or ¼ c. sunflower seeds, ground

Bring 1⅓ c. water to a boil in a saucepan. Add the rice and lentils. Cover and simmer for 20 minutes. Stir in the crushed Vegex cubes and seasonings (mace through onion powder). Simmer another 25 minutes, covered, until all liquid is absorbed. Mix in chopped parsley.

Peel the eggplant and slice it ¼-inch-thick lengthwise. Dredge the slices in the whole wheat flour to coat them thinly. To eliminate fat calories, toast the slices slowly in a large non-stick skillet over moderate heat without oil, until they are lightly browned and beginning to get tender. Turn and toast the other sides. Or use oil for more flavor, 1 T at a time for each batch of slices that will fit in the pan. More oil may be needed when turning the slices over. An electric skillet works especially well to get the slices slightly crisp outside, tender inside.

When the eggplant is prepared, layer half of it in the bottom of a lightly oiled large shallow casserole dish. Spread the slices with 6 T of tomato sauce. Place half the cheese slices over the sauce.

Spread half the lentil-rice mixture over the cheese. Spread another 6 T tomato sauce over the lentils.

Beat egg in a mixing bowl. Add the cottage cheese, ground soy nuts, and ground sesame or sunflower seeds. Mix well. Spread this mixture over the lentils and sauce. Spread the remaining lentils over the cottage cheese, then another 6 T of tomato sauce.

Put a final layer of eggplant slices on the casserole. Spread with the remaining tomato sauce. Top with the remaining cheese slices. Bake at 350° for 30 minutes.

4 to 6 servings
Average serving = approx. 12 grams balanced protein
28 to 34% of daily protein need

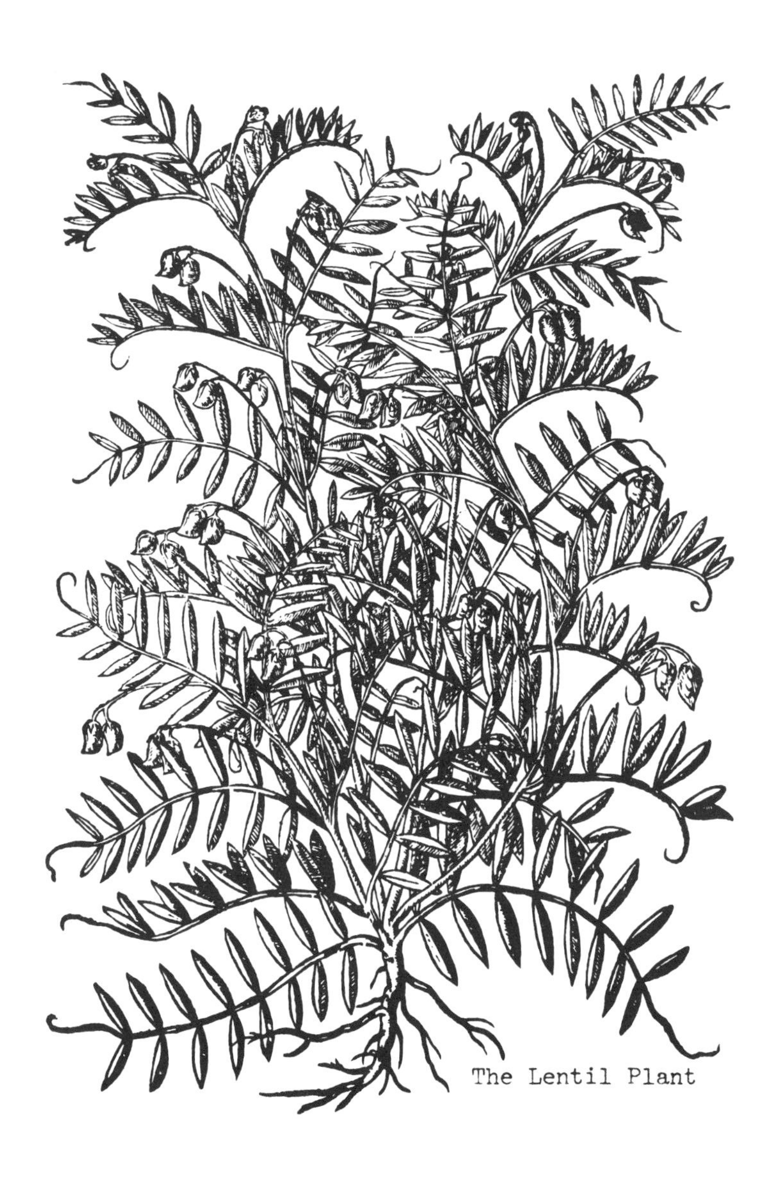
The Lentil Plant

Layered Eggplant With Soy Curd

Batter-dipped and browned eggplant slices spread with Italian-style tomato sauce, layered with seasoned soy curd, and baked with a topping of grated dairy cheese or nutritional yeast "cheese."

1 medium eggplant
1 recipe Seasoned Soy Curd*
1 recipe Italian-style Tomato Sauce*
1 recipe Seasoned Dipping Batter*
1 recipe Basic Sesameat* (dry mix)
Peanut oil
½-1 c. grated dairy cheese or Basic Vegetable Protein "Cheese" spread*

Prepare the seasoned soy curd, Italian-style tomato sauce, and dipping batter.

Prepare the Basic Sesameat dry mix, omitting egg and liquid. Set aside.

Peel the eggplant and slice it lengthwise ¼ inch thick. You will have oval shaped slices varying in size. Dip the slices in the seasoned batter, spreading the batter thinly over each side with a knife. Dredge the thinly-coated slices in the sesameat dry mix.

Heat 1 T of peanut oil in a large non-stick skillet over moderate heat, or in an electric skillet (350°). Brown the eggplant slices slowly on both sides, several slices at a time, until crispy outside and tender inside. Collect finished slices on a plate as the remaining ones cook. Use a tablespoon of oil per batch if necessary.

Lightly oil a shallow casserole dish with unrefined soy oil. Spread about ½ c. tomato sauce in the bottom of the dish. Place the slices of browned eggplant over the sauce.

Spread the eggplant slices with a thin layer of soy curd, about ¼ inch thick. Spread with tomato sauce.

Lay another layer of eggplant, then more soy curd and tomato sauce. Finish with eggplant, tomato sauce, and grated dairy cheese or nutritional yeast "cheese" spread.

Bake at 350° for 20 to 30 minutes, or until heated through.

4 to 6 servings
Average serving = approx. 16 grams balanced protein
37 to 44% of daily protein need

Layered Lima-Millet Casserole

Baby lima beans in tomato sauce complemented by millet and sesame seed meal, layered with cottage cheese and Cheddar cheese topping.

1 c. dried baby lima beans, washed
2 c. water
1 c. water
½ c. millet
1 can (8 ozs.) tomato sauce
½ c. sesame seeds, ground
2 c. (1 lb.) cottage cheese
1 c. coarsely grated Cheddar cheese

Bring 2 c. water to a boil in a saucepan. Drop the washed baby lima beans, a spoonful at a time, into the boiling water. Cover, lower heat, and simmer for 30 minutes.

Bring 1 c. water to a boil in pressure cooker. Pour in ½ c. millet. Add partially cooked lima beans and their water. Close, cover and bring up to pressure. Pressure cook for 5 minutes. Let the pressure drop naturally.

Mix 1 can tomato sauce (1 c.) into the bean-millet mixture. Heat to bubbling, lower heat, and simmer for 10 minutes, covered, so that most of the moisture can be absorbed.

Meanwhile, toast the ground sesame seeds by spreading the meal on a piece of aluminum foil in the oven tray of a small toaster-oven, or on a pie pan in the regular oven. Use moderate heat (350°) for 10 to 15 minutes. Stir occasionally.

Lightly oil a 2-quart shallow rectangular baking dish. Pour in half the lima-millet mixture and smooth it over the bottom of the casserole.

Spread half of the toasted sesame meal over the lima-millet mixture. Spread all of the cottage cheese next. Pour the remaining lima-millet mixture on the cottage cheese and even it out with the back of a large spoon. Sprinkle the remaining sesame meal over the beans. Spread the 1 c. of Cheddar cheese evenly over the top. Bake at 350° for 15 to 20 minutes.

4 to 6 servings
Average serving = approx. 15 grams balanced protein
35 to 42% of daily protein need

Burger-Vegetable Casserole

Chunked granule burger mixed with onion, chopped spinach and broccoli, topped with soy or egg custard.

Basic Recipe for Granule Burger,* cooked and chunked
1 large onion, chopped
1 T oil
½ c. tomato purée
1 package (10 ozs.) frozen chopped broccoli, or 2 c. chopped fresh broccoli
1 package (10 ozs.) frozen chopped spinach, or 1 lb. fresh cleaned spinach
Soy Custard or Egg Custard (see recipes below)

Sauté the onion in 1 T oil in a large non-stick skillet over moderate heat. Pour in the cooked chunked granule burger, breaking it up into smaller pieces as you stir it in. Stir in tomato purée. Cover and set aside.

Lightly steam the frozen broccoli and spinach in a steam rack over ½ inch of water. Bring the water to a boil, cover, and let simmer for 5 minutes, just until vegetables are defrosted. If the vegetables are fresh, steam them only until the spinach is barely wilted and the broccoli is still a little crisp. Chop the spinach.

Mix the steamed vegetables into the granule burger.

Oil a large shallow casserole dish with unrefined soy oil. Pour in the granule burger and vegetable mixture, spreading it flat over the bottom of the dish.

Pour the soy custard mixture or egg custard mixture from the blender container over the granule burger and vegetables. Bake at 350° for 45 minutes to 1 hour, or until the custard is firm and lightly browned. (For soy custard, a cake tester should come out clean from from the center.)

Makes 6 to 8 servings.

Soy Custard

1 c. soaked soybeans, drained
1 c. water
1 small onion, chopped
¼ c. tomato purée
1 T soy sauce
1 T oil
¼ t garlic powder
1 T nutritional yeast
2 T cashew nuts, ground
⅓ c. millet, ground to fine flour

Put the soaked soybeans, water, onion, tomato purée, soy sauce, and oil in a blender container. Blend until smooth. Add the garlic powder, yeast, ground cashew nuts, and ground millet. Blend again until mixed.

Egg Custard

3 eggs
1½ c. milk
½ t Vege-Sal
⅛ t ground nutmeg
⅛ t white pepper

Combine all ingredients in a blender container and blend until mixed.

6 to 8 servings
Average serving = approx. 12 grams balanced protein
28 to 34% of daily protein need

Millet and Burger Casserole

An easy oven dish with granule burger, onion, and tomato sauce between layers of millet and cheese.

2 c. whole millet
4 c. water or vegetable cooking water
1 t Vege-Sal
1 T oil
1 large onion, chopped
Basic Recipe for Granule Burger,* chunked and cooked
1t garlic powder
1 can (15 ozs.) tomato sauce
1 c. shredded Cheddar cheese

Pour the millet and Vege-Sal into boiling water in a large saucepan. Cover, reduce heat, and simmer for about 30 minutes, or until all liquid is absorbed.

Sauté the onion in oil in a skillet. Add the cooked granule burger, breaking up chunks with a fork, stirring until lightly browned, about 5 minutes. Sprinkle with garlic powder.

Use unrefined soy oil to oil a shallow rectangular 2-quart casserole dish. Pour in half the cooked millet and spread it over the bottom. Mix in half the cheese.

Pour the granule burger with onion over the millet. Spread the tomato sauce evenly over the burger. Top the burger with the remaining millet. Sprinkle the remaining cheese over a final layer of millet. Bake at 350° for 20 minutes, or until the casserole is heated through and the cheese is melted.

6 to 8 servings
Average serving = approx. 11 grams balanced protein
26 to 34% of daily protein need

Shepherd Pie

Delicious Granule Burger chunks in a savory sauce with carrots, peas and onions, topped with a layer of seasoned mashed potatoes, baked until golden.

Basic Recipe for One Pound of Soy Granule Burger,* or 2 cups of Convenience Mix*
2 T oil
2-3 carrots, thinly sliced (1 c. or more)
2 c. fresh peas
2 onions, chopped (about 1 c.)
2 T oil
1 t Vege-Sal
1 c. water
2 T whole wheat pastry flour
2 T Worcestershire sauce
1 c. potato cooking water
2½ c. cooked cubed potatoes, mashed and seasoned with butter, milk, Vege-Sal, as desired

Press the prepared Granule Burger into a firm mass and cut into 1-inch cubes on a cutting board. Firm the cubes with your fingers and brown them carefully on all sides over medium heat, using a large non-stick skillet. When done, remove them and set aside.

Heat the additional 2 T oil and sauté the carrots, onions, and peas for a few minutes, stirring constantly. Add the cup of water mixed with Vege-Sal, put in the burger chunks, allow to come to a boil, then lower the heat, and simmer for 10 minutes.

Mix the 2 T flour with the Worcestershire sauce and stir it into the cup of potato cooking water. Pour the mixture into the skillet, bring it to a boil again and let it bubble 1 minute.

Pour the contents of the skillet into a casserole dish oiled with unrefined soy oil. Top with the mashed potatoes. Bake at 375° for 20 minutes, or until the potatoes are golden.

4 to 6 servings
Average serving = approx. 10 grams balanced protein
23 to 28% of daily protein need

Tamale Pie

A yellow cornmeal-millet crusty topping covers beefy-looking chunks of soy granule burger, bits of crunchy corn and green peppers, tomatoes, and other vegetables with a savory taste.

Basic Recipe for One Pound of Soy Granule Burger*, or 2 cups of Convenience Mix*
½ c. stone-ground cornmeal
½ c. water
½ c. millet, ground fine
3 c. water
½ c. soy nuts, ground
2 T olive or other oil
1 onion, chopped
1 green pepper, chopped
½ c. 1-inch pieces fresh green beans
1 clove garlic, chopped
2 c. frozen corn
1 c. ripe pitted black olives
½ c. tomato sauce
1 T soy sauce
Drained tomatoes from a 16 oz. can

Have the Soy Granule Burger in a bowl prepared beforehand.

Mix cornmeal and millet together. Stir in the ½ c. of water and mix until smooth. Bring the 3 c. water to a boil. Gradually pour in the cornmeal-millet mixture. When the mixture bubbles, turn down the heat and let simmer for 15 minutes. Remove from the heat and allow to cool. Then stir in the ground soy nuts and mix well.

Cut the Soy Granule Burger into 1-inch chunks and set aside. In a large skillet, sauté the onion, green pepper, green beans, and garlic in the oil. Stir over medium heat for 1 minute. Add the burger chunks and stir all together for another minute. Stir in the frozen corn. Then add the olives, tomato sauce with soy sauce mixed in, and the broken-up drained tomatoes. Allow all to heat briefly, then remove the skillet from the heat and set aside.

Pour half of the cooked cornmeal mixture into a 6-quart shallow casserole dish which has been oiled with liquid lecithin and soy oil. Spread it to cover the bottom. Pour in the contents of the skillet and spread evenly over the cornmeal base. Cover the mixture with the remaining cornmeal mush, spread all over the top. Bake at 350° for 45 minutes to 1 hour.

4 to 6 servings
Average serving = approx. 11 grams balanced protein
26 to 34% of daily protein need

Chili-Tortilla Casserole

Granule Burger with onion, kidney beans, corn, and tomatoes in a special sauce layered between tortilla quarters with melted cheese.

1 Recipe Italian-style Tomato Sauce* (modified)
½ t oregano
¼ t ground cumin
1 t chili powder
1 Recipe Basic Granule Burger,* cooked and chunked
2 T oil, divided
1 medium onion, chopped
2 (14 oz.) cans stewed tomatoes, drained (reserve liquid)
1 (10 oz.) pkg. frozen corn, cooked
2½-3 c. cooked kidney beans
½ c. pitted ripe olives
1 Recipe Fortified Cornmeal Tortillas (see page 194)
1½ c. grated Cheddar cheese

Prepare the Italian-style Tomato Sauce but omit the Parmesan cheese, Italian herb seasoning, and basil. Substitute ½ t oregano, ¼ t ground cumin, and 1 t (more or less to taste) chili powder. (Use reserved liquid from the stewed tomatoes and liquid from cooking corn as part of the recipe.) Combine the ingredients of the recipe plus substitute seasonings in a blender container and blend until smooth. Set aside.

Heat 1 T oil in a large non-stick skillet. Sauté the onion until barely tender. Add another tablespoon of oil. Add the cooked granule burger chunks, stirring briefly until very lightly browned.

Add tomatoes, corn, kidney beans, and olives. Stir in tomato sauce.

Oil a 2½-3-quart casserole with unrefined soy oil. Spread half of the granule burger and vegetable mixture in the casserole.

Cut the prepared tortillas in quarters. Spread half the quarters over the granule burger mixture. Sprinkle with half the cheese.

Spread the remaining granule burger mix over the tortilla quarters. Arrange the remaining tortilla quarters on top, then sprinkle with the remaining cheese.

Bake at 350°, covered, for 15 minutes, then uncovered for another 5 minutes, or until heated through and cheese is melted. (If you prepare and refrigerate the casserole ahead of time, allow another 10 to 15 minutes of baking time.)

6 to 8 servings
Average serving = approx. 11 grams balanced protein
26 to 31% of daily protein need

Chopped Chicken-style Granule Burger Dish

Sauced chopped chicken-style granule burger on a bed of chopped broccoli and rice or millet.

Basic Recipe for Chopped Chicken-style Granule Burger,* cooked
3 c. cooked brown rice or millet (1 c. dry plus 2 c. water)
1 to 1½ pounds fresh broccoli or 2 packages (10 ozs.) frozen chopped broccoli

2½ c. vegetable cooking water
¼ c. whole wheat pastry flour
2 T oil
4 t low-sodium chicken-style soup base
2 t catsup
1 t Vege-Sal
¼ t tarragon
¼ c. instant powdered milk
½-⅔ c. grated cheese

Prepare the chopped chicken-style granule burger according to the basic recipe.

Simmer the brown rice or millet in water for 45 minutes, covered.

Trim the broccoli and cut into 1-inch pieces. Steam them until tender in a steam rack (15 to 20 minutes) or pressure cook exactly 1 minute and cool under running water.

In a blender container, mix the vegetable cooking water (use broccoli water plus enough additional water to total 2½ cups), flour, oil, soup base, catsup, Vege-Sal, tarragon, powdered milk, and grated cheese. Blend until smooth. Pour liquid into a non-stick saucepan over medium heat. Stir constantly until liquid thickens and bubbles. Remove from heat.

Mix the cooked rice and broccoli together in a lightly oiled 3-quart casserole. Gently fold in the cooked chopped chicken-style granule burger. Pour the sauce over all.

Cover and bake at 350° for 15 minutes, or 10 minutes longer if you have prepared the dish ahead and refrigerated it.

4 to 6 servings
Average serving = approx. 12 grams balanced protein
28 to 34% of daily protein need

Bulgar Wheat and Soy Hash

Bulgar wheat granule burger baked with diced potato, onion and celery, shredded carrots, and parsley, served with cream sauce.

Basic Recipe for Chopped Chicken-style Bulgar Wheat Granule Burger*
1 medium onion, chopped (⅔ c.)
1 scrubbed raw potato, diced (1 c.)
2 carrots, shredded (1 c.)
½ c. chopped celery
2 T chopped parsley
½ t poultry seasoning
1¾ c. vegetable cooking water
1 T chicken-style soup base
¾ t Vege-Sal
2 T cornstarch
¼ c. evaporated skim milk

Prepare the chopped chicken-style bulgar wheat granule burger.

Stir the chopped vegetables, parsley, and poultry seasoning into the granule burger mixture.

Make the sauce, blending the vegetable water, soup base, Vege-Sal, and cornstarch in a saucepan. Stir constantly over medium heat until the sauce is thick and bubbly. Stir in the evaporated skim milk.

Pour 1 c. of the sauce into the grain and vegetable mixture. Gently distribute the sauce through the mixture with a large spoon.

Pack the mixture into a 2-quart shallow casserole dish oiled with unrefined soy oil. Bake, covered, at 350° for 45 minutes. For a crisp top crust, uncover and bake another 15 minutes. Serve with remaining sauce.

4 to 6 servings
Average serving = approx. 11 grams balanced protein
26 to 31% of daily protein need

Double Corn, Cheese, and Granule Burger Casserole

A layer of textured granule burger sandwiched between two cornbread layers made with cornmeal, kernels of corn, and bits of sweet red pepper or pimiento, topped with cheese.

Basic Recipe for Bulgar Wheat Granule Burger,* cooked
½ c. Tomato Sauce*
1 medium onion, minced
2½ c. frozen corn, cooked in ½ c. water, or 1 can (17 ozs.) cream-style corn
½ c. whole wheat flour
¼ c. soy flour
½ c. cornmeal
½ t Vege-Sal
½ t baking powder
1 c. milk
2 eggs, slightly beaten
1 can (4 ozs.) pimientos, drained and diced or ½ c. diced sweet red pepper sautéed in 2 t oil
2 c. grated Cheddar cheese

Mix the cooked chunked granule burger with the tomato sauce and minced onion.

Purée ½ c. of cooked corn in a blender with the cooking water. Mix the purée with the remaining cooked corn.

Combine the flours, cornmeal, Vege-Sal, and baking powder in a mixing bowl. Stir in the milk and eggs. Stir in the corn mixture and pimientos or diced sweet red pepper.

Oil a 3-quart casserole with liquid lecithin and unrefined soy oil. Pour half of the corn batter into the casserole. Sprinkle half the cheese over the batter. Spread the soy granule mixture over the batter. Add the remaining batter, spreading it evenly. Sprinkle with remaining cheese.

Bake in a 400° oven for about 45 minutes.

6 to 8 servings
Average serving = approx. 12 grams balanced protein
28 to 34% of daily protein need

Baked Ham-style Hash

Chopped ham-style granule burger, diced cooked potatoes and onions with a topping of grated Cheddar cheese form this easy oven hash.

Basic Recipe for Chopped Ham-style Granule Burger,* cooked
4 large cooked potatoes, diced (4 cups)
2 large onions, diced (1½ cups)
2 T oil
1 c. vegetable cooking water
2 t low-sodium chicken-style soup base
½ t Vege-Sal
1 T cornstarch
1 T Worcestershire sauce
½ c. grated Cheddar cheese

Sauté the onion in oil over medium heat until nearly tender. Remove to a bowl. Combine the cooked chopped ham-style granule burger and cooked diced potatoes with the onion in the bowl.

Mix the vegetable cooking water, soup base, Vege-Sal, and cornstarch together in the skillet used for sautéing the onions. Heat, stirring constantly, until the mixture thickens and bubbles. Stir in Worcestershire sauce. Pour the sauce into the burger mix. Stir to mix thoroughly.

Oil a shallow 2-quart baking dish with liquid lecithin and unrefined soy oil. Pour the burger and potato mixture into the baking dish. Sprinkle with the cheese. Cover and bake in a preheated oven (375°) for 20 to 25 minutes. (Increase baking time 10 minutes if you have prepared the dish ahead and refrigerated it.)

4 to 6 servings
Average serving = approx. 11 grams balanced protein
26 to 34% of daily protein need

Vegetarian Indiana Bean Bake

Beans baked in tomato sauce with granule burger meatballs, onion, mustard, and molasses.

2 c. (1 lb.) dried lima, navy, or Great Northern beans
Water
Basic Recipe for One Pound of Soy Granule Burger*
2 T oil
1 large onion, chopped
¼ c. prepared mustard
1 T molasses
1 t Vege-Sal (optional)
1 can (15 ozs.) tomato sauce

Soak the beans overnight in 4 to 5 c. water. Next day, pressure cook for 10 minutes, adding enough water just to cover.

Make small meatballs from the granule burger. Brown them on all sides in 2 T oil using a very large skillet over medium heat.

Stir chopped onion, mustard, molasses, Vege-Sal, and tomato sauce into the beans. Pour the browned meatballs into the beans.

Transfer the bean and meatball mixture to an oiled 3-quart baking dish. Cover. Bake at 325° for 1 to 2 hours. The liquid will be absorbed by beans and meatballs.

8 to 10 servings
Average serving = approx. 11 grams balanced protein
26 to 34% of daily protein need

Barbecued Granule Meatballs, Lima Beans, and Rice

Little soy granule burger meatballs in barbecue sauce are combined with fresh lima beans and rice.

Basic Recipe for Soy Granule Burger*
¼ c. finely diced onion
2 c. cooked brown rice (⅔ c. dry plus 1⅓ c. water)
2 packages (10 ozs. each) frozen lima beans, thawed only enough to separate beans
1 or 2 T oil or butter
Barbecue Sauce (see recipe below)

Cook the brown rice, covered, in water for 45 minutes.

Prepare the dry mix for soy granule burger. Add ¼ c. minced onion to the dry mix and mix thoroughly before adding the liquid from the basic recipe. When the granule burger is firm, scoop out portions by teaspoons and make 1-inch balls by rolling them with your hands.

Place 1 c. water in the pressure cooker. Insert the rack that comes with the cooker. Separate the partially thawed lima beans and place them on the rack. Put the granule meatballs on top of the lima beans. Close the cooker, bring up to pressure, and pressure cook for 1 minute only. Cool cooker under running water.

Lightly oil a 12- x 8- x 2-inch baking dish. Mix the cooked brown rice and lima beans in the dish with 1 or 2 tablespoons of oil or butter. Stir the cooked meatballs into the prepared barbecue sauce, then pour balls and sauce into the dish with rice and beans. Cover the dish with a lid or foil and bake at 350° for 15 to 20 minutes, or until heated through.

The dish is easily prepared ahead and refrigerated until baking time, which should be increased by 10 minutes. If you are making the dish just before serving, baking may be omitted if the barbecue sauce is first heated and the meatballs stirred into it to flavor them for about 10 minutes.

Makes 4 to 6 servings

Barbecue Sauce

¼ c. oil
½ c. chopped onion
2 cans (8 ozs. each) tomato sauce
½ c. water
1 t Vege-Sal
¼ t cayenne pepper
2 t Worcestershire sauce
1 t prepared mustard
2 T honey
2 T lemon juice

Sauté the chopped onion in oil in a medium skillet over moderate heat. Stir in the tomato sauce, water, and remaining seasonings. Heat until sauce bubbles.

4 to 6 servings
Average serving = approx. 12 grams balanced protein
28 to 34% of daily protein need

The Rice Plant

Granule Burger Oven Pot With Vegetables

A big dish for a small crowd, this recipe combines little granule burger meatballs with diced potatoes, onions, and frozen mixed vegetables in a huge oven pot.

2 Basic Recipes of Soy Granule Burger* (2 pounds)
2-4 T oil
4 large potatoes, diced
2 large onions, diced
1 bag (20 ozs.) frozen diced mixed vegetables (peas, carrots, corn, lima beans)
1 t ground thyme
2 c. hot water
2 Vegex cubes, smashed
2 T soy sauce
2 T catsup
2 c. tomato juice
1 c. water (cold)
¼ c. cornstarch

Make small meatballs (1 inch in diameter) from the granule burger and brown them in the oil in a very large non-stick skillet over medium heat. (Do half or a third at a time if necessary.)

Put the diced potatoes, onions, and frozen mixed vegetables in the largest ovenproof covered pot you have—at least 6 quarts. (A turkey roaster is perfect.) Put granule burger meatballs on top of the vegetables. Sprinkle them with the ground thyme.

Dissolve the Vegex cubes in 2 c. hot water. Stir in the soy sauce and catsup. Pour the liquid mixture into the pot with the vegetables and meatballs. Pour in the tomato juice.

Cover the pot and bake at 375° for 30 minutes. Uncover, then add the 1 c. of the cold water in which the cornstarch has been dissolved. Stir to distribute it evenly, and mix the meatballs under the vegetables so that they will absorb liquid.

Cover and bake another 30 minutes, or until the vegetables are tender, the meatballs are cooked, and the thickened sauce is mostly absorbed.

8 to 12 servings
Average serving = approx. 10 grams balanced protein
23 to 28% of daily protein need

Persian-style Layered Granule Burger

A layer of spiced bulgar wheat, onion, spinach, tomatoes, and kidney beans between two layers of granule burger.

Basic Recipe for Granule Burger*
1 can (8 ozs.) tomato sauce
½ c. bulgar wheat
1 c. water
Sprinkle of Vege-Sal
1 T oil
1 small onion, chopped
1 package (10 ozs.) frozen chopped spinach, partially thawed
½ t curry powder
½ t crushed cardamom seeds
1 can (1 lb.) tomatoes, drained
1 can (1 lb.) kidney beans, drained

Prepare the basic recipe for granule burger, using ground sunflower seeds instead of chopped walnuts. Add ¼ c. tomato sauce to the granule burger mixture. Let stand for 10 minutes while you prepare filling.

Pour the bulgar wheat into 1 c. of boiling water in a saucepan with a sprinkle of Vege-Sal. Cover, lower heat, and simmer for 8 to 10 minutes.

Sauté the onion in oil over moderate heat in a non-stick skillet. Add the spinach and stir until there are no more frozen chunks. Sprinkle in the curry powder and crushed cardamom seeds. Mix in cooked bulgar wheat and ½ c. of the tomato sauce.

Coarsely chop the drained tomatoes and add to the bulgar wheat and vegetable mixture. Stir in the drained kidney beans.

Oil an 8-inch-square shallow (2-inch deep) baking dish with lecithin and unrefined soy oil. Spread half the granule burger mixture over the bottom of the dish in a thin layer (about ½ inch). Spread the mixture of bulgar wheat and vegetables over the layer of granule burger. Smooth the remaining granule burger evenly in a layer over the filling.

Bake at 350° for 45 minutes. Let the casserole rest for 10 minutes before cutting it into squares to serve. (Lift up entire square carefully with a wide spatula.) If desired, use tomato juice from canned tomatoes and remaining ¼ c. of tomato sauce to make a sauce to serve with squares. Measure 1 c. of tomato liquids and thicken in a saucepan with 1 T cornstarch.

4 to 6 servings
Average serving = approx. 12 grams balanced protein
28 to 34% of daily protein need

Mock Chicken Divan

Foil potato boats make unusual baking molds for mock chicken "breasts" made of soy curd batter with eggs and almond meal. The molds make a beautiful company dish served on a bed of cooked broccoli with a light cheese sauce over all.

1 pound fresh broccoli
1 c. Soy Curd*
2 eggs
2 T minced fresh onion
2 t low-sodium chicken-style soup base
½ t Vege-Sal
½ c. soy nuts, ground
½ c. almond meal

2 c. hot vegetable water (reserve broccoli cooking water)
¼ c. whole wheat pastry flour
2 T oil
¼ t–½ t Vege-Sal
¼ c. instant powdered milk
2 t low-sodium chicken-style soup base
½ c. Cheddar cheese cubes
Parmesan cheese (optional)

Beat the eggs in a mixing bowl. Stir in the soy curd. Mix in the minced onion, soup base, and Vege-Sal. Stir in the ground soy nuts and ground almonds. Divide the batter among six oval foil baked potato boats lightly oiled with liquid lecithin and soy oil. Bake the filled boats at 350° for 30 minutes.

Meanwhile, prepare the broccoli. Trim the broccoli and cut off the florets so that they have 3-inch stalks. Cut the clumps into single trees with ½-inch thick stems. Prepare the tougher stem portions by cutting them into ½-inch thick sticks. Place the prepared broccoli in a steam rack over ½ c. water in a pressure cooker. Pressure cook for 1 minute and cool immediately under running water. (Or steam the broccoli in a regular pot until tender, about 15 to 20 minutes.)

Lightly oil a shallow rectangular baking dish. Line the bottom of the dish with the cooked broccoli sticks and florets. After removing the mock chicken ovals from their tins, place them in a line centered over the broccoli.

Make a sauce by placing 2 c. of hot vegetable cooking water (use broccoli water plus 1½ c. more) in a blender container with whole wheat pastry flour, oil, Vege-Sal, powdered milk, soup base, and cheese cubes. Blend until smooth. Pour the mixture into a non-stick saucepan over medium heat. Stir constantly until thickened. Pour the sauce over the mock chicken, letting it seep down into the surrounding broccoli. Sprinkle with Parmesan cheese, if desired.

Place the dish under the broiler and broil until lightly browned, about 5 minutes. Or bake at 400° for 10 to 15 minutes.

Makes 3 to 4 servings.

Variation: Use slices of firm Chicken-Style Soyloaf* prepared ahead of time. Bake dish at 350° for 20 to 25 minutes, or until heated through.

For *Mock Chicken Supreme*, bake mock chicken as directed above in oval tins. Cook 1 c. raw brown rice in 2 c. water, simmering, covered, for 45 minutes. Make Mushroom Sauce.* Cook 2 c. of frozen diced mixed vegetables and stir them into the mushroom sauce.

Place the baked soy batter ovals in a line centered over the cooked brown rice spread on a heatproof platter. Pour mushroom and vegetable sauce over all. Heat at 400° for 10 minutes, or omit heating and serve immediately.

3 to 4 servings
Average serving = approx. 13 grams balanced protein
30 to 36% of daily protein need

Favorite Baked Soybeans

Inspired by New England baked beans, these baked soybeans are flavored with molasses, onion, and tomato sauce. A variation is baked with millet for complementarity to increase the quality of the protein.

1½ c. dry soybeans, soaked overnight in 3¾ c. water
Water to cover
1 can (8 ozs.) tomato sauce
1 large onion, chopped
2 T molasses
2 T oil

Place the drained soaked soybeans in a 4-quart pressure cooker. Add enough water or vegetable cooking liquid just to cover the beans. Bring up to pressure and pressure cook for 50 minutes. Let cooker cool naturally.

Drain the beans and place them in a mixing bowl. Mix in the tomato sauce, chopped onion, molasses, and oil.

Lightly oil a 1½-quart casserole dish with unrefined soy oil. Pour the bean mixture into it. Cover and bake at 325° for 3 to 5 hours. Add extra water if the beans become a little dry.

Makes 3 to 4 servings.

Variation: Before baking add to the above ingredients 1¾ c. cooked millet (½ c. dry millet cooked in 1½ c. water) and ½ c. tomato juice or tomato sauce. Use a 2-quart casserole dish.

3 to 4 servings (6 servings for variation)
Average serving = approx. 14 grams balanced protein
32 to 39% of daily protein need

Skillet Dishes

Skillet dishes in which the chunks of "protein" are mixed in with vegetables, and perhaps grains, make whole meals in one cooking utensil. This saves time and cleanup efforts for the cook. They are often quick to prepare, especially if some of their elements are done ahead of time.

For two very fast skillet dishes based on patties made of cottage cheese and ground soy nuts, try Cottage Cheese Fingers With Zucchini or Skillet Cacciatore. Other protein pieces made with ground soy nuts are included in Skillet Moussaka, and Soy Nut Slices with Mushrooms. Ground sesame seeds are used for Sesameat Balls in Tomato Sauce. If you make the basic soy-grain sausage and cook the beans ahead of time, the Vegetarian Sausage-Bean Skillet is very quick to put together.

For prepared soyloaf, try Chicken-style Soyloaf with Chinese Vegetables, Diced Ham-style Soyloaf and Beans, Ham-style Soyloaf Skillet, or Ham-style Soyloaf and Vegetable Medley.

We have many soy-granule burger dishes in this section. Granule Burger Chili and Western Skillet Dinner use chunks. Mini loaves are made in Skillet Loaves With Vegetables, Mini Skillet Loaves and Quick One-Pot Dinner. Steak-like forms of granule burger are made in Salisbury Skillet Meal, Swiss Steak-style Soy Granule Burger, Chinese Pepper Steak-Style Granule Burger, and Saucy Burger-Steak Skillet. Meatball Soup Pot, Soy Granule Meatballs Espagnol, Skillet Stew With Limas, Skillet "Sausage" Shepherd Pie, and Protein Patties Cantonese Style use various small round shapes.

Cottage Cheese Fingers With Zucchini

Soy nuts, oats, cottage cheese, and eggs make sausage-shaped fingers cooked with zucchini, mushrooms, and tomatoes.

1 c. soy nuts, ground
1 c. rolled oats
1 T nutritional yeast
2 t low-sodium chicken-style soup base
½ t ground thyme
1 t Vege-Sal
1 onion, minced
2 eggs, beaten
1 c. cottage cheese
2 T oil
4 small zucchini, thinly sliced
6 mushrooms, thinly sliced
2 tomatoes, sliced
2 c. tomato juice

Combine the ground soy nuts and oats in a bowl with yeast, soup base, thyme, Vege-Sal, and minced onion.

Stir in the beaten eggs and cottage cheese, mixing well. Form the mixture into 16 fat fingers by scooping up dough with a large spoon and squeezing it in your hand.

Heat 2 T oil in a large (12-inch) non-stick skillet. Brown the fingers on each side over moderate heat.

Add the zucchini, mushrooms, and tomatoes. Pour in the tomato juice. Bring to a boil, cover, lower heat and simmer for 20 minutes, or until vegetables are tender and much of the liquid has been absorbed.

4 to 6 servings
Average serving = approx. 12 grams balanced protein
28 to 34% of daily protein need

Skillet Cacciatore

Tender chicken-style cutlets browned in the skillet and simmered in tomato sauce with chopped green peppers, onion, and mushrooms, served with spaghetti or brown rice.

1 c. soy nuts, ground
1 c. rolled oats
¼ c. sunflower seeds, ground
1 T nutritional yeast
1 T low-sodium chicken-style soup base
1 t Vege-Sal
½ t Italian herb seasoning
1 medium onion, minced
2 eggs
1 c. cottage cheese

2 T oil, divided
4 medium green peppers, chopped
1 medium onion, chopped
1 large fresh tomato, chopped
2 c. tomato juice
⅓ c. tomato paste
1 t oregano, crushed
2 t soy sauce
1 can (8 ozs.) mushroom pieces
1 can (8 ozs.) tomato sauce (optional)

Combine the ground soy nuts, rolled oats, ground sunflower seeds, yeast, soup base, Vege-Sal, herb seasoning and minced onion in a bowl. Mix well.

Blend the cottage cheese and eggs in a blender container until smooth. Pour this liquid mixture into the bowl with the dry mixture. Stir until no dry particles remain and a uniform stiff dough results. Pack the dough down with a spoon to yield a level surface.

Heat 1 T oil over moderate heat in a non-stick skillet or electric skillet (350°).

Draw lines with a spoon to divide the dough in the bowl into 8 segments, then scoop out 16 parts. Shape them with your hands into irregular small cutlets, or place the scoops directly onto the heated skillet and flatten them with the back of the spoon. Brown the cutlets, about 2 minutes on each side. Remove them to a plate and set aside.

Heat 1 T oil again in the skillet. Stir-fry the green peppers and onions for 3 minutes. Add the chopped tomato.

Pour in the tomato juice. Stir in the tomato paste, oregano, and soy sauce. Add the browned cutlets. Bring to a boil, cover, lower heat and simmer for 10 minutes.

Stir in the mushroom pieces. Cover and simmer for another 10 minutes. Most of the liquid will be absorbed.

To serve, add extra tomato sauce (an 8 oz. can) if desired. Serve with whole wheat and soy spaghetti or brown rice.

4 to 6 servings
Average serving = approx. 13 grams balanced protein
30 to 36% of daily protein need

The Oat Plant

Skillet Moussaka

Moist and flavorful chunks of soy nut meat with tomatoes, eggplant cubes, and onion bits.

1 recipe Soy Nut Meat*
1 eggplant (1 lb.), cubed into ½-inch pieces
1 medium onion, chopped
1 T oil
1 can (1 lb.) whole tomatoes and liquid
½ c. fresh parsley, chopped
1 t leaf oregano

Use the recipe for Soy Nut Meat in the directions for Moussaka Supreme (Casseroles Section).

Turn the mass of soy nut meat out onto a piece of waxed paper or a cutting board, flatten it with your hands, and cut it into 20 to 25 small squares.

Brown the pieces of soy nut meat on both sides in a large non-stick skillet in 1 T oil over medium heat. Remove the pieces to a plate and set aside.

Heat an additional tablespoon of oil in the skillet and sauté the onion and eggplant over medium heat, stirring constantly for 2 to 3 minutes.

Pour in the tomatoes and liquid, breaking up the tomatoes with a spoon. Stir in the parsley and oregano. Stir in the soy nut meat pieces. Bring to a boil, cover, lower heat, and simmer for 20 minutes. The soy nut meat pieces absorb excess liquid from the vegetables, becoming moist and flavorful as the vegetables become tender.

4 servings
Average serving = approx. 14 grams balanced protein
32 to 39% of daily protein need

Soy Nut Slices with Mushrooms

Little soy nut meat slices with sautéed mushrooms in a tangy clear juice, garnished with yogurt and chopped parsley.

1 c. soy nuts, ground fine
¼ c. walnuts, ground to meal
¼ c. rolled oats
¼ t garlic powder
1 Vegex cube, ground
⅓ c. grated Swiss cheese
1 small onion, minced (¼ c.)
¼ of a 3 oz. pkg. of cream cheese
2 eggs, beaten

1 small onion, sliced
1 T oil
¼ t paprika
1 c. sliced fresh mushrooms
1 c. hot water or vegetable water
2 t low-sodium beef-style soup base
1 t lemon juice
½ t Vege-Sal, or to taste
1 c. yogurt
¼ c. chopped parsley
Dash of paprika

Mix the first five ingredients together in a bowl. Add the grated cheese and minced onion, distributing them throughout the mixture with a spoon.

Smash the cream cheese in a small bowl and mix in the beaten eggs. Add this liquid to the dry ingredients, blending thoroughly until no more dry particles remain in the bowl.

Turn out the mass onto a lightly floured board and roll it to a thickness of about ⅜ inch with a lightly floured rolling pin. Cut the mass into irregular rectangles about 1½ x 2 inches.

Brown the sliced onion in 1 T oil in a large non-stick skillet. Shake in some paprika. Push the onions aside and lightly brown the soy nut meat pieces gradually over medium heat, turning them carefully with a plastic or wooden fork.

Place the mushrooms in the pan, stir-fry a bit, then add the mixture of hot water, soup base, lemon juice, and Vege-Sal. Bring to a boil, cover, and simmer for 5 minutes, or until the mushrooms are tender and the soy nut meat pieces are done.

Pour all on a dish, including the sauce. Garnish with 1 c. yogurt, chopped parsley and paprika.

4 servings
Average serving = approx. 12 grams balanced protein
28 to 34% of daily protein need

Sesameat Balls in Tomato Sauce

Tiny sesameat balls browned in olive oil and simmered in a special tomato sauce, served over fine wheat-soy noodles or brown rice.

⅓ c. sesame seeds, ground
¼ c. soy nuts, ground
¼ c. soy powder
¼ c. raw wheat germ
2 T bran
1 T nutritional yeast
1 t gluten flour (or whole wheat)
¼ t garlic powder
¼ t paprika
⅛ t ground thyme
½ t marjoram, ground
½ t Italian herbs, ground
1 Vegex cube, ground
1 t dried parsley flakes, crushed
2 T grated Parmesan cheese
2 T minced onion
2 eggs, beaten
1 T oil
1 c. tomato purée
1 can (8 ozs.) tomato sauce
⅓ c. fresh parsley
1 small onion, chopped
1 small fresh tomato, chopped
Wheat-Soy Noodles or Brown Rice

Mix the dry ingredients (ground sesame seeds through gluten flour) together in a bowl. Stir in seasonings (garlic powder through ground Vegex cube). Add the parsley flakes, Parmesan cheese and minced onion. Mix in the beaten eggs, distributing the liquid well until no more dry particles remain and the mass of sesameat starts to firm up.

Form about 20 small balls from the sesameat mass by taking off chunks with a teaspoon, then rolling them on a lightly floured board. Brown the balls very carefully in 1 T oil in a large non-stick skillet over medium heat.

Put tomato purée, tomato sauce, parsley, onion, and fresh tomato in a blender container. Blend until smooth. Pour the sauce into the skillet with the sesameat balls. Bring to a boil, cover, lower the heat, and simmer for 20 minutes. Serve over fine wheat and soy noodles or brown rice.

4 servings
Average serving = approx. 14 grams balanced protein
32 to 39% of daily protein need

Vegetarian Sausage-Bean Skillet

Navy beans in tangy tomato sauce with vegetarian sausage slices, garnished with onion rings and parsley.

1 recipe Soy and Grain Sausage*
2 c. dried navy (pea) beans
1 can (15 ozs.) tomato sauce
¼ c. catsup
1 T prepared mustard
2 medium onions
1 T oil
2 T fresh parsley, minced

Prepare soy and grain sausages ahead of time. Form it into 12 links and cook as directed.

Have beans soaked overnight or use 1-hour soaking method described under cooking beans (Cooking Hints Section). Cook beans in soaking water for 2 hours or more, or until very tender. Or pressure cook for 30 minutes.

Place the drained beans in a large skillet on top of the stove. Stir in the tomato sauce, catsup, and mustard. Bring to a boil, cover, lower heat, and simmer for 10 minutes.

Cut the onions into rings. In a separate skillet, sauté the onion rings in oil until tender.

Slice cooked soy-grain sausage links into ¼-inch-thick little rounds. Stir them into the beans with sauce and simmer for another 5 minutes.

Place the onion rings on top of beans. Sprinkle with minced parsley.

4 to 6 servings
Average serving = approx. 13 grams balanced protein
30 to 36% of daily protein need

Chicken-style Soyloaf With Chinese Vegetables

Diced chicken-style soyloaf with bean sprouts, shredded cabbage, mushrooms, bamboo shoots, water chestnuts, and shredded green beans served over brown rice.

1½ c. fresh green beans, thinly sliced lengthwise and chopped in 1-inch pieces (or frozen French-cut green beans)
1 T oil
2 T water
4 c. shredded cabbage
1 large onion, sliced
2 c. sliced mushrooms
1 can (1 lb.) bean sprouts, drained; or 1½ c. fresh, steamed
1 can (8 ozs.) bamboo shoots, drained
1 can (8 ozs.) water chestnuts, drained and sliced
2½ c. water or vegetable liquid
1 T low-sodium chicken-style soup base
1 t Vege-Sal
¼ t ground ginger
2 T cornstarch
5 c. cubed Chicken-style Soyloaf*

Heat 1 T oil in an electric skillet over moderate heat. Stir-fry the green beans. Add 2 T water, cover, lower heat, and steam until barely tender. Raise heat, then add cabbage and onion. Stir-fry until they start to become tender. Stir in the mushrooms.

Add the drained bean sprouts, bamboo shoots, and water chestnuts.

Mix 2½ c. vegetable liquid or water with soup base, Vege-Sal, ginger, and cornstarch. Pour into the skillet, bring to a boil, and boil for one minute.

Add the soyloaf cubes. Mix them in. Cover, lower heat, and let cubes heat through. Serve with brown rice.

6 to 8 servings
Average serving = approx. 12 grams balanced protein
28 to 34% of daily protein need

Diced Ham-style Soyloaf and Beans

A one-pot meal of beans and a savory tomato sauce with diced hamloaf and sautéed onion.

½ recipe of Ham-style Soyloaf*
2 c. dried navy (pea) beans, soaked overnight
1 medium onion, chopped
1 T oil
¼ c. tomato paste
1 T Worcestershire sauce
1 t prepared mustard
1 t Vege-Sal

Prepare half the recipe of Ham-style Soyloaf and place the uncooked batter in a small metal bowl lightly oiled with unrefined soy oil. Seal the bowl with a square of aluminum foil. Place the bowl in the middle of the pressure cooker on the flat pressure cooker rack.

Place the soaked beans with soaking water around the bowl in the pressure cooker. Make sure that there is enough water to cover the beans. Close the cooker, bring up to pressure, lower heat, and pressure cook for 25 to 30 minutes. Cool cooker naturally.

Meanwhile, sauté the chopped onion in oil in a separate skillet.

Remove the bowl and rack from cooker. Dice the ham-style soyloaf into ½-inch or 1-inch cubes. Stir the tomato paste, Worcestershire sauce, mustard, and Vege-Sal into the beans and bean liquid. Place the cooker over moderate heat and allow the sauce to bubble. (Add a little more water if you want more sauce.) Stir in the sautéed onion and diced ham-style soyloaf. Let soyloaf heat through.

Makes 4 to 6 servings.

Variations: Use other kinds of beans with about the same cooking time as navy beans. Use Chicken-style or Beef-style Soyloaf. Omit tomato paste, season with soup base, soy sauce, thyme, or marjoram. Purée half a cup of cooked beans in the blender to thicken the bean cooking liquid for sauce.

4 to 6 servings
Average serving = approx. 12 grams balanced protein
28 to 34% of daily protein need

Ham-style Soyloaf Skillet

Brown rice, diced ham-style soyloaf, cut green beans, mushrooms, diced onions, and green pepper in a chicken-style sauce make this easy skillet dish.

3 c. cubed Ham-style Soyloaf*
3 c. cooked brown rice
1 T oil
¾ c. chopped onion
⅓ c. diced green pepper
1 can (8 ozs.) sliced mushrooms, drained
2½ c. cooked green beans (1-inch pieces) or 1 package (9 ozs.) frozen cut green beans
2 c. water or vegetable water
2 T low-sodium chicken-style soup base
1 t Vege-Sal
2 T cornstarch
¼ c. diced pimiento
½ c. grated sharp cheese (optional)

Prepare ham-style soyloaf ahead of time. Cut into chunks or cubes about 1 x ½ inches.

Cook the brown rice using 1 cup of raw rice and 2 cups of water. Prepare the green beans if you are using fresh ones.

Heat the oil in a very large non-stick skillet over moderate heat. Sauté the diced onion and green pepper. (If using frozen green beans, add them and stir until no frost remains.) Add the mushrooms.

Combine the water with the soup base, Vege-Sal, and cornstarch. Pour the mixture into the skillet. Bring to a boil, stirring until liquid thickens and becomes clear.

Add the cooked stringbeans if using fresh ones. Add the rice and cubed soyloaf. Stir in diced pimiento. Mix so that the sauce is well distributed. Sprinkle on grated cheese. Cover, lower heat, and simmer very briefly (or until frozen string beans are cooked).

4 to 6 servings
Average serving = approx. 11 grams balanced protein
26 to 31% of daily protein need

Ham-style Soyloaf and Vegetable Medley

Diced ham-style soyloaf in a white sauce with mixed vegetables.

3 c. cubed Ham-style Soyloaf*
1 T oil
4 c. frozen mixed vegetables, or 1 package (20 ozs.)

1¾ c. vegetable cooking water
2 T cornstarch
1 t Vege-Sal
3 T powdered skim milk
¼ c. evaporated skim milk or buttermilk

Prepare the cooked soyloaf in advance. Make ¾-inch cubes.

Heat the oil in a large (12-inch) non-stick skillet over moderate heat. Add the vegetables, stirring until there is no more frost.

Mix the cornstarch and Vege-Sal with water and powdered skim milk. Pour into the skillet with the vegetables. Bring to a boil and stir until thickened. Cover, lower heat, and simmer for 10 minutes.

Stir in the soyloaf cubes and evaporated skim milk or buttermilk. Simmer for another few minutes, covered, until soyloaf is heated through.

4 servings
Average serving = approx. 10 grams balanced protein
23 to 28% of daily protein need

Granule Burger Chili

Mildly seasoned chunks of granule burger with tomatoes, sauce, kidney beans, and vegetable bits served over brown rice.

Basic Recipe for One Pound of Soy Granule Burger,* or 2 cups of Convenience Mix*
2 T oil
2 large onions, chopped
1 green pepper, chopped
2 stalks celery, chopped
2 cloves garlic, minced
2 T oil
2 c. fresh or canned tomatoes
1 c. tomato purée
½ c. catsup
2 t chili powder
1 t Vege-Sal, or to taste
2 c. home-cooked kidney beans, just barely done
Cooked brown rice

Press Granule Burger mass into a 1-inch-thick square and cut it into 1-inch chunks. Press the chunks firmly with your fingers, then brown them carefully in 2 T oil over medium heat in a large non-stick skillet. Remove them to a plate and set aside.

Heat another 2 T oil in the skillet and sauté the chopped onions, peppers, celery, and garlic, stirring for several minutes. Stir in the tomatoes, purée, catsup, and seasonings, mixing well. Then mix in the kidney beans. Fold in the burger chunks, bring to a boil, cover, lower heat and let simmer 20 minutes. Serve over cooked brown rice.

4 to 6 servings
Average serving = approx. 12 grams balanced protein
28 to 34% of daily protein need

Western Skillet Dinner

A skillet combination of chunked granule burger with brown rice, peas, onion, tomato, and grated cheese.

¾ c. raw brown rice
1½ c. water or vegetable liquid
Basic Recipe for Granule Burger*
1 T oil
1 onion, chopped
2 c. fresh or frozen peas
1 can whole tomatoes, chopped or 3 fresh tomatoes, chopped
¾ c. water, vegetable liquid or liquid from canned tomatoes
1 t Vege-Sal
1 T cornstarch
2 T cold water
½ c. grated Cheddar cheese

Bring 1½ c. water to a boil in a saucepan. Add the rice, cover, lower heat, and simmer for 45 minutes, or until all liquid has been absorbed.

Prepare the granule burger and cook, chunked, in a pressure cooker for 5 minutes using a metal bowl on a steam rack in 1 inch of water.

Sauté onion in oil over moderate heat in a large (12-inch) skillet. Add peas and keep stirring until frost disappears (or until fresh peas start to become tender).

Add the chopped tomatoes, ¾ c. vegetable cooking liquid or juice from tomatoes, Vege-Sal, brown rice, and chopped granule burger.

Bring to a boil, cover, then lower heat, and simmer for 5 to 10 minutes, or until peas are tender and all ingredients are heated through.

Stir in the cornstarch mixed with cold water, bring to a boil, stirring in the mixture, and boil a minute to thicken the juices.

Add the grated cheese and cover until it melts.

4 to 6 servings
Average serving = approx. 12 grams balanced protein
28 to 34% of daily protein need

Skillet Loaves With Vegetables

Top-of-the-stove granule burger loaves with lima beans, sliced carrots, onion and celery.

Basic Recipe for Granule Burger*
¼ c. whole wheat flour
¼ c. oil, divided
4 carrots, sliced
3 stalks celery, sliced
1 large onion, chopped
2 c. water or vegetable water
2 Vegex cubes, smashed
2 T catsup
2 c. frozen lima beans
2 T whole wheat pastry flour
¼ c. water

Cut prepared granule burger mass in half and form 2 loaves, firming them with your hands. Roll them in whole wheat flour. Brown them well on all sides in 2 T of the oil over medium heat in a large skillet or electric skillet. Remove loaves and set them aside.

Sauté the onion, carrots, and celery in the remaining 2 T oil in the skillet. Return the loaves to the skillet. Pour in 2 c. water in which Vegex cubes have been dissolved. Stir in catsup. Bring to a boil, cover tightly, lower heat, and simmer for 10 minutes.

Bring liquid to a boil again, add lima beans, and when liquid boils again cover, lower heat, and simmer for 15 minutes. (Turn and baste the loaves with the liquid in the skillet several times during the cooking.)

Mix 2 T whole wheat pastry flour with ¼ c. water. Stir into the skillet, raise heat, and keep stirring until the broth bubbles and thickens.

Makes 4 to 6 servings.

Variation: Omit frozen lima beans, but add 2 c. cooked dried lima beans 5 minutes before the dish is finished, or long enough for them to heat through.

4 to 6 servings
Average serving = approx. 11 grams balanced protein
26 to 31% of daily protein need

Mini Skillet Loaves

Basic granule burger seasoned with sage, thyme, and minced onion makes six little loaves with tomato soup sauce.

⅔ c. soy granules
⅔ c. soy nuts, ground
⅔ c. whole wheat flour
⅔ c. rolled oats
⅔ c. sunflower seeds, ground
½ c. wheat germ
½ c. bran
½ t sage
½ t thyme leaves, crushed
½ c. minced onion
1⅔ c. hot water
2 Vegex cubes, smashed
2 T soy sauce
1 can (10¾ ozs.) condensed tomato soup, divided
2 T oil
⅔ c. water

Mix together dry ingredients (soy granules through bran) in a bowl. Stir sage, thyme, and minced onion into the dry ingredients.

Dissolve 2 Vegex cubes in 1½ c. hot water. Add 2 T soy sauce and stir in ⅓ c. condensed tomato soup. Pour liquid into dry ingredients; mix well, so that all parts are moistened. Allow mixture to stand for 10 minutes for moisture to be absorbed.

Make 6 mini oval loaves from the mixture, molding them with your hands.

Heat 2 T oil in a large non-stick skillet and brown the mini loaves well on all sides, using moderate heat.

Mix the remaining condensed soup with ⅔ c. water. Pour into the skillet with the loaves. Bring to a boil, cover, lower heat, and simmer for 30 minutes. (Baste the mini loaves with the tomato sauce occasionally during the cooking.)

6 servings
Average serving = approx. 13 grams balanced protein
30 to 36% of daily protein need

Quick One-Pot Dinner

Firm little individual loaves with brown gravy, whole carrots, potatoes, and onions.

Basic Recipe for One Pound of Soy Granule Burger,* or 2 cups of Convenience Mix*
1 onion, minced
2 T fresh chopped parsley
2 T catsup
Whole wheat flour
2 T oil
8-12 new potatoes, scrubbed
6-8 medium carrots, scrubbed
4-6 medium whole onions, peeled
1 c. water
½ t Vege-Sal
½ t Kitchen Bouquet (optional)
2 T whole wheat pastry flour

Add the minced onion and chopped fresh parsley to the Soy Granule Burger Mix before stirring in the liquid, to which the catsup is added.

Form 6 little meat loaves (about 3 inches long x 2½ inches wide) from the Soy Granule Burger. Roll them in the whole wheat flour.

Put the 2 T oil in a pressure cooker, and using medium heat, brown the little loaves on all sides, turning carefully with tongs. Remove them and set aside.

Put the whole carrots and potatoes on the bottom of the cooker with the onions. Place the little loaves on top of the vegetables. Mix the water, Vege-Sal, and Kitchen Bouquet together; pour it into the cooker.

Close the cooker as instructed with your model, bring up to pressure, and cook for 7 minutes. Reduce the pressure under cold running water.

After removing the food to a serving platter, thicken the remaining cooking liquid by adding 2 T whole wheat pastry flour, stirring while it comes to a boil and bubbles for 1 minute. Pour the gravy over the loaves and vegetables.

4 to 6 servings
Average serving = approx. 10 grams balanced protein
23 to 28% of daily protein need

Salisbury Skillet Meal

Granule burger forms oval patties browned in a skillet and simmered with sliced potatoes, onions, and peas in onion soup sauce.

Basic recipe for Granule Burger*
2 T oil, divided
4 medium potatoes, sliced ¼ inch thick
1 large onion, sliced
1½ c. frozen peas
1 envelope dehydrated onion soup mix (from a 2.75 oz. pkg), or about ⅓ c.
3 c. hot water
2 T cornstarch
2 T cold water

When the granule burger mass is firm, separate it into 6 equal portions. Shape them with your hands into 6 oval patties, about ½ inch thick. Brown them on both sides in 1 T oil using moderate heat (350°) in an electric skillet. Remove them to a plate.

Heat another tablespoon of oil in the skillet. Add the potato and onion slices. Stir them until they are heated on all sides. Pour in the frozen peas. Stir briefly.

Mix the dried onion soup with 3 c. hot water. Pour the liquid into the skillet and let it come to a boil. Place the patties on top of vegetables. Cover and lower the heat to 250°. (The vents should be closed.) Simmer for 15 minutes.

Uncover, turn the patties, cover, and simmer for another 15 minutes, or until the potatoes are tender.

Mix the cornstarch with cold water. Stir the mixture into the liquid in the skillet. Turn up the heat so that sauce thickens and bubbles for 1 minute.

Makes 4 to 6 servings.

Variation: Substitute ⅓ c. sunflower seeds, ground, for ⅓ c. walnuts, chopped, in Basic Granule Burger Mix.

4 to 6 servings
Average serving = approx. 10 grams balanced protein
23 to 28% of daily protein need

Swiss Steak-style Soy Granule Burger

Chunks of tender soy granule burger in a savory tomato sauce with peas, carrots, potatoes, and onions.

Basic Recipe for One Pound of Soy Granule Burger*, or 2 cups of Convenience Mix*
½ t onion powder
Whole wheat flour
1 c. fresh peas or more
3 large carrots, thinly sliced
2 large potatoes, cut in ½ inch cubes
1 large onion, chopped
1 c. tomato juice
1 c. hot water
1 Vegex cube, crushed
1 T soy sauce
1 T catsup
½ c. cold water
2 T cornstarch or 4 t arrowroot
Oil for sautéing

Add ½ t. onion powder to the dry ingredients of the Basic Soy Granule Burger Mix, if desired, before stirring in the liquid.

When the burger mass is firm, turn it out onto a cutting board, press it into a ¾-inch-thick rectangle, and cut it into 18 small rectangles about 1 x 2 inches. Firm the dough pieces by pressing and compacting them with your fingers. If desired, roll them in whole wheat flour for crustier chunks. Then brown them over medium heat in 1 to 2 T oil in a large (12-inch) non-stick skillet, turning them carefully so that all sides are done. Remove them and set aside.

In the same skillet, sauté the vegetables in another tablespoon of oil over medium heat, stirring for about 2 minutes.

Mix together the hot water and Vegex cube, tomato juice, soy sauce, and catsup. Pour this liquid into the skillet, add the browned granule burger pieces, and bring to a boil. Cover, lower the heat, and simmer for 20 minutes.

Dissolve the cornstarch in the cold water and stir it into the skillet, distributing it well. Bring the contents of the skillet to a boil again, and let bubble for 1 minute. Serve.

4 to 6 servings
Average serving = approx. 11 grams balanced protein
26 to 34% of daily protein need

Chinese Pepper Steak-style Granule Burger

Slices of soy-granule burger with stir-fried green peppers, onions, water chestnuts, and a savory sauce, served over brown rice.

Basic Recipe for One Pound of Soy Granule Burger,* or 2 cups of Convenience Mix*
2-3 large green peppers
2-3 medium onions, sliced
2 cloves garlic, minced
1 T oil
4 green onions, chopped
1 can (8 ozs.) water chestnuts, sliced
2 c. hot water or vegetable liquid
2 t low-sodium "beef" soup base
1 t Vege-Sal
2-3 T soy sauce
¼ t ground ginger
½ c. cold water
2 T cornstarch
Cooked brown rice

Prepare the basic mix for Soy Granule Burger. When the mass is firm, divide it into 6 small loaves, compacting them with your hands. Place the loaves on a rack over ½ c. of water in a pressure cooker. Cover, bring up to pressure, and cook for 5 minutes. Cool the cooker under the cold water faucet before opening it. Allow the loaves to cool while preparing the vegetables for this recipe. When they are cool enough to handle, cut the loaves into ½-inch-thick slices.

Have the green peppers trimmed, seeded, and cut into 1-inch pieces. Heat the oil in a very large skillet or electric skillet over moderate heat. Add the green peppers, sliced onions, and garlic and stir-fry them for 3 minutes.

Combine the 2 c. hot water and seasonings (soup base through ginger). Pour this liquid into the skillet. Add the green onions and water chestnut slices. Carefully fold in the cooked granule burger slices. Dissolve the cornstarch in the cold water and stir this liquid into the skillet, distributing it in several places. Bring to a boil and simmer for 5 minutes, covered. Serve over cooked brown rice.

4 to 6 servings
Average serving = approx. 11 grams balanced protein
26 to 34% of daily protein need

Saucy Burger-Steak Skillet

Steaklet-shaped granule burger with onions, green beans, and sliced potatoes in a savory sauce.

Basic Recipe for Granule Burger*
½ c. whole wheat flour
¼ c. oil, divided
1 onion, chopped (½ c.)
1 stalk celery, chopped (½ c.) (1-inch pieces)
8 new potatoes, sliced
2 c. water or vegetable liquid
1 Vegex cube, crushed
1 T Worcestershire sauce
1 t Vege-Sal
½ t marjoram, crushed
¼ c. catsup
2 T cornstarch
¼ c. cold water
2 ozs. pimiento, chopped (optional)

Prepare the granule burger as directed in the Basic Recipe. Divide the mass in half, then press each half to a ½-inch thickness and cut each into 4 irregular steak shapes. Dredge them in the whole wheat flour. Brown all 8 pieces well on both sides in 2 T oil, using a large non-stick skillet over medium heat. Remove the burgers to a plate.

Sauté the onion, celery, green beans, and sliced potatoes in the remaining 2 T oil.

Have Vegex cube dissolved in the 2 c. vegetable water. Add Worcestershire sauce, Vege-Sal, marjoram and catsup to the liquid. Pour this mixture into the skillet with the vegetables. Bring to a boil.

Put burger steaks on top of the vegetables. Cover tightly, lower heat, and simmer for 20 minutes. (Turn the burger steaks over after 10 minutes.)

At the end of the cooking time, dissolve the cornstarch in the ¼ c. cold water. Stir the mixture into the broth in the skillet, raise the heat, and keep stirring until the broth bubbles and thickens. Add chopped pimiento, if desired.

4 to 6 servings
Average serving = approx. 10 grams balanced protein
23 to 28% of daily protein need

Meatball Soup Pot

A hearty tomato soup with granule burger meatballs, kidney beans, cabbage, carrots, celery, and onion.

Basic Recipe for One Pound of Soy Granule Burger,* or 2 cups of Convenience Mix*
1 T oil
Whole wheat flour
1 c. dried kidney beans, soaked overnight in 2 c. water
1 quart vegetable cooking water
1 can (6 ozs.) tomato paste
1 T low-sodium "beef" soup base
2 t Vege-Sal, or more, to taste
1 bay leaf
½ small cabbage, chopped in 2-inch pieces
1 c. sliced carrots
1 c. sliced celery
1 onion, coarsely chopped

Make the Basic Soy Granule Burger Recipe and set it aside to firm up.

Cook the kidney beans in the soaking water, or in fresh water to cover them, in the pressure cooker for 20 minutes. Allow the cooker to cool naturally before opening the lid.

Divide the granule burger mix into 14 meatballs, making them firm with your hands. Dredge them in the whole wheat flour, then brown them well in the oil in a skillet over moderate heat.

When the pressure cooker has cooled, add the vegetable cooking water to the kidney beans. (If your vegetable cooking water is frozen, remove the kidney beans to a Pyrex bowl, them melt the frozen water over medium heat in the pressure cooker before putting the beans back in.) Stir in the tomato paste, soup base, and Vege-Sal, and add the bay leaf. Mix in all the chopped and sliced vegetables, then put the browned meatballs on top of all the vegetables. Cover, bring up to pressure, and cook for 1 minute only. Cool the cooker under cold running water before opening it.

4 to 6 servings
Average serving = approx. 12 grams balanced protein
28 to 34% of daily protein need

Soy Granule Meatballs Espagñol

Granule balls in a tomato-herb sauce with crunchy vegetable bits and zucchini rounds, served over brown rice.

Basic Recipe for One Pound of Soy Granule Burger,* or 2 cups of Convenience Mix*
2 T oil plus 2 T oil
1 green pepper, chopped
2 stalks celery, finely cut
1 large onion, minced
4 medium zucchini, thinly sliced
2 c. fresh or canned tomatoes
1½ c. liquid from tomatoes or other vegetable water
2 t low-sodium vegetarian "beef" soup base
2 t Worcestershire sauce
¼ t Gravy Master (optional)
1 t Vege-Sal
½ t garlic powder
½ t oregano
½ t basil
4 t cornstarch or 2½ t arrowroot
¼ c. water
Cooked brown rice

Have Granule Burger Mix prepared. To make 18 meatballs about 1½ inches in diameter, divide the burger mass into three parts, divide these also into three, then cut all the parts in half. Roll the chunks in your hands to make balls.

Heat the 2 T oil in a large non-stick skillet, using medium heat. Brown the meatballs carefully on all sides. Remove them from the pan and set aside.

Heat the additional 2 T oil and sauté the minced vegetables a few minutes, stirring constantly. Add the tomatoes and zucchini.

Have the seasonings (from soup base through basil) all mixed into the tomato or other vegetable liquid, then pour the liquid into the skillet with the vegetables. Put the meatballs on top of the vegetables, bring to a boil, cover, lower heat and simmer for 20 minutes.

Mix the cornstarch or arrowroot in the ¼ c. of water, stir it into the skillet liquid, and bring the liquid to a boil again, letting it bubble 1 minute. Serve with brown rice.

4 to 6 servings
Average serving = approx. 10 grams balanced protein
23 to 28% of daily protein need

Skillet Stew with Limas

Small granule burger meatballs combine with onions, lima beans, and carrots in a spicy tomato sauce.

Basic Recipe for Granule Burger*
1 medium onion, chopped
¼ c. chopped parsley
1 t dry mustard
2 T oil
6 small white onions
6 medium carrots
1 package (12½ ozs.) frozen lima beans
2¼ c. tomato juice
½ c. water
1 clove garlic, minced
1 bay leaf
½ t to 1 t chili powder

Prepare the granule burger using ground sunflower seeds instead of chopped walnuts. Add the chopped onion, parsley, and dry mustard to the granule burger dry mix before stirring in liquid ingredients. When granule burger is firm, make 1-inch meatballs from it by scooping it up with a teaspoon. Roll the balls in your palms to firm them up.

Heat 2 T oil in a large (12-inch) non-stick skillet or electric skillet, using moderate heat. Brown the meatballs well on all sides. Remove the meatballs to a plate and set aside.

Peel the onions and carrots. Cut the carrots into 1-inch pieces and halve the onions.

Put the tomato juice and water in the skillet with garlic, bay leaf, and chili powder. Bring to a boil. Add the carrots, onions, and lima beans. Cover, lower heat. When bubbling subsides, put the granule burger meatballs on top of the vegetables. Cover again and simmer for 20 to 25 minutes, or until vegetables are cooked. Turn meatballs occasionally so that they absorb liquid evenly.

4 to 6 servings
Average serving = approx. 11 grams balanced protein
26 to 31% of daily protein need

Skillet "Sausage" Shepherd Pie

Granule burger sausage pieces and mixed vegetables in a light brown sauce, surrounded by a ring of mashed potatoes.

Basic Recipe for Granule Burger Sausage*
2 T oil
4 c. frozen mixed vegetables, or 1 package (20 ozs.)
2 c. vegetable cooking water, divided
2 Vegex cubes
3 T whole wheat pastry flour
2-3 c. cooked cubed potatoes, mashed and seasoned

Prepare the granule burger sausage. Form small balls or little links from the mixture, rolling them with your hands to firm them up. Brown the granule burger shapes in the oil over moderate heat in a large non-stick skillet. Add 1 c. vegetable cooking water plus one Vegex cube. Bring to a boil, lower heat, cover, and simmer for 10 minutes.

Add the remaining 1 c. liquid mixed thoroughly with whole wheat pastry flour and remaining Vegex cube, crushed. Bring to a boil. Add the frozen vegetables. Cover, lower heat, and simmer for 10 minutes.

Spoon mashed potatoes around the edge of the skillet and serve, or pour granule burger sausage and vegetable mixture into a serving dish and surround with a ring of mashed potatoes.

4 to 6 servings
Average serving = approx. 11 grams balanced protein
26 to 31% of daily protein need

Protein Patties Cantonese-style

An Oriental-inspired dish of granule-burger patties with stir-fried vegetables—green beans, peppers, onions, mushrooms, and bamboo shoots—in a delicious sause, served over brown rice.

Basic Recipe for One Pound of Soy Granule Burger,* or 2 cups of Convenience Mix*
2 T oil
½ pound green beans, in 1-inch pieces
1 medium red pepper, chopped
2 green onions, chopped
½ pound mushrooms, sliced
1 can (5½ ozs.) bamboo shoots, drained
1-2 T vegetable oil
2 c. water or vegetable liquid
2 t low-sodium chicken-style soup base
1 t Vege-Sal
3 T soy sauce
¼ t ground ginger
½ c. water
2 T cornstarch or 4 t arrowroot
Cooked brown rice

Have the Soy Granule Burger prepared and let stand while you are preparing the vegetables. When firm, turn out the lump of burger onto a cutting board and pat it down to a cake about 1 inch thick and 5 inches square. Cut it into 25 one-inch squares. Press each square into a small patty (about 1½ inches in diameter) with your fingers.

Heat 2 T oil in a large non-stick skillet and brown the patties about 2 minutes on each side, using medium heat. Remove the patties to a plate and set aside.

Heat the additional 1 to 2 T oil in the skillet. Stir in the beans, pepper, and onions. Stir-fry for 3 minutes. Put the patties over the beans. Pour in the 2 c. water to which you have added the soup base, Vege-Sal, soy sauce, and ginger. Bring to a boil, cover, and simmer for 10 minutes, or until the beans begin to become tender. Add the mushrooms and bamboo shoots. Cover and cook for another 5 minutes.

Blend the 2 T cornstarch with ½ c. water in a cup. Stir it into the skillet, distributing it through the hot liquid. Bring to a boil again, stirring constantly, until the mixture thickens and bubbles 1 minute. Serve with cooked brown rice.

4 to 6 servings
Average serving = approx. 11 grams balanced protein
26 to 34% of daily protein need

Stuffed Vegetables

One of the nicest of vegetarian main dishes is the stuffed vegetable. Certain vegetables like green peppers, cabbage leaves, zucchini, and eggplant lend themselves readily to stuffing with meat substitutes such as granule burger or vegemeat. Try Sesameat Stuffed Green Peppers, Granule Burger Stuffed Cabbage Rolls, Stuffed Zucchini and Granule-Burger Stuffed Eggplant.

Other not so common stuffed vegetable ideas are Yellow Squash Boats (stuffed with ham-style granule burger), Soy-Millet Stuffed Pumpkin, and Stuffed Acorn Squash. You can also use tomatoes, potatoes, and large onions: Soy Curd Stuffed Tomatoes, Soy Curd or Granule Burger Stuffed Potato Shells, Granule Burger and Spinach Stuffed Onions.

Vary the stuffings by using ham-style granule burger (Ham-style Granule Burger Stuffed Peppers) or sausage-style granule burger (Soy Curd and Burger ''Sausage'' Stuffed Acorn Squash). You can also use chopped seasoned soybeans (Soybean-Millet Stuffed Peppers) or other beans in combination with granule burger (Italian-style Stuffed Peppers).

Another attractive idea is to make eggplant rolls with oval eggplant slices spread with soy curd or granule burger (Soy Curd Stuffed Eggplant Rolls; Granule Burger Eggplant Rolls).

Sesameat Stuffed Green Peppers

Brown rice and grated cheese are added to the basic sesameat recipe for stuffing baked or steamed green pepper halves topped with tomato slices.

⅔ c. raw brown rice
1⅓ c. water
4 medium green peppers
1 recipe for Basic Sesameat*
½ t basil, crushed
1 medium onion, minced
½ c. tomato juice
½ c. grated cheese
1 large tomato, sliced

Cook the rice in water in a covered saucepan, simmering for 30 to 45 minutes, or until all water is absorbed.

Halve the green peppers lengthwise and remove the cores. Using a steam rack in a pot over 1 inch of water, steam the green pepper halves, covered, until tender crisp, about 10 minutes.

To dry ingredients for Basic Sesameat recipe, add ½ t basil, crushed. Substitute medium minced onion for small one called for in the basic recipe. Dissolve the Vegex cube for the basic recipe in ½ c. tomato juice instead of water. Mix in egg or chickpea flour and water. Let stand for liquid to be absorbed.

Mix cooked rice into the sesameat. Stir in the grated cheese.

Stuff the pepper halves with the sesameat-rice mixture. Place a slice of tomato on top of each half. Bake at 350° for 30 minutes in an oiled casserole dish, uncovered.

Makes 4 servings.

Alternate cooking method: Do not steam green pepper halves. Fill them raw. Place filled peppers with tomato slices on a steam rack in a large (6-quart) pressure cooker and pressure cook for 5 minutes over 1 c. of water. Cool under running water. (If this recipe is halved, a 4-quart pressure cooker may be used.)

Note: Baking gives a firm stuffing, and pressure cooking results in a soft stuffing.

4 servings
Average serving = approx. 11 grams balanced protein
26 to 31% of daily protein need

Soy Granule Burger Stuffed Peppers

Green pepper halves stuffed with a mixture of soy granule burger, brown rice, and tomato sauce, served on a platter of brown rice and garnished with additional sauce.

Basic Recipe for One Pound of Soy Granule Burger,* or 2 cups of Convenience Mix*
1 medium onion, chopped
2 c. tomato sauce
½ t basil, crushed
½ c. grated Cheddar cheese
3 large green peppers
3 c. cooked brown rice (1 c. dry plus 2 c. water)

Have the brown rice cooked about 30 minutes. Mix the basil with the tomato sauce.

Add the chopped onion to the dry Soy Granule Mix before adding the liquid. Along with the liquid, put in ½ c. of the 2 c. of tomato sauce.

Cut the cleaned green peppers in half lengthwise. Remove and discard the stem ends and seeds. Steam the halves for 10 minutes in a steam rack over 1 inch of water in a covered pot.

Put ½ c. of the cooked brown rice and the grated cheese into the Granule Burger mixture and stir together. (Allow the remaining brown rice to cook another 15 minutes.) Stuff the green pepper halves with the Granule Burger mixture.

Oil a shallow casserole dish with unrefined soy oil. Put the stuffed peppers in it, and pour another ½ c. of the tomato sauce around them. Bake, covered, at 350° for 40 minutes. Serve with the brown rice and remaining tomato sauce.

Variation: Use Bulgar Wheat Granule Burger.*

6 servings
Average serving = approx. 10 grams balanced protein
23 to 28% of daily protein need

Burger Stuffed Pepper Halves

Green pepper halves stuffed with bulgar wheat granule burger, brown rice, onion, and tomato sauce, topped with Parmesan cheese.

6 medium green peppers
Basic Recipe for Bulgar Wheat Granule Burger,* cooked
2 cans (8 ozs. each) tomato sauce
1½ c. cooked brown rice (½ c. dry plus 1 c. water)
¼ c. catsup
1 medium onion, finely chopped and sautéed in 2 t oil
Parmesan cheese

Wash and cut the peppers in half lengthwise. Scoop out the seeds and membranes. Steam the halves on a steam rack in a large covered pot over ½ inch of water for about 10 minutes, or until just tender.

Mix the cooked granule burger and 1 can of tomato sauce in a bowl. Stir in cooked rice, catsup, and sautéed onion. Stuff the pepper halves with the mixture, heaping them high.

Bake the pepper halves in an oblong baking dish (oiled with unrefined soy oil) at 350° for 20 to 25 minutes. Ten minutes before the end of the baking time, pour the remaining tomato sauce over the top of each stuffed pepper, and sprinkle with Parmesan cheese.

6 servings
Average serving = approx. 10 grams balanced protein
23 to 28% of daily protein need

Vegemeat Stuffed Peppers

Green pepper halves filled with a savory burger-like mixture of Basic Vegemeat with cooked brown rice, served with tomato sauce.

½ c. raw brown rice
1 c. water
4 medium green peppers
1 recipe for Basic Vegemeat*
Tomato Sauce*

Cook rice in water in a covered saucepan, simmering for 30 to 45 minutes, or until all water is absorbed.

Halve the green peppers lengthwise and remove the cores. Using a steam rack in a pot over 1 inch of water, steam the green pepper halves, covered, until tender-crisp, about 10 minutes.

Mix the cooked brown rice into the Basic Vegemeat recipe.

Stuff the pepper halves with the vegemeat mixture.

Bake at 350° for 30 minutes in an oiled casserole dish, uncovered. Serve with Tomato Sauce.

Alternate cooking method: Do not steam the green pepper halves. Fill them raw. Place the filled peppers on a steam rack in a large (6-quart) pressure cooker and pressure cook for 5 minutes over 1 c. of water. Cool under running water. (If this recipe is halved, a 4-quart pressure cooker may be used.)

Note: Baking gives a firm stuffing, and pressure cooking results in a soft stuffing.

4 servings
Average serving = approx. 10 grams balanced protein
23 to 28% of daily protein need

Granule Burger Stuffed Cabbage Rolls

Cabbage leaves rolled around a seasoned granule burger and brown rice mix, spread with special tomato sauce.

Basic Recipe for One Pound of Soy Granule Burger,* or 2 cups of Convenience Mix*
½ t ground thyme
1 medium onion, chopped
¼ c. catsup
1 c. 30-minute cooked brown rice (⅓ c plus ⅔ c. water plus 1 t soy sauce)
1 c. water or vegetable cooking water
12 outer cabbage leaves
Tomato Sauce (see recipe below)

Place the rice, water. and soy sauce in a saucepan. Bring to a boil, cover tightly, and simmer for 30 minutes. Drain off any remaining water for later use.

Before adding the seasoning liquid (to which you also add the catsup) to the Granule Burger dry mix, add the ground thyme and chopped onion, mixing in well. Add the drained partially cooked rice to the granule formula.

Have the cabbage leaves steamed for 5 minutes in a covered pot, using a steam rack over 1 inch of water.

Divide the top of the granule burger mass in the bowl into 6 pie-shaped segments. Scoop each one out, divide it in half, and fill one cabbage leaf with it. Cover the granule ball with the top part of the leaf, fold in the sides of the leaf, then bring the coarser stem side up, forming a roll. Place the rolls in the steam rack, stem side down.

Put the 1 c. of water or vegetable water in the bottom of the pressure cooker. Add the rack of cabbage rolls. Close cooker as instructed with your model. Bring up to pressure and pressure cook for 8 to 10 minutes. Cool cooker under cold running water. Remove the cabbage rolls to a serving platter. Make the Tomato Sauce and pour some over the rolls.

Tomato Sauce

2 T tomato paste
1 T whole wheat pastry flour
2 T water
1 t soy sauce or dash Vege-Sal

Stir the tomato paste into the cooking water remaining in the pressure cooker. Mix the flour with the 2 T water, blending to a smooth paste. Add the paste to the cooking water mixture, stir well and bring to a boil. Allow to bubble for 1 minute. Season with soy sauce or Vege-Sal. Serve over cabbage rolls.

Variations: Use Bulgar Wheat Granule Burger.* Or use *cooked* granule burger, omitting catsup. Stir in a beaten egg, 2 T minced fresh parsley, ¾ t poultry seasoning, and Vege-Sal to taste. Add a small onion and some mushrooms, chopped and sauteed, if desired. Stuff the cabbage leaves as directed above. Place the rolls in a baking dish with 1 can (8 ozs.) of tomato sauce. Bake, covered, 40 minutes to 1 hour, or until cabbage leaves are tender.

4 to 6 servings
Average serving = approx. 11 grams balanced protein
26 to 31% of daily protein need

Vegemeat-stuffed Cabbage Leaves

Brown rice and savory mushroom vegemeat with onion, soy, sesame, oats, and walnuts fill these cabbage leaf rolls that are quickly cooked in the pressure cooker.

2 Recipes of Basic Vegemeat*
1 c. partially cooked brown rice (⅓ c. dry plus ⅔ c. water)
12 outer cabbage leaves
2-3 tomatoes, sliced
Extra chopped cabbage

Prepare the basic vegemeat and set aside.

Cook brown rice about 30 minutes instead of 40.

Steam the cabbage leaves, carefully cut and separated from the head, about 5 minutes on a steam rack in a covered pot over ½ inch of water.

Thoroughly mix the partially cooked brown rice and basic vegemeat together in a bowl. Stuff the cabbage leaves with the mixture. Cover the ball of vegemeat with the top part of one leaf, tuck in the sides of the leaf, then roll, with the coarser stem end on the outside of the roll.

Place ½ c. water or tomato juice in a pressure cooker and insert the flat steam rack that comes with the cooker. Fill the bottom of the cooker over the rack with extra raw chopped cabbage from the core of the cabbage. Place the stuffed rolls on the chopped cabbage, then top them with sliced tomatoes. Pressure cook for 5 minutes. Cool cooker under running water.

Note: This recipe is easily halved to serve 3 people.

6 servings
Average serving = approx. 12 grams balanced protein
28 to 34% of daily protein need

Persian-style Stuffed Cabbage

Cabbage leaves rolled around a stuffing of bulgar wheat granule burger, split peas, chopped onion, parsley, and cinnamon, served with a lemon-honey sauce.

½ c. split peas
1 cup water
Basic Recipe for Bulgar Wheat Granule Burger,* cooked
1 c. chopped onions
½ c. chopped parsley
½ t cinnamon
Dash of pepper (optional)
1 large head of cabbage

½ c. vegetable water
1 t low-sodium beef-style soup base
½ t soy sauce
2 t cornstarch
1½ c. vegetable water
1 Vegex cube
1 t soy sauce
¼ c. lemon juice
2 T honey

Bring 1 c. water to a boil. Add the washed split peas. Cover, lower heat, and simmer for 30 minutes.

Wash the cabbage. Place it on a steam rack over 1 inch of water in a large covered pot. Bring the water to a boil, lower heat, and simmer for 15 minutes to steam cabbage enough so that leaves become just pliable enough to be removed easily. Remove outer leaves and continue steaming if inner leaves are still stiff. Carefully remove 24 leaves.

In a mixing bowl combine cooked bulgar wheat granule burger, chopped onions, chopped parsley, cinnamon, and a dash of pepper, if desired.

Make the sauce by combining ½ c. vegetable water with 1 t soup base, ½ t soy sauce, and 2 t cornstarch in a non-stick saucepan. Bring to a boil, stirring constantly until mixture thickens. Pour sauce into granule burger stuffing. Mix well.

Place about ¼ c. of filling in the middle of each cabbage leaf. Fold in the opposite ends, then roll into sausage shapes, having the stem end on the outside.

Line the bottom of a deep skillet with cabbage leaves and arrange the rolls in it, in layers, placing more leaves between the layers. Coarsely chop remaining cabbage and add it to the pot, easing it underneath the layers toward the bottom of the pot.

For cooking broth, combine 1½ c. hot vegetable cooking water (use water from steaming cabbage and add to it if necessary) with lemon juice, honey, and Vegex cube. Stir until honey and Vegex cube are dissolved. Pour this broth into the deep skillet. Cover, bring to a boil, lower heat, and simmer for about 45 minutes. (Or arrange stuffed cabbage as directed above in the pressure cooker and cook for 8 to 10 minutes. Cool under running water.)

Remove the cabbage rolls and extra cabbage to a serving platter. Mix 1 T cornstarch with 2 T water and stir the mixture into the liquid left in the pot, if there is about 1 c. remaining. Heat until sauce bubbles and thickens, stirring constantly. Serve the sauce over cabbage rolls.

If much of the cooking liquid has evaporated with the skillet method, make more sauce by adding 1 T plus 1½ t cornstarch dissolved in 2 T cold water to another recipe of the broth mixture given above. Cook, stirring constantly, until thickened.

4 to 6 servings
Average serving = approx. 12 grams balanced protein
28 to 34% of daily protein need

Stuffed Zucchini

Tender zucchini halves stuffed with granule burger "sausage," chopped onion, and seasoned sauce, topped with Parmesan cheese.

Basic Recipe for Bulgar Wheat Granule Burger "Sausage"*
4-5 medium zucchini (about 6 inches long and 1½ inches wide)
¾ c. finely chopped onion
1 small clove garlic, minced
2 T olive oil
¼ c. chopped parsley
1 c. vegetable cooking water
2 t low-sodium beef-style soup base
½ t Vege-Sal
1 t rosemary, crumbled
1 T cornstarch
Parmesan cheese

Prepare bulgar wheat burger sausage, using ¼ c. sunflower seeds, ground, as directed in the Basic Recipe. Precook in pressure cooker.

Wash the zucchini and cut off the stem ends. Cut them in half lengthwise and steam them for 5 minutes on a steam rack in a large covered pot over 1 inch of water. Reserve the steaming water.

Scoop out the pulp from the centers of the zucchini halves, leaving a ¼-inch-thick shell. Chop the pulp and reserve.

Sauté the onion and garlic until tender in the olive oil over moderate heat. Stir in the zucchini pulp. Add the cooked granule burger. Mix in the chopped parsley.

Using 1 c. of water from the steamed zucchini, make a sauce with the soup base, Vege-Sal, rosemary, and cornstarch. Combine the ingredients in a small non-stick saucepan and heat until bubbling, stirring constantly. Pour the sauce into the zucchini and granule burger mix. Stir to combine ingredients thoroughly.

Place the zucchini halves in a lightly oiled shallow rectangular casserole dish or lasagna pan. Fill the cavities with the granule burger mixture. Sprinkle the stuffed zucchini halves with Parmesan cheese.

Bake at 350° for 15 to 20 minutes, or 10 minutes longer if the recipe has been prepared ahead and refrigerated.

4 to 6 servings
Average serving = approx. 12 grams balanced protein
28 to 34% of daily protein need

Granule Burger Stuffed Eggplant

Eggplant halves stuffed with bulgar wheat granule burger, chopped green pepper, onion, garlic, eggplant pulp, tomato sauce, and spices, topped with bread crumbs and Parmesan cheese.

1 eggplant, about 1½ lbs.,
or 2 (12-oz.) eggplants
Vege-Sal
2 T oil
1 clove garlic, minced
½ c. chopped onion
½ c. chopped green pepper
1 T oil
¼ c. chopped parsley
¼ t ground allspice
1 c. Tomato Sauce*
Basic Recipe for Bulgar Wheat
Granule Burger,* cooked
¼ c. whole wheat bread crumbs
Grated Parmesan cheese

Cut the eggplant in half lengthwise. Make lengthwise cuts in center of pulp, cutting lines for a ⅜-inch-thick shell border. Sprinkle with Vege-Sal. Let stand for 20 minutes.

Heat 2 T oil in a large (12-inch) skillet. Place the eggplant halves, cut side down, in skillet. Cover and cook for 10 minutes over medium-low heat. Turn and cook for another 5 minutes, or until tender.

Remove eggplant halves to a lightly oiled shallow baking dish. Score the pulp crosswise and scoop it out, leaving ⅜-inch-thick shells. Chop the pulp.

Heat another tablespoon of oil in the same skillet. Sauté the garlic, onion, and green pepper until they start to become tender.

Stir in the parsley, allspice, and tomato sauce. Add the cooked granule burger, tossing gently to mix. Fill the eggplant shells with burger and vegetable mixture, dividing it evenly between the two large shells or among the four smaller ones, heaping it high so that all of it is used. Sprinkle bread crumbs and Parmesan cheese over the fillings.

Bake at 375° for 20 minutes, or until hot and lightly browned.

6 servings
Average serving = approx. 9 grams balanced protein
21 to 25% of daily protein need

Yellow Squash Boats

Tender yellow squash halves stuffed with chopped ham-style granule burger, onion, and seasoned sauce, topped with grated Cheddar cheese.

Basic Recipe for Chopped Ham-style Granule Burger,* cooked
4-5 medium yellow squash (about 6 inches long and 1½ inches wide)
¾ c. finely chopped onion
1 small clove garlic, minced
2 T oil
1 small carrot, grated
¼ c. chopped parsley
1 c. vegetable cooking water
2 t low-sodium chicken-style soup base
½ t Vege-Sal
½ t tarragon, crumbled
1 T cornstarch
½ c. grated Cheddar cheese

Prepare the chopped ham-style granule burger as directed in the basic recipe.

Wash the squash and cut off the stem ends. Cut the squash in half lengthwise and steam them for 5 minutes on a steam rack in a large covered pot over 1 inch of water. Reserve the steaming water for the sauce.

Scoop out the pulp from the centers of the squash halves, leaving ¼-inch-thick shells. Chop the pulp and set aside.

Sauté the onion and garlic until tender in the oil over moderate heat. Stir in the grated carrot. Add the chopped squash pulp, then cooked granule burger. Mix in the chopped parsley.

Using 1 c. of water from the steamed squash, make a sauce with soup base, Vege-Sal, tarragon, and cornstarch. Combine the ingredients in a small non-stick saucepan and heat until bubbling, stirring constantly. Pour the sauce into the squash and granule burger mix. Stir to combine the ingredients thoroughly.

Place the squash halves in a lightly oiled shallow rectangular casserole dish or lasagna pan. Fill the cavities with the granule burger mixture. Sprinkle each stuffed squash half with 1 T grated Cheddar cheese.

Bake at 350° for 15 to 20 minutes, or 10 minutes longer if the recipe has been prepared ahead and refrigerated.

4 to 6 servings
Average serving = approx. 10 grams balanced protein
23 to 28% of daily protein need

Soy-Millet Stuffed Pumpkin

A whole baked pumpkin stuffed with a savory mixture of millet, soy granules, chopped celery and onion, kidney beans, and roasted pumpkin seeds.

1 small pumpkin, 3-4 lbs., about 7 inches in diameter
⅓ c. water
⅓ c. millet
½ c. soy granules
Dash Vege-Sal
1 T oil
½ c. chopped celery
1 c. chopped onion
Dash ground thyme
¼ c. roasted pumpkin seeds (pepitas)
¼ c. chopped parsley
1 c. cooked kidney beans, seasoned to taste

Cut the top off the washed pumpkin, making a circular lid with the stem as the handle. Scoop out the seeds and pulp. Oil the pumpkin outside. Sprinkle the inside cavity with soy sauce or Vege-Sal. Set aside while you prepare stuffing.

Bring 1⅓ c. water to boiling and add millet. Cover, lower the heat, and simmer for 20 minutes. Put the soy granules into the pot, stir, and let them absorb the excess water. Add a dash of Vege-Sal.

Sauté the chopped celery and onion in 1 T oil in a small non-stick skillet. Add a dash of ground thyme. Stir the vegetables into the millet mixture. Stir in the pumpkin seeds and chopped parsley. Add the cooked kidney beans and mix well.

Fill the pumpkin with the stuffing and replace the lid. Place the pumpkin in a lightly oiled shallow baking dish or baking pan. Bake at 350° for about 1½ hours, or until the pumpkin is tender and the skin browns and starts to blister. (Moisture from the pumpkin will be absorbed by the stuffing.)

To serve, scoop out stuffing and some of the cooked pumpkin at the same time.

Note: This recipe can be doubled to fill a larger pumpkin serving more people.

4 servings
Average serving = approx. 10 grams balanced protein
23 to 28% of daily protein need

Stuffed Acorn Squash

Acorn squash halves filled with a savory pudding of bulgar wheat, soy granules, chopped onion, apple cubes, walnuts, and nutmeg.

2 medium acorn squashes
1 medium onion, chopped
2 t butter or oil
½ c. bulgar wheat
2 c. vegetable cooking water
1 T low-sodium chicken-style soup base
1 t Vege-Sal
½ c. soy granules
1½ c. diced apple
¼ t nutmeg
2 eggs, beaten lightly
½ c. chopped walnuts

Clean and wash the squash. Cut in half lengthwise. Scoop out the seeds. Place squash halves on a rack in pressure cooker with ½ c. water. Pressure cook for 10 minutes and cool cooker under running water. Or steam the halves, cut side down, in a covered pot in 1 inch of water for about 25 minutes, or until tender. Reserve the cooking water for cooking the bulgar wheat.

Heat the butter or oil in a saucepan. Add the onions and bulgar wheat. Sauté until the onions start to tenderize. Pour in the water, soup base, and Vege-Sal. Bring to a boil. Cover, lower heat, and simmer for another 5 minutes. Remove from heat. Stir in egg and walnuts.

Scoop out some of the centers of the acorn squash halves to make wider cavities for the filling—about 2 tablespoons from each half. Stir the squash pulp into the stuffing. Stuff each squash cavity with a quarter of the stuffing.

Place the stuffed squash halves in an oiled baking dish. Bake at 350° for 15 to 20 minutes.

4 servings
Average serving = approx. 10 grams balanced protein
23 to 28% of daily protein need

Soy Curd Stuffed Tomatoes

Tomato shells filled with seasoned soy curd, bulgar wheat, chopped celery, onion, and mushrooms, topped with bread crumbs and Parmesan cheese.

6 large tomatoes
Vege-Sal
1 or 2 T oil
¼ c. chopped onion
1 stalk celery, chopped
¾ c. bulgar wheat
1½ c. reserved tomato juice and water
2 t low-sodium chicken-style soup base
3 or 4 mushrooms, chopped
1½ c. Soy Curd*
¼ c. chopped parsley
¼ c. chopped green onions
¼ c. bread crumbs
Parmesan cheese (optional)

Wash the tomatoes and cut thin slices from the stem ends. Scoop out the seeds and pulp, leaving shells ½ inch thick, and reserve the shells for the filling. Sprinkle with Vege-Sal and let stand upside-down for 10 minutes.

Strain the tomato pulp and reserve the tomato juice. Measure the reserved juice, and add enough water to total 1½ c. if necessary.

Chop the tomato pulp. Heat 2 t oil in a skillet. Sauté the onion and celery. Add the bulgar wheat and stir until the grains are coated with oil. Pour in the tomato juice and soup base. Bring to a boil. Add the chopped tomato and mushrooms. Cover, lower heat, and simmer for 15 minutes.

Stir the soy curd into the bulgar mixture. Taste for seasoning and add additional Vege-Sal if desired. Stir in the parsley and green onion.

Stuff the tomato shells with the mixture, heaping it high. Top with bread crumbs and Parmesan cheese, if desired. Place the stuffed shells in a shallow lightly oiled baking dish. Bake at 350° for 20 minutes.

6 servings
Average serving = approx. 10 grams balanced protein
23 to 28% of daily protein need

Soy Curd Stuffed Potato Shells

Baked potato shells heaped with seasoned soy curd, mashed potatoes, minced onion, and parsley, topped with bread crumbs.

4 large baking potatoes
2 T oil or butter
1 t Vege-Sal
¼ c. grated onion
2 T chopped green onion
2 T minced parsley
1 recipe (1½ cups) for Soy Curd*
1 T soy sauce
¼ c. whole wheat bread crumbs
½ c. grated Cheddar cheese

Scrub the potatoes very well in water. Dry them and rub a little oil over the skins. Bake them at 400° for about 1 hour, or until they are easily pierced with a fork. (Prick the potatoes with a fork after 20 minutes of baking.)

Split the potatoes in half lengthwise and carefully scoop out the pulp, leaving ½-inch-thick shells.

Mash the pulp with a potato masher or with an electric mixer. Add 2 T oil or butter, 1 t Vege-Sal, grated onion, chopped green onion, and minced parsley.

Mix the soy curd thoroughly with soy sauce, checking for taste. Stir the soy curd into mashed potatoes, mixing thoroughly. Taste for seasoning.

Stuff the potato shells with the mixture, heaping it high so that all is used. Sprinkle the stuffed shells with bread crumbs. Dot with oil or butter, if desired. Sprinkle with grated Cheddar cheese.

Bake at 400° until browned and heated through, about 10 to 15 minutes.

Variation: Substitute 1½ c. of Deviled Sandwich Spread* for soy curd. Omit the soy sauce.

4 to 6 servings
Average serving = approx. 12 grams balanced protein
28 to 34% of daily protein need

Granule Burger-stuffed Baked Potatoes

Baked potato shells stuffed with mashed potato, bulgar wheat granule burger, onion, mushrooms, and Cheddar cheese.

6 medium baking potatoes, or 3 large Idaho potatoes (about 3 lbs.)
Basic Recipe for Bulgar Wheat Granule Burger* (made with ground walnuts), cooked
1 c. vegetable water
2 t low-sodium beef-style soup base
1 T cornstarch
½ t Vege-Sal
⅔ c. chopped mushrooms
1 medium onion, chopped and sautéed in 2 t oil
⅓ c. yogurt or milk
1 c. shredded Cheddar cheese

Wash, dry, lightly oil, and bake the potatoes in a 400° oven about 1 hour, or until tender. (Very large potatoes may take up to half an hour longer.)

Meanwhile, make the sauce for cooked granule burger by combining water, soup base, cornstarch, and Vege-Sal in a small non-stick saucepan. Heat until bubbling, stirring constantly. Mix into the cooked granule burger.

Sauté the onion in 2 t oil over medium heat. Add the chopped mushrooms and stir until the vegetables are barely tender. Stir them into the granule burger mixture.

For medium potatoes, slice off a side of each potato. Scoop out the pulp carefully, leaving sturdy shells. Mash the pulp in a bowl with yogurt or milk. (For large Idaho potatoes, cut them in half lengthwise and carefully scoop out the centers, leaving ⅜-inch-thick shells.)

Stir the mashed potatoes into the granule burger mixture. Place the potato shells in a lightly oiled baking pan. Stuff the shells, heaping the filling into high mounds so that all of it is used. Sprinkle stuffing with shredded cheese.

Broil the stuffed potatoes for 3 to 5 minutes, or until lightly browned and hot. If they have been prepared ahead and refrigerated, bake them at 350° for 20 to 30 minutes, or until heated through.

Garnish with parsley.

Variation: Use Chopped Ham-style Granule Burger.*

6 servings
Average serving = approx. 11 grams balanced protein
26 to 31% of daily protein need

Granule Burger and Spinach Stuffed Onions

Scooped out onion halves stuffed with bulgar wheat granule burger, chopped onion, and spinach, garnished with cream sauce or cheese sauce.

4 large onions
1 recipe Bulgar Wheat Granule Burger,* cooked
1 package (10 ozs.) frozen chopped spinach
1 T oil
1 large clove garlic, minced
½ c. vegetable water
1 t low-sodium beef-style soup base
½ t soy sauce
2 t cornstarch
1 c. Cream Sauce or Cheese Sauce (see recipe below)

Cook the unpeeled onions in boiling salted water for 15 minutes. Drain. Let stand until cool enough to handle, then peel and cut in half. Or pressure-cook peeled onions, cut in half, 5 minutes. Cool cooker under faucet of running water.

Carefully scoop out the inside portion of each onion half, leaving shells about ½ inch thick. (Reserve the scooped out portions—some for this recipe, the rest for another meal.)

Heat 1 T oil in a non-stick skillet. Sauté ½ c. of reserved onion, diced, and the minced garlic. Add the frozen spinach. Cook, breaking up spinach as it thaws. Push the vegetables to one side of skillet.

Combine the vegetable water, soup base, soy sauce, and cornstarch. Pour the mixture into the skillet and cook, stirring constantly, until bubbling. Stir sauce into vegetables.

Stir cooked granule burger into the skillet with the vegetables, mixing well.

Place the onion shells in a lightly oiled rectangular baking dish. Fill the shells with scoops of granule burger-spinach stuffing, heaping it high so that all is used. Pour a tablespoon of Cream Sauce or Cheese Sauce over the top of each stuffed onion. Bake at 350° for 25 to 30 minutes.

Makes 4 to 6 servings.

Variation: Omit the spinach. Chop all of the reserved scooped out onion centers and sauté until translucent in place of spinach. Season with Vege-Sal to taste.

Cream Sauce or Cheese Sauce

1 T oil
2 T whole wheat pastry flour
1 c. milk
½ t Vege-Sal
¼ c. grated Cheddar cheese (optional)

Heat the oil in a small non-stick saucepan over medium heat. Stir in the flour, mixing well. Gradually stir in the milk. Cook, stirring constantly, until the mixture thickens and bubbles 1 minute. Add Vege-Sal. Stir in cheese, if desired.

4 to 6 servings
Average serving = approx. 11 grams balanced protein
26 to 31% of daily protein need

Ham-style Granule Burger Stuffed Peppers

Green pepper halves stuffed with chopped ham-style bulgar wheat granule burger, brown rice, onion, and cheese sauce or tomato sauce.

6 medium green peppers
Basic Recipe for Chopped Ham-style Granule Burger,* cooked
1½ c. cooked brown rice (½ c. dry rice plus 1 c. water)
½ c. chopped onion, sautéed in 2 t oil
¼ t marjoram, crushed
2 t prepared mustard
2 c. Cheese Sauce, divided (see recipe below) or 2 cans (8 ozs. each) tomato sauce

Wash the green peppers and prepare by cutting in half lengthwise for 12 pepper halves. Remove seeds and membranes. Steam the green peppers for 10 minutes on a steam rack over ½ inch of boiling water in a covered pot. Vary steaming time according to the degree of tenderness you desire.

Mix chopped ham-style granule burger, cooked rice, sautéed onion, marjoram, and mustard together in a bowl. Stir in 1 c. of the Cheese Sauce or tomato sauce.

Fill pepper halves with the granule burger mixture, heaping them high so that all the filling is used.

Place the stuffed pepper halves in a lightly oiled shallow baking dish. Bake at 350° for 25 to 30 minutes, or 10 minutes longer if they have been prepared ahead of time and refrigerated. Ten minutes before the end of baking time, pour some of the remaining 1 c. of Cheese Sauce or tomato sauce over the top of each stuffed pepper half.

Makes 6 servings.

Cheese Sauce

¼ c. whole wheat pastry flour
2 T oil
½ c. tomato juice
1½ c. hot vegetable cooking water
¼ c. instant powdered milk
¼ c.-½ c. grated Cheddar cheese
¼ t Vege-Sal, or to taste

Put the flour, oil, and tomato juice in a blender container and mix on low speed. Slowly add the hot vegetable water (use the water from steaming the peppers) while blending. Add the powdered milk and cheese, cover and blend on regular speed. Pour the mixture into a saucepan and stir over moderate heat until it bubbles and thickens.

6 servings
Average serving = approx. 10 grams balanced protein
23 to 28% of daily protein need

The Rice Plant

Soy Curd and Burger "Sausage" Stuffed Acorn Squash

Acorn squash halves stuffed with soy curd and granule burger "sausage" with minced green pepper and onion, topped with grated cheese.

2 medium acorn squash
1 T oil
¼ c. minced onion
¼ c. minced green pepper
½ recipe Bulgar Wheat Granule Burger "Sausage,"* cooked
2 T minced fresh parsley
1 recipe (about 1½ c.) Soy Curd*
Vege-Sal to taste
½ c. grated Cheddar cheese

Wash, halve lengthwise, and remove the seeds from the squash. Pressure-cook for 10 minutes using ½ c. water and the round perforated rack that comes with the cooker. Let the cooker cool naturally. Or cook squash halves until tender on a steam rack in 1 inch of water in a covered pot for about 25 minutes. (Save water for cooking)

Heat 1 T oil in a large non-stick skillet. Sauté the onion and green pepper until tender. Stir in prepared granule burger "sausage," minced parsley, and then the soy curd, which has been seasoned to taste with Vege-Sal.

Stuff the squash halves with the granule burger-soy curd mixture. Sprinkle each stuffed half with 2 tablespoons of grated cheese.

Place the squash under the broiler, 2 inches from the heat, for 4 or 5 minutes, or until the cheese is melted. If you have refrigerated this recipe after preparing it ahead, bake the squash in a lightly oiled shallow baking dish at 375° for 25 to 30 minutes.

4 servings
Average serving = approx. 13 grams balanced protein
30 to 36% of daily protein need

Soybean-Millet Stuffed Peppers

Green pepper cups stuffed with chopped soybeans, millet, cottage cheese or seasoned soy curd, onion, and mushrooms, topped with tomatoes.

4 medium green peppers
1 c. cooked soybeans, chopped
1 c. cooked millet
½ c. cottage cheese or seasoned soy curd*
1 small onion, chopped and sautéed in 2 t oil
3 mushrooms, chopped (½ c.)
2 T chopped parsley
¼ t oregano
¼ t basil
⅛ t garlic powder
1 t soy sauce
1 T catsup
Fresh tomato slices or canned stewed tomato halves

Wash the green peppers and open them at the top. Scoop out the seeds and membranes. Steam the peppers on a steam rack in a large covered pot over ½ inch of water for about 10 minutes, or until just tender.

Mix the chopped cooked soybeans with the cooked millet and cottage cheese or seasoned soy curd in a bowl. Stir in the sautéed onion and mushrooms. Mix in seasonings (parsley through catsup).

Oil a small shallow square baking dish, just the right size to support the four pepper cups standing up. Place the peppers in the dish and spoon the filling into them, dividing it evenly among them. Top the pepper halves with sliced fresh tomatoes or canned stewed tomato halves.

Bake at 350° for 20 to 25 minutes.

4 servings
Average serving = approx. 11 grams balanced protein
26 to 31% of daily protein need

Italian-Style Stuffed Peppers

Green peppers stuffed with granule burger, chick-peas, onion, chopped tomatoes, and mozzarella cheese.

6 medium green peppers
Basic Recipe for Bulgar Wheat Granule Burger,* cooked
1 t fennel seeds, crushed
1 medium onion, chopped (½ c.) and sautéed in 2 t oil
2 c. cooked chick-peas, drained
1 can (16 ozs.) tomatoes, drained and chopped
1 egg
1 t oregano, crumbled
¼ c. minced parsley
1 c. diced mozzarella cheese

Cut off the tops of the green peppers. Scoop out the seeds and membrane. Steam the peppers on a steam rack in a large covered pot over ½ inch of water for about 10 minutes, or until just tender. Drain them well. Stand the peppers in an oiled shallow baking dish that supports them close together.

Before cooking the bulgar wheat granule burger according to the basic recipe, add the crushed fennel to the dry mix.

Mix the cooked granule burger, sautéed onion, chick-peas and drained chopped tomato in a bowl. Stir in the egg, oregano, parsley, and diced cheese. Spoon the mixture into the pepper cups.

Bake at 350° for 20 to 25 minutes.

6 servings
Average serving = approx. 12 grams balanced protein
28 to 34% of daily protein need

Soy Curd Stuffed Eggplant Rolls

Eggplant slices dipped in batter and crumbs, browned in oil, spread with savory soy curd, rolled, and baked with tomato sauce and grated cheese.

1 medium eggplant (about 1 lb.)
1 recipe Seasoned Dipping Batter*
1 c. whole wheat bread crumbs
½ c. sunflower seeds, ground
⅓ c. wheat germ
¼ c. bran, ground fine
1 t oregano, crumbled
Olive oil
1 recipe (1½ cups) Soy Curd*
1 onion, chopped
1 T oil
1 T soy sauce
2 T minced parsley
1 c. Italian-style Tomato Sauce*
Grated Cheddar or Parmesan cheese

Peel eggplant and slice it thin lengthwise into 12 to 16 slices about ⅛ inch thick.

Combine the bread crumbs, ground sunflower seeds, wheat germ, ground bran, and oregano in a wide shallow bowl.

Dip the eggplant slices in the dipping batter (made in another wide shallow bowl), coating them thinly but uniformly. Next dip the slices into the crumb mixture.

Heat a tablespoon of olive oil in a very large non-stick skillet over moderate heat, or in an electric skillet at 350°. Place as many eggplant slices as will fit in the pan and let cook until nicely browned on the underside. Cover the pan while doing this, to let the eggplant steam through. Turn and brown the other side. (This process can be shortened by using two skillets at once.)

Set the slices aside on a plate until all are finished. You may wish to add another tablespoon of oil to the skillet before adding each new set of slices.

Sauté chopped onion in 1 T oil in a small skillet. Mix the soy curd, sautéed onion, soy sauce, and minced parsley in a bowl.

Spread each slice of prepared eggplant with about ¼ c. of the soy curd mixture (more or less, depending on the size of the slice). Roll up the slice starting from the narrow end, and place the roll, seam side down, in a lightly oiled casserole dish. Continue until all the slices have been filled and rolled. Cover rolls in the dish with 1 c. of Italian-style tomato sauce. Sprinkle with grated cheese, if desired.

Bake at 350° for 25 minutes.

4 to 5 servings
Average serving = approx. 11 grams balanced protein
26 to 31% of daily protein need

The Sunflower

Granule Burger Eggplant Rolls

Eggplant slices rolled around a mixture of browned granule burger, chopped onion, and grated zucchini, sauced with celery soup, sprinkled with grated cheese and baked until tender.

1 large eggplant (about 1½ lbs.), or 2 medium eggplants
⅓ c. oil
1 recipe for Granule Burger*
2 t Worcestershire sauce
1 medium onion, chopped
1 small zucchini, shredded (about 1½ c.)
2 T oil
1 can (10¾ ozs.) condensed cream of celery soup, or 1 recipe for Celery Cream Sauce (see page 119)
¾ c. milk
2 T grated Parmesan cheese

Remove the stem end of the eggplant. (Peel the eggplant if it has been waxed.) Cut the eggplant lengthwise into ¼-inch-thick slices. With a very large eggplant, have at least 8 wide, long slices. With 2 smaller eggplants, make 16 smaller ones.

Brush the slices with the oil on both sides. Lay them on a broiler pan, as many as will fit at one time. Broil 4 inches from the heat, for about 2 or 3 minutes per side, only until barely tender and very lightly browned. Repeat until all slices are done. Set aside.

Add 2 t Worcestershire sauce to the liquid for basic granule burger mix. Pour the liquid into dry granule burger mix and stir thoroughly, until all liquid is uniformly absorbed by dry mix. Stir in the chopped onion. Let stand until granule burger is firm.

Heat 2 T oil in a large (12-inch) non-stick skillet. Put the granule burger and onion mix in skillet. Stir over moderate heat with a nylon spatula, breaking up any large lumps. Keep stirring until burger becomes slightly browned and onions start to become tender. Remove from heat. Stir in shredded zucchini, distributing it throughout the burger mixture.

Oil a large casserole dish with unrefined soy oil. With a big spoon, take mounds of burger mixture and place them horizontally on the wide bottom end of each eggplant slice. Roll up the eggplant, squeezing the filling to compact it. Place each roll in the casserole dish. (The number of eggplant slices you have will vary with the size and shape of your eggplant.)

In a bowl, mix condensed soup and milk (or Celery Cream Sauce* and milk). Pour it over the eggplant rolls. Sprinkle them with the grated cheese. Bake, covered, at 350° for 30 minutes.

4 servings
Average serving = approx. 12 grams balanced protein
28 to 34% of daily protein need

The Soybean Plant

Pasta Dishes

People are fond of pasta. It cooks quickly and is easy to turn into a simple or fancy dish. We prefer whole wheat or whole wheat and soy pasta. If we can't buy it, we often make our own. You can find the recipes for homemade whole-grain pasta in this section.

Even if you can't find whole-grain pasta, you should be able to find high-protein white pasta, fortified with soy flour, even in a supermarket. If you want to use it, but would like to replace the vitamins, minerals, and fiber removed in milling the flour, then add a tablespoon or two each of wheat germ and bran to every cup of cooked pasta. Or put wheat germ and bran in your sauce to thicken it nicely and provide better nourishment. If you use ordinary pasta, to increase the protein value we recommend adding soy granules to your spaghetti sauce (see Cooking Hints Section under Sauces) and topping the pasta with cheese in addition to using wheat germ and bran.

You don't have to give up spaghetti and meatballs or "meaty" lasagna though you are eliminating meat. Granule burger meatballs and "sausage" slices are so satisfying that you will never miss what they are replacing.

Various diced soyloaves are good served over cooked pasta with sauce and vegetables. See Ham-style Soyloaf with Stir-Fried Cabbage and Noodles, or Tetrazzini-style Soyloaf. Or try Whole Wheat Straw and Hay Pasta With Hamloaf, using green and regular noodles.

Do you want to make a special company meal? Try Homemade Ravioli, Stuffed Shells, Macaroni Burger Pie, Granule Burger Lasagna, Lasagna Rollups, or Granule Burger "Sausage" Balls With Pasta.

For serviceable family meals, try Baked Soy Curd Casserole, Granule Burger and Spinach Pasta, Ragout With Olives, Soy Granule Meatballs and Macaroni Supper, or Spaghetti and Soy Granule Meatballs—all are good choices.

Are you happy with a simple meal of pasta, vegetables, and complementary beans? Easy-to-make Zucchini With Macaroni and Beans or Macaroni and Eggplant With Beans are right for you. Or try Garden-Style Spaghetti complemented with soy granules.

HINTS ON COOKING PASTA

Most of us have been taught that pasta needs to cook in "lots and lots" of boiling water—something like 6 or 7 quarts per pound of pasta. We have also been told that the water should be boiling for the 5 to 8 minutes (timed exactly) required to cook the pasta. This information applies to pasta made with white flour.

We used to cook pasta in lots of water, but have found that whole-grain pasta cooks just as well in only twice its volume of water, like rice or other cereals. B vitamins and minerals pass into the cooking water, and are lost with the large quantities of water that are thrown away when the pasta is done. In a smaller amount of water, the liquid dissolving those nutrients is actually absorbed by the pasta. Usually very little water needs to be drained when the pasta is cooked this way. It can be saved in a freezer container, like your vegetable cooking water, to be used in soups. Or use it in your pasta sauce recipe.

To cook pasta this nutrient-conserving way, bring 2 cups of water to a boil for every 1 cup of pasta. (For spaghetti, estimate its volume, then use twice as much water.) Add the pasta a bit at a time so that the boiling doesn't stop. This cooks the starch grains quickly so that the cooking time is shortened and the starch doesn't soak out to thicken the cooking liquid. Boil for a minute or two, then lower heat and let the pasta simmer a few more minutes, covered, until it is tender and the water is mostly absorbed. Dry whole wheat pasta, especially if stored long, will take at least 10 minutes or even up to 20 minutes for large pieces like jumbo shells. Fresh homemade whole grain pasta takes much less time—only 5 to 8 minutes. Fresh pasta made without eggs may take even less than 5 minutes.

Suppose you are giving a pasta party with lots of whole wheat and soy spaghetti, plenty of tomato sauce and granule burger meatballs. You will have no problem keeping the sauce and granule burger warm and ready for serving, using a hot tray or chafing dish. But the pasta needs some special treatment. Here's what to do:

Use three quarts of boiling water for every pound of spaghetti or other pasta. (This is three times the volume of the pasta instead of twice the volume.) Add a tablespoon of oil to prevent the water from boiling over. When the water has come up to a rolling boil, add the pasta. Let the pasta boil gently only one-half the total time it normally requires to cook. Then you can let the pasta stand in the hot water for 10 minutes or more to finish cooking. As the water cools gradually it has its own thermostat and automatic cooking cutoff point. The pasta can be scooped up with a big strainer to be served nice and warm without drying out. If the pasta becomes too cold, heat once again to boiling and serve at once. Pasta cooked this way makes a nice party food because it does not stick together and is perfectly cooked for the people arriving early and for those who may be late.

Homemade Whole Wheat Pasta

Basic homemade pasta with variations will make any shape flat noodle from whole wheat flour, with or without egg, with complementary soy powder if desired, or even with spinach for green noodles.

2 c. whole wheat flour	**2 eggs**
½ t Vege-Sal	**½ c. water**

Mix the flour and Vege-Sal in a mound on a very clean bread board or counter. Make a well in the mound and break the eggs into it. Add a little water to the eggs, then beat them with a fork for 1 or 2 minutes, gradually drawing the flour from inside the well, adding the rest of the water a bit at a time.

Working with the palms, squeeze the mixture together until a crumbly paste is formed. Start kneading the dough, folding it over and over until it is well mixed, smooth and elastic, for 10 to 15 minutes. (If the dough remains too dry and flaky, add more water, only a tablespoon at a time. If it stays too wet, gradually knead in more flour by the tablespoon.)

When the dough has become shiny, smooth, and elastic, cover it with an inverted bowl or put it in a plastic food storage bag and allow it to rest for ½ to 1 hour.

Divide the dough into two or four sections on a lightly floured board. Roll each piece of dough as flat as possible with a sturdy rolling pin. Start from the center of the piece and work out. Roll the dough lengthwise, turn, then roll crosswise. Repeat until the dough is as thin as possible—⅛ inch or less. (To prevent the dough from sticking to the board, carefully lift it and sprinkle a little more flour on the board.)

Thinly rolled pasta may now be cut into various widths or shapes. For lasagna noodles, cut strips 1½ to 2 inches wide and about 12 inches long. For fettuccini, make narrow strips ⅛ to ¼ inch wide. (Fold the pasta strips accordion-style, or roll them up as if you were rolling paper, then shred with a sharp knife at the desired interval for the width of noodles you need.) You can also cut 4½- × 5-inch rectangles to make flat cooked noodles for stuffed rolled manicotti or cannelloni (instead of using crepes). Or follow the directions for Homemade Ravioli given later in this section. (This dough may also be used in a regular pasta machine.)

You can cook the pasta immediately while it is still fresh, or air-dry it on clean towels. Uncooked noodles may be refrigerated in an airtight container for several days, or they may be frozen.

To cook fresh pasta, drop it into a kettle of boiling water, using about twice the volume of water as the amount of pasta. Allowing the pasta to simmer gently is better for preserving nutrients than hard boiling. (Using less water means less dissolving of vitamins and minerals.) Cover the pot and stir several times during the simmering. The pasta will take 8 or 10 minutes to cook *al dente*, or still firm enough to bite. Larger pieces take longer. Dried fresh pasta may take longer also, so time and test it by biting.

Makes 4 to 6 servings.

Pasta Variations

Whole Wheat and Soy Egg Pasta. Substitute 1 c. of natural soy powder for 1 c. of whole wheat flour. Substitute 2 t soy sauce for Vege-Sal.

Whole Wheat and Spinach Pasta. Substitute ½ c. puréed cooked spinach for water in the recipe.

Eggless Whole Wheat Pasta. Substitute 2 T oil for egg and add ¼ c. more of water.

Eggless Whole Wheat and Soy Pasta. Use 1⅔ c. whole wheat flour and ⅓ c. natural soy powder. Use 2 t soy sauce instead of Vege-Sal, if desired. Use 2 T oil instead of eggs, and increase water to ⅔ cup. (Moisture content of soy powder varies, so more tablespoons of whole wheat flour may have to be kneaded in.)

Torchio Machine Homemade Pasta

This recipe works for the inexpensive plastic machine that looks like a meat grinder and works like a meat grinder to extrude pasta shapes from a ball of dough.

¾ c. whole wheat flour	**1 egg**
¼ t Vege-Sal	**1 t olive oil**

Mix together the flour and Vege-Sal. Beat the egg and oil separately, then pour into flour and mix thoroughly. Knead dough for 10 minutes on a lightly floured board. (There is no water in this recipe because the machine requires a firm dough.)

Put the dough ball into the Torchio machine and grind out the desired pasta shapes. Cut the extruded pasta into the desired lengths and cook immediately or let the pieces dry on clean towels for about 1 hour.

To cook, place in boiling water (twice the volume of the pasta), lower the heat and let simmer. Undried fresh pasta may take less than 10 minutes to cook *al dente*, so watch it carefully and test by biting.

Makes 2 to 4 servings.

Ham-style Soyloaf With Stir-fried Cabbage

Ham-style soyloaf cubes with shredded cabbage, chopped onion, sliced mushrooms, and fine wheat and soy egg noodles.

1 package (8 ozs.) wheat and soy egg noodles, cooked and drained (reserve water)
1 T oil
½ Basic Recipe (3 c.) for Ham-style Soyloaf,* cooked and cubed
1 T oil
1 large onion, chopped
1 pound Chinese celery cabbage, or green cabbage, finely shredded
4-5 mushrooms, sliced
2 T soy sauce
1 c. noodle cooking water
1 T cornstarch

Mix the oil into cooked noodles and keep them warm in a bowl.

Brown the cubed soyloaf in 1 T oil in a large non-stick skillet. Remove to a plate and set aside.

Heat 1 T oil in the same large skillet and stir-fry the onion and cabbage until just tender-crisp. Stir in mushrooms. Mix in soyloaf cubes.

Have the soy sauce, cornstarch, and water mixed together. Pour into the vegetables. Allow to come to a boil and let bubble 1 minute.

Stir cooked noodles into the skillet.

4 servings
Average serving = approx. 12 grams balanced protein
28 to 34% of daily protein need

Tetrazzini-style Soyloaf

A dish of wheat and soy egg noodles spread with mushrooms, diced chicken-style soyloaf, and cream sauce, topped with melted cheese and paprika.

1 T olive oil
½ pound fresh mushrooms, sliced (3 c.)
2 T non-fat dry milk
1½ t cornstarch
2 t low-sodium chicken-style soup base
1 t Vege-Sal
¼ t garlic powder or ½ t onion powder
Pinch of nutmeg
2 c. cold water or vegetable water
8 ozs. wheat and soy egg noodles, cooked
3 c. diced Chicken-style Soyloaf*
½ c. grated cheese
Paprika

Heat the oil in a skillet. Sauté the mushrooms until they are barely tender.

Mix the powdered milk, cornstarch, chicken-style seasoning, Vege-Sal, garlic powder, and nutmeg into the cold water in a saucepan. Cook over medium heat, stirring, until sauce bubbles and thickens.

Oil a 2-quart shallow baking dish with unrefined soy oil. Place the cooked noodles in the dish. Spread the mushrooms over noodles. Spread the soyloaf cubes over mushrooms. Pour the sauce over all.

Sprinkle grated cheese evenly over the top of the dish. Garnish with paprika.

Bake at 350° for 15 to 20 minutes, or until the casserole is heated through and the cheese is melted.

4 to 5 servings
Average serving = approx. 11 grams balanced protein
26 to 31% of daily protein need

Whole Wheat "Straw and Hay" Pasta With Hamloaf

A blend of whole wheat ribbon egg noodles and green (spinach) noodles in a creamy sauce, topped with sautéed mushrooms, onion and diced soyloaf or sausage granule burger topped with additional sauce.

1½-2 c. diced cooked Ham-style Soyloaf* or cooked Granule
5 c. Burger Sausage*
8 ozs. fresh white mushrooms, sliced (about 2½ cups); or 1 package (10 ozs.) frozen tiny peas
1 small onion, diced
1 clove garlic, minced
2 T oil or butter
1 package (5 ozs.) narrow whole wheat egg noodles, or homemade pasta
1 package (5 ozs.) narrow green (spinach) noodles, or homemade pasta
Creamy Sauce (see recipe below)
½ c. freshly grated Parmesan cheese

Prepare ham-style soyloaf or granule burger sausage ahead of time.

Sauté the onion and garlic in butter or oil. Add mushrooms. Sauté until tender. (Or stir-fry partially thawed peas until no frost remains.) Gently stir in diced ham-style loaf or granule burger sausage. Pour in 2 tablespoons of water, cover, and steam briefly to heat. (Or steam long enough for the peas to cook through, if you are using them.) Lower heat and keep warm.

Cook pastas separately in twice their volume of water. Bring water to a boil. Add pasta, allow to boil a minute, lower heat, then cover (leaving the cover slightly ajar) and let the pasta simmer until tender and the water is nearly all absorbed. Stir several times during cooking to prevent pasta from sticking to the pan.

Make Creamy Sauce.

Pour the drained pasta, mixed together, onto a heated platter. Mix half the Creamy Sauce into the noodles. Top with sautéed vegetables and ham-style loaf or granule burger sausage. Pour the remaining sauce over the topping.

Makes 4 to 6 servings.

Creamy Sauce

¾ c. vegetable cooking water
1 T cornstarch
½ t Vege-Sal
½ t olive oil (optional)
¼ t dried basil
¼ t tarragon
Pinch each of thyme, oregano, sage, nutmeg

2 T powdered milk
¼ c. evaporated skim milk
2 T cashew nuts, ground
2 T grated Parmesan cheese
1 T minced fresh parsley

In a small non-stick saucepan, mix the cornstarch with water, Vege-Sal, oil, and herbs. Stir constantly over moderate heat until sauce thickens and bubbles for 1 minute. Stir in remaining ingredients.

4 to 6 servings
Average serving = approx. 11 grams balanced protein
26 to 31% of daily protein need

Homemade Ravioli

Little pillows of homemade whole wheat or whole wheat and soy pasta, stuffed with any of a number of fillings: seasoned soy curd, ricotta and Parmesan cheeses, granule burger, or one of these three combined with spinach.

Many variations of homemade ravioli can be put together with the basic pasta recipes at the front of this section and the fillings described later in this recipe. Here are some possibilities that are good for their protein complementarity:

Whole Wheat Pasta With Seasoned Soy Curd
Whole Wheat Pasta With Ricotta Cheese and Parmesan Cheese
Wheat and Soy Pasta With Granule Burger
Wheat and Soy Pasta With Granule Burger and Spinach
Whole Wheat Pasta With Seasoned Soy Curd and Spinach
Whole Wheat Pasta With Ricotta Cheese and Spinach

To make ravioli dough, choose and prepare one of the homemade pasta recipes, using about 2 cups of flour. Knead as directed.

(If you have a pasta machine you will not have to roll out the dough by hand. Just make wide strips and proceed as directed below.)

Roll out the dough as thin as possible on a floured surface. Cut long strips 5 inches wide with a fluted pastry wheel. Place teaspoonfuls of filling, 1½ inches apart, down the center of each strip. Fold over the long edge of the strip, covering the little mounds of filling, to meet the other long edge, and press together with your fingers along the edge to seal. Press between mounds with your index finger to seal the pieces of dough around the fillings. Cut between the mounds with the pastry wheel. (If dough becomes too dry to stick together, dip the pastry wheel into warm water before cutting, then pinch the edges of the dough with your fingers to seal.) Repeat until all dough and all filling are used. You will have little squares like plump cushions.

Cook the ravioli for 8 to 10 minutes in a pot of boiling water. Lift them out onto a plate with a slotted spoon. Serve with Italian Tomato Sauce* and grated Parmesan cheese, if desired.

A 2 c. flour recipe for pasta will make about 50 ravioli, or enough for 4 to 6 servings.

Seasoned Soy Curd Filling

2 c. Soy Curd*
1 large onion, minced
1 T oil
1 T soy sauce

Heat oil in a skillet and sauté the onion until tender. Stir in the soy curd and soy sauce, mixing everything together well. Remove from heat. Use a teaspoon to fill ravioli dough squares with this mixture.

Average serving ravioli = approx. 15 grams balanced protein
35 to 42% of daily protein need

Ricotta Cheese With Parmesan Cheese Filling

1 c. ricotta cheese
⅓ cup grated Romano cheese
⅔ c. grated Parmesan cheese
1 egg yolk

Mix cheeses together in a bowl with the egg yolk. Fill ravioli dough with the mixture.

Average serving ravioli = approx. 17 grams balanced protein
39 to 47% of daily need

Granule Burger Filling

2 c. cooked chopped Granule Burger*
½ c. tomato sauce
2 T grated Parmesan cheese (optional)
1 large onion, minced
1 T oil

Heat the oil in a skillet and sauté onion until tender. Remove from the heat. Stir in the chopped granule burger, tomato sauce, and Parmesan cheese. Use a pastry blender to mash up the larger granule burger chunks. The mixture should be blended enough to hold together into small balls when placed by heaping teaspoonfuls on the ravioli dough.

Average serving ravioli = approx. 13 grams balanced protein
39 to 47% of daily protein need

Granule Burger and Spinach Filling

1 c. cooked chopped Granule Burger*
1 large onion, minced
1 clove garlic, minced
1 T oil
1 T soy sauce
1 package (10 ozs.) frozen spinach
⅛ t each thyme and marjoram
1 egg, beaten
2 T grated Parmesan cheese

Heat the oil in a skillet and sauté onion and garlic until tender. Have spinach cooked, drained, and chopped fine. Stir into the skillet with onion. Stir in cooked chopped granule burger and soy sauce. Add thyme and marjoram, (crushed), beaten egg, and grated cheese. Mix well. Remove from the heat. Fill ravioli dough by heaping teaspoons.

Average serving ravioli = approx. 12 grams balanced protein
28 to 34% of daily protein need

Seasoned Soy Curd and Spinach Filling

1 c. Soy Curd*
1 large onion
1 T oil
1 T soy sauce
1 package (10 ozs.) frozen spinach
⅛ t ground nutmeg

Heat the oil in a skillet and sauté the onion until translucent. Add the cooked, drained, chopped spinach. Stir to absorb oil. Stir in soy curd and soy sauce. Mix in nutmeg. Remove from heat. Fill ravioli dough by heaping teaspoons.

Average serving ravioli = approx. 12 grams balanced protein
28 to 34% of daily protein need

Ricotta Cheese and Spinach Filling

2 T minced onion
2 T oil or butter
1 package (10 ozs.) frozen spinach, cooked, drained, chopped
1 egg yolk
½ c. ricotta cheese
½ c. grated Parmesan cheese
⅛ t ground nutmeg

Cook onion in oil or butter over medium heat in a skillet. Stir in spinach to absorb fat. Stir in egg yolk, cheeses, and nutmeg. Use teaspoonfuls of filling to stuff ravioli.

Average serving ravioli= approx. 13 grams balanced protein
30 to 36% of daily protein need

The Soybean Plant

Stuffed Shells

Jumbo whole wheat macaroni shells stuffed with a savory soy curd or ricotta cheese and chopped soyloaf filling, baked with tomato sauce and cheese sauce.

1 package (12 ozs.) jumbo whole wheat shells, cooked and drained
2½ c. seasoned Soy Curd*
2 T chopped parsley
1 t leaf oregano, crumbled
2 c. finely chopped Ham-style* or Chicken-style Soyloaf*
1 recipe Italian Tomato Sauce* or Tomato-Vegetable Sauce (see recipe below); or 1 c. Tomato Sauce and 1 c. Cheese Sauce (see recipe below)
Grated Parmesan cheese (optional)

Jumbo whole wheat macaroni shells will take about 20 minutes of simmering to become tender.

Mix the seasoned soy curd with chopped parsley, crumbled oregano, and finely chopped soyloaf. Stuff each macaroni shell with about 1 T of the soy curd mixture.

Spoon ½ c. Tomato Sauce into a 13- × 9-inch baking dish. Arrange stuffed shells over sauce in one layer. Spoon remaining sauce over shells. (Or pour remaining tomato sauce and cheese sauce alternately over shells in a ribbon-like design.)

Sprinkle sauced shells with grated Parmesan cheese, if desired.

Bake for 20 minutes at 350° , or until shells are heated through and sauce bubbles.

Makes 6 to 8 servings.

Variation: Instead of using soy curd, stuff shells with a mixture of ricotta cheese (2 c.), cottage cheese (½ c.), and diced soyloaf.

Tomato-Vegetable Sauce

1 c. chopped onion
½ c. chopped celery
1 T oil
½ c. chopped mushrooms
1 t leaf basil, crumbled
1 can (16 ozs.) Italian tomatoes, crushed
1 t Vege-Sal

Sauté the chopped onion and celery in oil over moderate heat. Stir in the mushrooms. Stir in the basil, tomatoes, and Vege-Sal. Bring to a boil, cover, lower heat, and simmer for 10 minutes.

Cheese Sauce

1½ T whole wheat flour
1 T butter or oil
1 c. milk (or skim milk)
¼ c. grated Parmesan cheese
Sprinkle of Vege-Sal (optional)

Place the flour, butter, or oil and milk in a blender container. Blend until smooth. Pour the liquid into a small non-stick saucepan over moderate heat. Cook, stirring constantly, until thickened and bubbly. Stir in cheese and Vege-Sal.

6 to 8 servings
Average serving = approx. 10 grams balanced protein
23 to 28% of daily protein need

Macaroni Burger Pie

Wheat and soy macaroni with a rich cheese sauce forms the crust and top of a pie filled with granule burger and tomato sauce.

Basic Recipe for Granule Burger,* cooked and chunked
2 T oil
1 medium onion, chopped
1 clove garlic, minced
1 can (8 ozs.) tomato sauce
2 T oil
¼ c. whole wheat pastry flour
½ t Vege-Sal
2 c. milk
2 eggs
1 c. grated Parmesan cheese, or half Parmesan and half Cheddar
2 c. wheat and soy macaroni, cooked and drained (4 c.)
1 c. whole wheat bread crumbs (2 slices, crumbed)

Heat 2 T oil in a large non-stick skillet. Add the onion and garlic, stirring. Pour in the chunked cooked granule burger, breaking it up into smaller pieces as you stir it in. Add the tomato sauce, mixing it in well. Cover the skillet and remove from the heat.

Combine 2 T oil, ¼ c. pastry flour, and ½ t Vege-Sal in a non-stick saucepan. Heat and cook for 1 minute, stirring to mix. Gradually add 2 c. milk, stirring until mixture thickens and bubbles.

Beat the eggs in a small bowl. Pour half the sauce into the eggs and mix thoroughly. Pour the egg mixture into remaining white sauce. Stir in the cheese.

Have cooked macaroni, drained, in a large bowl. Pour cheese sauce into the macaroni, removing all of the sauce from the pan with a flexible spatula. Mix sauce well with the macaroni.

Oil a 9-inch pie plate with unrefined soy oil. Put half the bread crumbs in the plate, sprinkling the bottom and sides. Pour two-thirds of the macaroni mixture into the pie plate, spreading it on the bottom and up the sides.

Spoon the burger mixture into the center of the macaroni in the pie plate. Cover with the rest of the macaroni. Sprinkle the top of the pie with the remaining bread crumbs.

Bake at 375° for 20 to 30 minutes, or until the pie is lightly browned on top. Let stand for 15 minutes before cutting to serve.

6 to 8 servings
Average serving = approx. 14 grams balanced protein
32 to 39% of daily protein need

Granule Burger Lasagna

Layers of whole wheat lasagna noodles, ricotta cheese, granule burger "sausage," tomato sauce, and mozzarella cheese. A perfect dish for a party or special company dinner, it can be assembled ahead of time and baked the hour before serving.

Basic Recipe for One Pound of Soy Granule Burger*
½ t sage
½ t marjoram
¼ t ground thyme
¼ t garlic powder
8 ozs. whole wheat or wheat and soy lasagna noodles
1 can (8 ozs.) tomato sauce
1 can (1 lb.) tomatoes and liquid
1 can (6 ozs.) tomato paste
1 handful of fresh parsley
1 small onion, quartered
2 cloves garlic
2 T soy sauce
1 t oregano
1 carton (15 ozs.) ricotta cheese
1 package (12 ozs.) mozzarella cheese
¼-⅓ c. grated Parmesan cheese

Add seasonings (sage through garlic powder) to dry granule burger mix before adding the liquid for the basic recipe. Form granule burger into 8 small sausage-shaped rolls. Pressure cook on a steam rack over 1 c. water for 5 minutes. Let pressure drop naturally.

Cook lasagna noodles in boiling water for 10 minutes, or until firm-tender. Drain and set aside.

To make sauce, combine tomato sauce, tomatoes with liquid, tomato paste, parsley, onion, garlic, soy sauce and oregano in a blender container. Purée. (Makes 4 cups.)

Oil a lasagna pan (8½ × 12 × 2¼ inches) with unrefined soy oil. Place three lasagna noodles on the bottom. Spread them with half the ricotta cheese.

Take 4 "sausages" and slice them ¼ inch thick. Place the slices evenly over the layer of ricotta. Spread 1½ c. of sauce over these slices.

Slice the mozzarella cheese thinly with a cheese slicer and spread one-third of it evenly over the sauce layer. (Or grate the cheese and use one-third of it.)

Spread another layer of 3 noodles, the rest of the ricotta, the remaining "sausages," sliced, and another 1½ c. of sauce. Layer another one-third of the mozzarella cheese over the sauce.

Place a last layer of noodles on top. Spread them with the remaining 1 c. of tomato sauce, then with the last one-third of the mozzarella cheese. Sprinkle with grated Parmesan cheese.

Bake at 350° for 30 to 45 minutes (longer if the casserole has been refrigerated).

9 to 12 servings
Average serving = approx. 15 grams balanced protein
35 to 42% of daily protein need

Wheat

Lasagna Rollups

Whole wheat or wheat and soy lasagna noodles spread with a savory chicken-style soyloaf and spinach filling, rolled and baked in tomato sauce with strips of mozzarella cheese topping.

1½ c. cooked Soft Chicken-style Soyloaf*
1 package (10 ozs.) frozen chopped spinach; or 1½ c. cooked fresh spinach, chopped
1 onion, minced
1 T oil
½ t ground nutmeg
1 package (16 ozs.) whole wheat or wheat and soy lasagna noodles (preferably with fluted edges)
1 recipe Italian Tomato Sauce*
1 package (6 ozs.) sliced mozzarella cheese

Partially thaw the frozen spinach, or prepare fresh spinach.

Sauté the onion in oil until tender in a skillet over medium heat. Add spinach, stirring until no frost remains. Stir in nutmeg. Cover, lower heat, and let steam for 5 minutes. (Omit steaming with fresh cooked spinach.)

Meanwhile, cook lasagna noodles in a kettle. Drain. Spread them out lengthwise on a platter. (You should have 12 wide noodles.)

Stir spinach mixture into soyloaf in a mixing bowl. Blend together well. Spread ¼ c. of soyloaf mixture over each lasagna noodle in a thin, even layer. Roll up the noodle, jelly-roll fashion, starting at the narrow end.

Spread 1 c. tomato sauce over the bottom of a 13- × 9- × 2-inch baking dish. Place lasagna rolls in the pan, seam side down. Spoon the remaining tomato sauce over the rolls.

Bake at 375° for 15 minutes.

Place the mozzarella cheese on rollups in lengthwise strips. Bake 10 minutes longer, or until cheese is melted and sauce bubbles.

6 to 8 servings
Average serving = approx. 13 grams balanced protein
30 to 36% of daily protein need

Granule Burger Sausage Balls With Pasta

Tiny granule burger sausage balls in tomato sauce served over tubular pasta with dollops of ricotta cheese or seasoned soy curd.

Basic Recipe for Granule Burger Sausage*
2 T olive oil
Double recipe Italian Tomato Sauce*
1 c. sliced fresh mushrooms
12-16 ozs. tubular pasta (preferably homemade wheat and soy)
1 c. ricotta cheese
⅓ c. grated Romano cheese
⅓ c. grated Parmesan cheese or Seasoned Soy Curd*
Additional Parmesan cheese (optional)

Shape granule burger sausage in ¾-inch balls. Using a very large non-stick skillet, heat oil over moderate heat. Brown "sausage" balls on all sides. Remove to a dish.

Use the skillet to make a doubled recipe of Italian Tomato Sauce. Just before simmering the sauce, add the cooked granule burger balls and sliced mushrooms to skillet with the sauce. Bring to a boil, cover, lower heat, and simmer for 20 minutes.

Cook the pasta, putting it in twice its volume of boiling water. Lower heat and simmer, covered, until nearly all the water is absorbed, about 10 minutes. Drain pasta.

In a large skillet heat pasta in a cup of plain tomato sauce taken from the skillet of sauce and "sausage" balls.

Mix cheeses together in a bowl. Or prepare one recipe of Seasoned Soy Curd to use instead of cheeses.

Turn hot pasta out onto a large serving dish. Ladle on the granule burger sausage balls in sauce. Top with dollops of cheese mixture or seasoned soy curd. Serve with additional Parmesan cheese, if desired.

6 to 8 servings
Average serving = approx. 16 grams balanced protein
37 to 44% of daily protein need

Granule Burger and Spinach Pasta

Layers of granule burger with tomato sauce, whole wheat and soy elbow macaroni, cheese, and seasoned soy curd with spinach.

1 recipe Bulgar Wheat Granule Burger,* cooked
1 medium onion, chopped
1 T oil
1 can (15 ozs.) tomato sauce
1 t Italian herbs, crumbled
8 ozs. whole wheat and soy elbow macaroni, cooked
8 ozs. diced mozzarella cheese
1 medium onion, chopped
1 T oil
1 recipe (1½ c.) Soy Curd*
1 T soy sauce
1 package (10 ozs.) frozen chopped spinach, thawed
Parmesan cheese

Prepare the bulgar wheat granule burger and cook as directed in the basic recipe.

Heat 1 T oil in a large non-stick skillet and sauté the chopped onion. Add the cooked bulgar wheat granule burger chunks and sauté briefly. Stir in the tomato sauce and herbs.

Combine the mozzarella cheese and cooked macaroni. Place half the mixture in the bottom of a 3-quart casserole oiled with unrefined soy oil. Cover the macaroni with half of the sauce mixture.

Sauté the second onion in 1 T oil. Stir in the soy curd and soy sauce. Stir in the thawed chopped spinach. Mix well. Spread the spinach mixture over layer of sauce and burger mixture. Layer with remaining macaroni and then remaining sauce mixture. Sprinkle with Parmesan cheese.

Cover the casserole and bake at 350° for 20 to 30 minutes.

Variation: Substitute 1 package (15 ozs.) ricotta cheese for soy curd. Combine spinach, 2 eggs, and ricotta. Season to taste.

4 to 6 servings
Average serving = approx. 15 grams balanced protein
35 to 42% of daily protein need

Baked Soy Curd Casserole

Whole wheat noodles or macaroni with soy curd, chopped onion, green pepper, celery, and carrot with sesame meal and grated cheese.

1 recipe Soy Curd*
1 T soy sauce
2 c. cooked whole wheat noodles or macaroni (1 c. dry)
1 T oil
1 large onion, chopped
1 green pepper, chopped
½ c. chopped celery
1 c. grated carrot
½ t basil, crushed
¼ c. sesame seeds, ground
½ c. grated Cheddar cheese (optional)

Prepare soy curd according to the basic recipe. Stir soy sauce into finished soy curd.

Cook noodles or macaroni.

Meanwhile, heat the oil in a non-stick skillet. Sauté the onion, green pepper, and celery until barely tender. Stir in the grated carrot and crushed basil. Cover and steam briefly over low heat. Sprinkle with Vege-Sal, if desired.

Mix cooked drained noodles and vegetables into soy curd. Stir in all the ground sesame seeds except a tablespoon. Stir in all the grated cheese except two tablespoons. Spread the soy curd mixture into an 8-inch-square shallow casserole dish lightly oiled with unrefined soy oil. Sprinkle with the remaining sesame meal and grated cheese.

Bake at 375° for 20 minutes.

Variation: Use whole wheat spinach noodles; substitute 1 c. sliced mushrooms for the green pepper. Use 1 c. thinly sliced carrots instead of grated carrots.

4 to 6 servings
Average serving = approx. 11 grams balanced protein
26 to 31% of daily protein need

Ragout With Olives

Bulgar wheat granule burger and spaghetti mixed with chopped celery, onions, green peppers, peas, and tomatoes, sprinkled with Parmesan cheese and garnished with a circle of black olives.

Basic Recipe for Bulgar Wheat Granule Burger,* cooked
1 c. broken wheat-soy spaghetti, cooked in 2 c. water
2 T oil
2 c. thinly sliced celery
2 green peppers, chopped
2 medium onions, chopped
1 c. chopped mushrooms
2 c. frozen peas
1 can (1 lb.) tomatoes and liquid
½ c. pecans, ground
½ c. tomato juice
¼ c. grated Parmesan cheese
1 can (4 ozs.) pitted ripe olives

Prepare the bulgar wheat granule burger and cook the spaghetti.

Sauté the celery, green peppers, and onion briefly. Stir in mushrooms, then peas, stirring until no frost remains. Remove from heat. Add the tomatoes and liquid.

Add the cooked spaghetti. Stir the ground pecans into cooked bulgar wheat granule burger. Mix the granule burger into the vegetables. Pour all into an oiled 3-quart casserole.

Pour ½ c. tomato juice over all. Sprinkle with Parmesan cheese. Bake at 350° for about 1 hour, or until slightly browned and hot in the center. Before serving, circle the edge of the dish with pitted black olives.

4 to 6 servings
Average serving = approx. 13 grams balanced protein
30 to 36% of daily protein need

Soy-Noodle Confetti Bake

A casserole of whole wheat ribbon noodles, complementary soy granules, mixed vegetables, diced onion and celery, and chopped tomatoes in a Cheddar cheese sauce.

1 package (6 ozs.) whole wheat ribbon noodles
1 c. soy granules
1¾ c. water
2 T soy sauce
1 T oil
1 large onion, diced
1 clove garlic, minced
1 stalk celery, diced
2 c. frozen mixed vegetables
¼ c. chopped parsley
Vege-Sal to taste
1 can (1 lb.) tomatoes (reserve liquid)
Cheddar Cheese Sauce (see recipe below)
½ c. grated Cheddar cheese (optional)
Parmesan cheese

Cook the noodles in only 2½ c. water. Bring water to a boil. Add the noodles and stir gently. Allow to boil a minute, then lower heat, cover, and simmer for 5 to 8 minutes. Stir several times during cooking. The water should be all absorbed, and the noodles tender.

Cook the soy granules with the water and soy sauce over moderate heat until the water is absorbed, about 5 minutes. Set aside.

Heat the oil in a large non-stick skillet. Sauté the onion, garlic and celery. Add the frozen mixed vegetables and stir until no frost remains. Add a tablespoon of water. Cover, lower heat, and steam until the vegetables are tender, 5 or 10 minutes. Sprinkle with a little Vege-Sal to taste.

Drain tomatoes and reserve ¼ c. of the liquid for the cheese sauce. Make the sauce as directed.

Mix together the soy granules and cooked noodles. Stir in the vegetables, chopped tomatoes, and cheese sauce. Stir in additional grated cheese, if desired. Pour the mixture into a lightly oiled 2-quart (10 inches square × 2 inches deep) casserole. Sprinkle with Parmesan cheese.

Bake at 350° for 20 minutes.

Makes 4 to 6 servings.

Cheddar Cheese Sauce

1 T oil
2 T whole wheat pastry flour
¼ c. tomato liquid
¾ c. milk
¼ c. Cheddar cheese cubes

Put oil, flour, and juice in a blender container. Mix on low speed. Shut off blender. Add milk and cheese cubes. Blend again until smooth. Pour mixture into a non-stick saucepan. Stir over moderate heat until sauce bubbles and thickens.

4 to 6 servings
Average serving = approx. 11 grams balanced protein
26 to 31% of daily protein need

Soy Granule-Meatballs and Macaroni Supper

Toasty-coated meatballs in tomato sauce, surrounded by wheat-soy elbow macaroni with chopped fresh tomatoes and grated cheese.

Basic Recipe for One Pound of Soy Granule Burger,* or 2 cups of Convenience Mix*
1 medium onion, chopped
½ t dried oregano, crushed
½ c. whole wheat flour
2 T olive or other oil
1 can (6 ozs.) tomato paste
1 c. hot water
2 t honey
1 t Vege-Sal
2 c. cooked wheat-soy elbow macaroni
Chopped fresh tomatoes
Grated cheese

Put the dry soy granule burger mix in a bowl and stir in the chopped onion and crushed oregano. Pour in the soy granule burger liquid, stirring well until all dryness has disappeared. Allow to stand a few minutes for all the liquid to be absorbed.

Divide the top of the mixture in the bowl by flattening it with the back of a mixing spoon, then drawing intersecting lines with the spoon to make 8 pie-shaped portions. Scoop out each one, divide it in half, and roll the chunks into balls with your hands. You will have 16 balls. Roll them in the whole wheat flour.

Heat the oil in a large non-stick skillet and brown the balls on all sides, using medium heat.

Mix the tomato paste with the hot water, honey, and Vege-Sal. Pour this liquid around the meatballs and spoon some of it over them. When the liquid bubbles, lower the heat, cover, and simmer for 20 minutes. The meatballs puff up and cook by steaming in the sauce. Just before they are done, add the wheat-soy macaroni to the skillet around the meatballs, and put in the chopped tomatoes. Cover just till the tomatoes are heated. Garnish with grated cheese and serve from the skillet.

4 to 6 servings
Average serving = approx. 11 grams balanced protein
26 to 31% of daily protein need

Spaghetti and Soy-Granule Meatballs

High-protein soy-granule meatballs in a thick tomato sauce, served on a bed of wheat-soy spaghetti, topped with grated cheese.

Basic Recipe for One Pound of Soy Granule Burger,* or 2 cups of Convenience Mix
1 onion, minced fine
2 T fresh chopped parsley
2 T olive or other oil
Cooked wheat-soy spaghetti (about 12 ozs., dry)
½-1 c. grated cheese
Spaghetti Sauce (see recipe below)

Add the minced onion and chopped parsley to the dry soy granule burger mix before adding the liquid. When the mass is firm, place it on a cutting board, press it into a firm rectangle about 5 × 4 inches. Cut it into 5 vertical strips, then cut each strip into four 1-inch chunks. Roll the chunks in your hands, making 20 balls about 1 inch in diameter.

Brown these balls in 2 T olive oil in a large non-stick skillet over medium heat, turning carefully so that all sides are done. Put the balls into the simmering spaghetti sauce, and continue to simmer for 15 minutes. Serve the sauce and balls over the cooked spaghetti and top with grated cheese.

Spaghetti Sauce

1 can (16 ozs.) tomatoes
1 can (8 ozs.) tomato paste
1 onion, quartered
½ c. fresh parsley
1 T olive oil
2 T soy sauce
1 t Italian herbs
½ t oregano
½ t garlic powder

Put all the ingredients in a blender container and purée until smooth. Pour the sauce into a large saucepan, bring to a boil, and simmer for 20 minutes. (Granule balls simmer along with sauce.)

4 to 6 servings
Average serving = approx. 13 grams balanced protein
30 to 36% of daily protein need

Soy Granule-Meatballs Stroganoff

A sumptuous dish of meaty soy granule burger balls or cubes in a creamy thick mushroom-laden sauce, served over buttered noodles and garnished with parsley.

Basic Recipe for One Pound of Soy Granule Burger,* or 2 cups of Convenience Mix*
1 T oil
2 c. water or vegetable water
1 Vegex cube, smashed
2 t low-sodium vegetarian "beef" soup base
1 T soy sauce
1 T catsup
1 small onion, minced, or ½ t onion powder
1 c. sliced fresh mushrooms
½ c. water
2 T cornstarch or 4 t arrowroot
⅓ c. sour cream or yogurt
Buttered noodles
Parsley

Mix the minced onion or onion powder with the dry ingredients for the basic soy granule burger before stirring in the liquid.

When the mass of burger is firm, turn it out onto a cutting board. Press it down to a ¾-inch thickness in a square shape about 6 × 6 inches. Cut it into 5 vertical strips, then 5 horizontal ones, making 25 cubes. Separate the cubes and roll each one in your hands into a firm ball. Or press them into firm chunk shapes.

Heat 1 T oil in a large non-stick skillet. Brown the balls or chunks on all sides over moderate heat, turning carefully.

Have the Vegex cube dissolved in the 2 c. water into which you have also mixed the soup base, soy sauce, and catsup. Pour this sauce liquid into the skillet with the burger pieces, bring to a boil, cover, and simmer for 10 minutes. Stir in the fresh mushrooms, cover, and continue to simmer for 10 more minutes.

Stir in the cornstarch dissolved in ½ c. cold water, bring again to a boil, and let bubble for 1 minute. Remove from heat. Just before serving stir in sour cream or yogurt. Serve over noodles. (Broccoli is a good vegetable accompaniment.)

4 to 6 servings
Average serving = approx. 12 grams balanced protein
28 to 34% of daily protein need

Zucchini, Macaroni, and Beans

Spiral whole wheat macaroni served with a topping of sauced diced zucchini, tomatoes, and seasoned white beans for protein complementarity.

2 c. dried white beans, cooked and seasoned (4 c., cooked)
1 large onion, chopped
6 small zucchini
2 T oil (olive preferred)
¼ t oregano, crushed
2 cans (1 lb. each) tomatoes plus liquid
2 T cornstarch
Vege-Sal to taste
1 lb. dry spiral whole wheat macaroni
Grated cheese (optional)

Prepare the beans ahead of time. Pressure-cook the soaked beans for 25 minutes, or simmer them in a regular pot until tender, 1½ to 2 hours. When beans are cooked, season with Vege-Sal, if desired. Keep beans warm or re-heat when ready to serve.

Cook macaroni at the same time you are cooking the vegetables. Large whole wheat spirals will take about 15 to 20 minutes to become tender.

Quarter the washed zucchini lengthwise, then cut the pieces into ½-inch chunks.

Heat the oil in a large skillet over moderate heat. Sauté the onion for a few minutes, then add the zucchini and keep stirring until the vegetables start to become tender. Sprinkle with crushed oregano. Add 2 T water, lower heat, cover, and simmer for 8 to 10 minutes. Add tomatoes, broken up. Mix cornstarch with tomato liquid and add to the skillet. Raise the heat and stir the contents of the skillet until the liquid bubbles and thickens. Season with Vege-Sal, if desired.

To serve, place the drained macaroni on the plate. Top with a portion of vegetables and sauce, then a portion of seasoned beans. Sprinkle with grated cheese, if desired.

5 to 6 servings
Average serving = approx. 11 grams balanced protein
26 to 31% of daily protein need

Macaroni and Eggplant Sauce with Beans

Whole wheat elbow macaroni served with a topping of diced eggplant in tomato sauce, beans and grated cheese.

2 c. dried pinto beans or other beans, cooked and seasoned (4 c., cooked)
2 T oil
1 large onion, chopped
1 large eggplant, peeled and chopped
¼ t oregano, crushed
Vege-Sal
2 cans (8 ozs. each) tomato sauce
1 lb. whole wheat elbow macaroni
Grated cheese

Cook soaked beans in pressure cooker for 25 minutes, or in a regular pot about 2 hours. Season with Vege-Sal, if desired. Keep beans warm or reheat before serving.

Cook macaroni while you are cooking the eggplant sauce. Whole wheat macaroni, especially if stored a long time, needs about 15 to 20 minutes of simmering to become tender.

Sauté the chopped onion in oil. Add eggplant, stirring constantly until chunks are heated throughout. Sprinkle on crushed oregano and Vege-Sal. Add tomato sauce. Cover, lower heat, and simmer about 20 minutes.

To serve, place portions of drained elbow macaroni on plates. Top each with a serving of eggplant sauce, then with a serving of drained beans. Sprinkle with grated cheese.

5 to 6 servings
Average serving = approx. 11 grams balanced protein
26 to 31% of daily protein need

Garden Spaghetti

Whole wheat spaghetti complemented with soy granules and Parmesan cheese, topped with broccoli, cauliflower, asparagus, and mushrooms in a creamy sauce.

1 T olive oil
1 clove garlic, minced
4 c. broccoli florets
4 c. cauliflower florets
2 c. asparagus pieces
1 c. sliced mushrooms
1 c. vegetable cooking water
1 T cornstarch
½ t Vege-Sal
¼ t garlic powder
¼ t basil, crushed
Dash of nutmeg
2 T instant powdered milk
¼ c. evaporated skim milk
8 ozs. dry whole wheat spaghetti
¾ c. soy granules
1 T soy sauce
1 T butter (optional)
¼ c. grated Parmesan cheese
¼ c. minced fresh parsley

Heat the oil in a large non-stick skillet over moderate heat. Sauté the garlic. Add the florets, stirring for about 2 minutes. Add the asparagus pieces and stir another minute. Add the mushrooms and stir half a minute.

Mix the vegetable cooking water (or plain water) with cornstarch, Vege-Sal, garlic powder, basil, and nutmeg. Add the liquid to vegetables and stir until the sauce bubbles. Cover, lower heat, and simmer until vegetables are tender, about 10 to 15 minutes. Stir in the powdered milk and evaporated milk.

Meanwhile, cook the whole wheat spaghetti in 1 qt. of water. Bring water to a boil, add spaghetti and let boil a minute. (Add a trace of oil to prevent boiling over.) Lower the heat, cover, and simmer for 10 to 15 minutes. When the spaghetti is done, pour the soy granules into the pot to absorb the cooking liquid. Add 1 T soy sauce to the pot. When the soy granules are soft, drain the spaghetti and granules in a colander and place on a serving plate. Toss with butter and Parmesan cheese.

Pour the vegetable mixture over the cooked spaghetti. Garnish with minced parsley.

Variations: Use pieces of green beans or peas instead of asparagus. Use 6 c. of other vegetables, such as diced eggplant, zucchini, and green pepper, with oregano instead of basil.

4 servings
Average serving = approx. 12 grams balanced protein
28 to 34% of daily protein need

Appendix 1

In this appendix we give an idea of just what the computer accomplished. We begin by looking at the basic role of amino acids, the elements balanced by the computer to get good protein. They are, to the body, "units of construction." We can use a little analogy: The amino acids are like letters of the alphabet. The body uses these letters to make different words and these words, or combinations of letters, are *proteins*. On the average, the body uses letters in certain *specific proportions*. If some of these letters are in short supply, after a time the body will have difficulty in piecing together all the words that it needs. (In any protein food, the amino acid which is in shortest supply is called the "limiting amino acid.")

Now, when we eat some protein, we are in a sense ingesting a "book of words." No matter how simple or varied the vocabulary in the book is, the body always does the same thing: It begins at once to break down as many of the words as it can into the constituent letters. (In our body, this takes place in the digestive tract. The proteins which our digestive tract can't break down are "dietary fiber" proteins.) The body's protein-splitting or "proteolytic" enzymes are like little electric scissors which speedily but ever so carefully and accurately separate the words into individual letters; that is, they break down the ingested protein into amino acids. These amino acids pass into the blood stream and protein-*constructing* enzymes re-group them into new proteins (that is, re-group the letters into new words). These are specific proteins for the body which are used to replace worn-out muscle tissue cells, nerve cells, enzymes, and the like.

Various *plant* proteins are like children's books—the vocabulary is not quite so extensive, but they surely contain plenty of letters, and letters are what our bodies require. Their simpler vocabulary results in different ratios of letters used in them. By mixing together various plant proteins in the right proportions, we can end up with just the proportions of letters our bodies need.

Here is a specific example, using actual numbers; it indicates the kind of work the computer did. We choose peanuts and sesame seeds. We need look only at the eight essential amino acids. Their names are: tryptophan, leucine, lysine, methionine, phenylanaline, isoleucine, valine, and threonine. For any plant food, we can represent the relative amounts of the amino acids in it by a bar graph. For instance, a pound of peanuts or peanut butter gives us this bar graph:

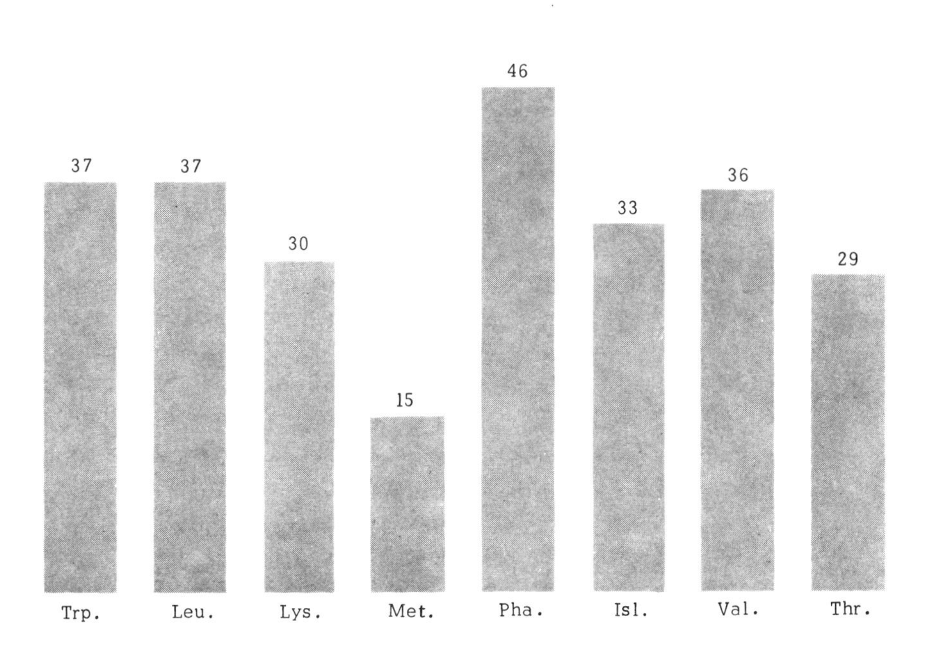

Note that the amino acid in shortest supply is the fourth one—methionine. That is, methionine is the limiting amino acid.

Here is the bar graph for one pound of sesame seeds:

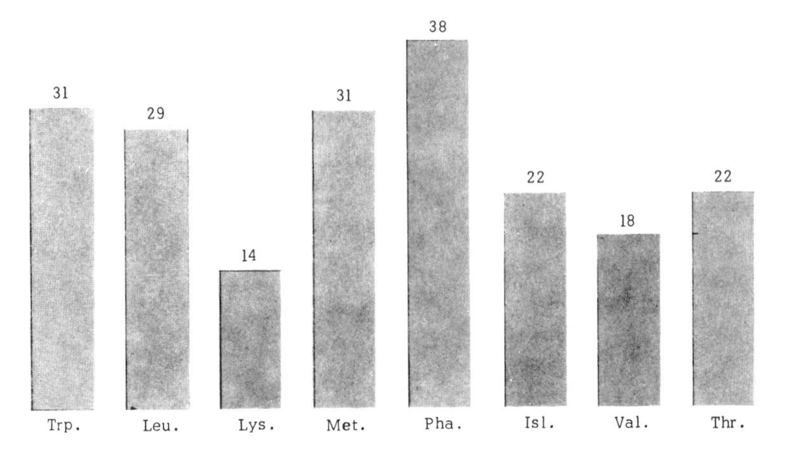

Note that the limiting amino acid in this case is lysine.

Now any combination, such as three-quarters of a pound of peanuts and one-quarter of a pound of sesame seeds, is a protein, and it, therefore, has its own bar graph. The object is to find that particular combination of these two ingredients so that the shortest bar in the corresponding bar graph is as *long* as possible. We do this because it is the shortest bar—the limiting amino acid—which measures how much usable protein we have. (In analogy, a box of printer's type with very few "e's" in it would be of limited use to the printer, and the "e's" would be the limiting letter.) By a special technique known as "linear programming," the computer found that particular combination. For peanuts and sesame seeds, the proportion is 55% peanuts to 45% sesame seeds. The associated bar graph looks like this:

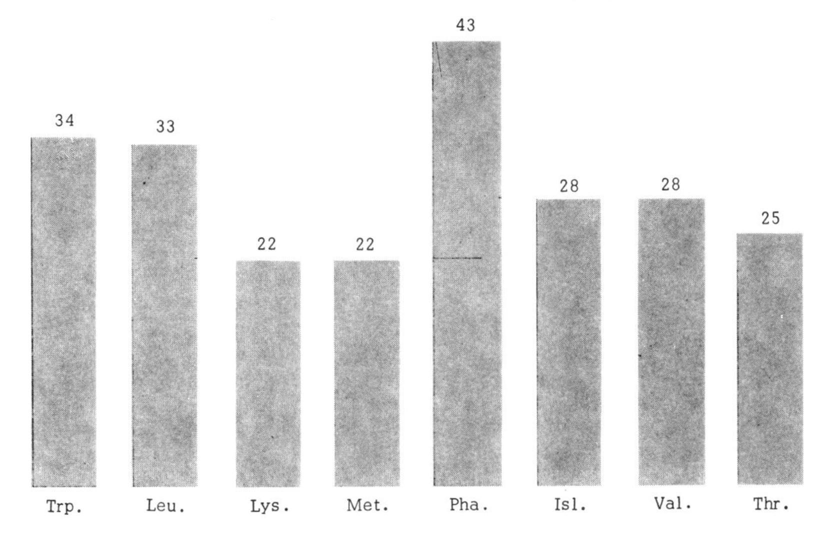

Note that the shortest bar is 22. This is over 50% longer than 14 (the shortest bar in sesame seeds), and almost 50% longer than 15 (the shortest bar in peanuts). This combination thus has a protein approximately 50% better than either peanuts or sesame seeds alone. In any other combination of peanuts with sesame, the shortest bar will be less than 22 and the corresponding increase in protein quality, less than 50%. On a weight-for-weight basis such a combination has more usable protein than a T-bone steak.

What the computer did for this book, then, was to carry out an extensive search to find the ideal combinations of all our basic ingredients. Even fairly good protein like cottage cheese can be made to yield protein closer to the body's needs. For instance, a handful of cashew nuts or sunflower seeds eaten with cottage cheese improves the protein of the cottage cheese.

ADDENDUM

Here are a few additional facts. There are altogether twenty-two amino acids in the body. The body can synthesize all of these but the essential eight. These amino acids are themselves molecules, containing mostly from 10 to 30 atoms each. The proteins, or "words," are quite long. They may contain anywhere from about 50 amino acids or "letters" (insulin has 51), to giant spiral-shaped proteins containing several *hundred thousand* amino acids. These words in turn form larger units like chapters of a book, for the proteins are arranged into cells—nerve cells, blood cells, and so on. There are typically over a *hundred million* of these "giant words" or proteins in a single cell. (In addition, each cell also contains hundreds of millions of molecules of water, fats, and carbohydrates, all encased in the cell walls.) Finally, these chapters link together to make a whole book—a truly incredible book of many trillions of chapters. In fact, there are approximately 60 trillion cells in the human body.

Appendix 2

In addition to the dietary changes suggested by the following chart, the Senate's *Dietary Goals* report also recommends that daily cholesterol intake, which currently averages about 600 mg. per day per person in the U.S., be decreased to around 300 mg. per day. And salt, which averages around 12 grams per day, should be reduced to about 5 grams per day. The report also recommends eating more fruits, vegetables and whole grains. It points out that high levels of fat, saturated fat and cholesterol, so typical in the American diet, usually enter our diet by eating animal protein, and suggests that a more vegetarian diet (that is, a diet containing more vegetable protein) will greatly help to reduce the percentage of calories coming from fat as well as the levels of saturated fat and cholesterol.

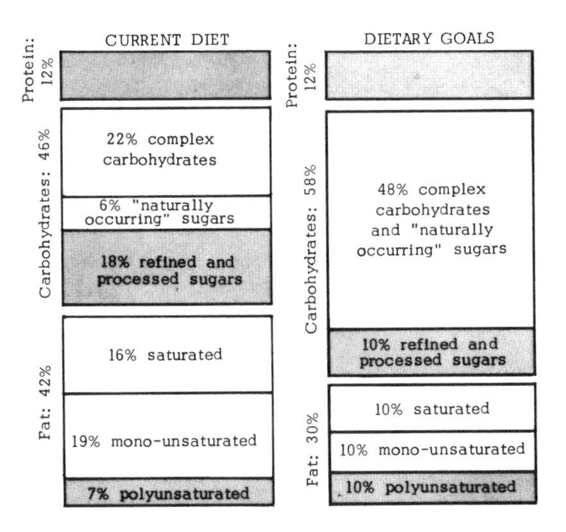

The report includes a summary of health benefits to be expected from an improved diet, and even its relatively conservative estimates are truly dramatic. Here are some of them:

- Over 6 billion dollars saved each year from heart and other vascular problems.
- 80% fewer obese persons.
- 20% less cancer.
- 50% fewer dental problems—a savings of over 3 billion dollars in annual dental fees.

- One billion dollars saved each year from various digestive disorders.
- 15% to 20% fewer days of work and school lost each year from colds and other infectious diseases. That's a savings of 20 million dollars each year in cold remedies and tissues alone!
- 33% less alcoholism.
- 50% fewer people afflicted with arthritis.
- 50% of all diabetes cases avoided or improved.
- 50% fewer infant deaths.

An even tighter and more persuasive case could be made for the advantages of a better diet if it could be shown that diet changes can actually *reverse* progress of various disorders.This has been noted in various whole *populations* (for instance in Denmark and Norway during the World Wars) who experienced declining death rates and generally improved health. But a real "acid test" is: Can a changed diet actually reverse the progress of diseases—particularly the "killer diseases"—on *individuals*? To draw a valid conclusion, we would need information based on closely monitored progress reports on large numbers of individuals over substantial periods of time.

The Pritikin Longevity Center (based in Santa Monica, California) has been carrying out a program along these lines. The Center's dietary changes may be thought as being closer to the "ideal" than those outlined in the *Dietary Goals* report. Fat intake is restricted to 5% to 10% (*Dietary Goals* allows 30%); refined sugar is 0% (*Dietary Goals* allows 10%); salt, 1 to 2 grams per day (*Dietary Goals* allows 5); cholesterol, less than 100 mg. per day (*Dietary Goals* allows 300 mg. per day). Animal protein is limited to at most 1½ pounds a week—just a third of the American average.

The Center's dietary changes are coupled with an exercise program as well. The results are extremely encouraging. For example, a women 81 years old with extreme circulation problems, unable to walk 50 feet without becoming totally exhausted, has now won several gold medals in Senior Citizens' half-mile and mile races.

In a group of the first 1,000 people given 26-day diet and exercise program, 85% experienced much lowered blood pressure and ceased taking medication. 50% of maturity-onset diabetics left insulin-free, with controlled glucose-tolerance levels. (In the case of diabetics, high levels of complex, unrefined carbohydrates and very low amounts of fat in the diet were emphasized.) Many angina patients left with greatly reduced pain and most left with significantly lower cholesterol levels. Of those who were overweight, the average weight loss was 13 pounds.

Index